ANNA MARIA FALCONBRIDGE

NARRATIVE OF TWO VOYAGES
TO THE RIVER SIERRA LEONE
DURING THE YEARS 1791–1792–1793

ALEXANDER FALCONBRIDGE

AN ACCOUNT OF THE SLAVE TRADE
ON THE COAST OF AFRICA

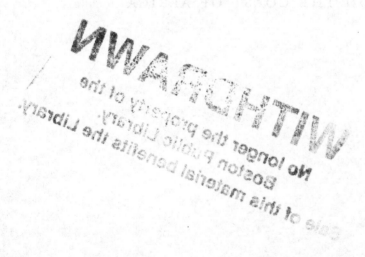

Anna Maria Falconbridge

NARRATIVE OF TWO VOYAGES
TO THE RIVER SIERRA LEONE
DURING THE YEARS
1791–1792–1793

and
THE JOURNAL OF ISAAC DUBOIS

with
Alexander Falconbridge

AN ACCOUNT OF THE SLAVE TRADE
ON THE COAST OF AFRICA

Edited by Christopher Fyfe

LIVERPOOL UNIVERSITY PRESS

First published 2000 by
LIVERPOOL UNIVERSITY PRESS
4 Cambridge Street,
Liverpool L69 7ZU

British Library Cataloguing-in-Publication Data
A British Library CIP record is available.

ISBN 0 85323 643 7 *paperback*

Typeset by Carnegie Publishing, Lancaster
Printed and bound in European Union by
Bell and Bain Ltd, Glasgow

Table of Contents

List of Illustrations

* The author and publishers have been unable to trace the copyright holders of these illustrations, which previously appeared in *The Loyal Blacks* and *John Clarkson and the African Adventure* by Ellen Gibson Wilson.

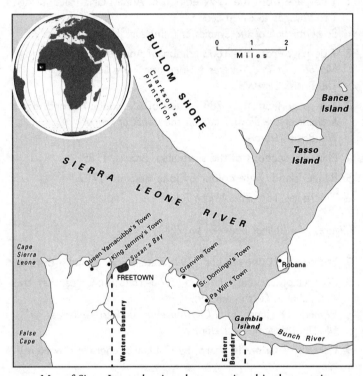

Map of Sierra Leone showing places mentioned in the narrative.

INTRODUCTION

Anna Maria Falconbridge was the first Englishwoman to publish an eye-witness narrative of her experiences in West Africa. She went out to Sierra Leone in 1791, went home briefly later in the year, then returned in February 1792, and stayed there until June 1793, recording her experiences in a series of letters.

She was born, Anna Maria Horwood, in Bristol, in 1769, the youngest of the five children of Charles and Grace Horwood (née Roberts). Her father was a watchmaker and goldsmith in All Saints Lane. When she was four years old her mother died. Her father eventually remarried, and had another family, most of whom died in childhood.[1] He died of apoplexy in 1787.[2] She then left home, and in the following year, at the age of nineteen, she married Alexander Falconbridge.[3] Her fluent, lucid style of writing, and her felicitous choice of words, show that she had been given a remarkably good education.

Falconbridge had played a crucial role in the campaign to abolish the Atlantic slave trade. Thomas Clarkson, the initiator of the campaign, having founded in London in June 1787 a Committee for the Effecting the Abolition of the Slave Trade, at once began collecting evidence of its horrors.[4] He started in Bristol, one of the main slave-trading ports. There he found people ready to give evidence privately, but no one who dared give it publicly. Then he met Falconbridge, a ship's surgeon, who, after a year's medical training at the Bristol Infirmary, had been employed between the years 1780 and 1787 on four successive voyages to West Africa on board slave ships. He had now left the slave trade for ever, disgusted by his experiences, and was only too glad to supply evidence of its cruelties.

When Clarkson moved on from Bristol to Liverpool, the heart of the slave trade, Falconbridge went with him to back up his moral arguments with fearlessly outspoken eye-witness accounts. When Clarkson was threatened with violence, he acted as his armed bodyguard. Clarkson then introduced him to his committee in London, and he agreed to substantiate what he had

---

[1] Information derived from Bristol Record Office, All Saint's Parish Registers. She was baptised on 13 July.

[2] *Sarah Farley's Bristol Journal*, 4 August 1787.

[3] Information supplied by Michael Browning, Bristol and Avon Family History Society.

[4] Clarkson gave a full account of his involvement with Falconbridge in his *The History . . . of the Abolition of the Slave Trade by the British Parliament*, London, 1806, vol. I, pp. 348–463.

said in print. A Quaker lawyer, Richard Phillips, helped him to reduce it to publishable form, and in 1788 his *An Account of the Slave Trade on the Coast of Africa* (added on pp. 191–230) appeared. Three thousand copies were printed by the committee, to circulate as propaganda.

He also gave evidence to a Committee of the Privy Council reporting on the slave trade, and in 1790 was subjected to four days of gruelling, chiefly hostile, questioning by a House of Commons Committee.[5] A cautious Quaker member of the abolition committee recorded in a confidential report, "His zeal and activity are wonderful, but I am really afraid he will at times be deficient in caution and prudence, and lay himself open to imposition, as well as incur much expense, perhaps sometimes unnecessarily."[6]

He then returned to Bristol and set up in medical practice at the neighbouring village of Lodway. Anna Maria Horwood was living nearby. "An athletic and resolute-looking man" (so Clarkson described him),[7] he won her heart. On 16 October 1788 they were hastily married, contrary to the wishes of her friends and relations (so she tells us in her first letter), who may well have been dismayed at her marrying a notorious abolitionist.

* * *

Clarkson realised that moralistic arguments against the slave trade must be supplemented by economic. During his visits to the seaports he had collected samples of African produce, arguing that once the slave trade was abolished it could be replaced by an even more profitable produce trade. He was therefore interested in a project initiated by an active opponent of slavery and the slave trade, Granville Sharp, who had already, in Somerset's Case (1782), extracted from the courts a judgment that a slave resident in England could not be returned to slavery overseas – a judgment that was widely (though inaccurately) taken to imply that slavery was henceforth illegal in England.

After the end of the War of American Independence many black refugee Loyalists who had liberated themselves from American slavery found their way to London. Destitute on the streets, the "Black Poor", as they were known, roused public sympathy, and Sharp sponsored a proposal to settle them, as free people, in West Africa. Sierra Leone, at the mouth of a wide estuary, some six hundred miles north of the equator, was chosen as the site for what he called, "The Province of Freedom", a self-governing settlement of free people. Many of the Black Poor agreed to enroll as settlers, and the government agreed to defray the expense of sending them out, under naval escort, to found a settlement. After various delays, 459 men,

[5] *Report of the Lords of the Committee of Council ... concerning ... the Trade in Slaves*, London, 1798; *House of Commons Papers* [reprinted S. Lambert (ed.), Wilmington, 1975], vol. 72, 1790, pp. 293–344.

[6] Quoted in Ellen Gibson Wilson, *Thomas Clarkson*, London, 1989, pp. 34–5.

[7] Clarkson, *History*, p. 388.

women, and children (some of the men had white English wives), embarked, and reached Sierra Leone in May 1787.[8]

The country where they landed had been known to Europeans since the mid-fifteenth century when the Portuguese reached it and named it, from its lion-shaped mountains, Serra Lyoa – a name eventually adopted into English usage in the hispanicised style of Sierra Leone. The mountains, jutting spectacularly out from the flat Atlantic coast, form the southern shore of a wide estuary, making a safe harbour on a surf-bound coast, which attracted ships to trade, and to take on water and firewood. It also gave the African rulers who controlled it access to overseas trade, and enabled them to collect customs duties. By this time it was controlled by rulers of the Temne people who, with their Bulom (or Sherbro) neighbours inhabited most of the surrounding country.

Over the centuries a well-organised import-export trade had grown up, chiefly in slaves, exchanged against imported manufactured goods. At first the Portuguese Crown had tried to establish a monopoly, and Portuguese traders settled along the coast, often marrying and leaving Afro-Portugese descendants. But from the seventeenth century onwards British traders came to dominate the trade. The Royal African Company, established by royal charter, which built trading posts a few miles up the Sierra Leone estuary on Bance (today Bunce) Island, and on York Island in the Sherbro estuary to the south, also tried to enforce a monopoly. But it too failed, and after 1728 traders were able to trade freely in the area, settling on islands or along the nearby river banks. The Bance Island premises passed into the hands of a London firm, Messrs John and Alexander Anderson. But the country was still under African sovereignty, and Europeans had to pay rent for the trading premises they occupied to the ruling kings and chiefs.[9]

So before the settlers could establish themselves on land, a treaty had to be negotiated with King Tom, the Temne ruler of a peninsula on the southern shore of the estuary, adjoining the land where they wanted to settle. And when he died a year later, another treaty had to be negotiated with his superior, Naimbana, who lived a few miles inland. A settlement was laid out on a hill near the waterside and named Granville Town. But the project was a disaster. The settlers had arrived at the beginning of the long rainy season and many of them fell ill and died. The survivors had no adequate means of livelihood, and depended on relief supplies from England. Inevitably they faced the hostility of the resident slave traders who incited King Tom's successor, King Jemmy, against them. They sought help against him from a passing naval ship which intervened on their behalf, and in the ensuing fracas King Jemmy's town was burnt. When the ship had gone, King Jemmy gave

[8] For an authoritative account of the Black Poor and the Province of Freedom, see Stephen J. Braidwood, *Black Poor and White Philanthropists: London's Blacks and the Foundation of the Sierra Leone Settlement 1786–1791*, Liverpool, 1994.

[9] See Christopher Fyfe, *A History of Sierra Leone*, London, 1962, pp. 1–12.

the settlers three days notice to quit. They scattered over the countryside and then, in retaliation, he had their town burnt down.[10]

Sharp, unable to finance the settlement further himself, persuaded wealthy friends in the City of London to form a company, the St George's Bay Company, to take it over. But though he was a director, he no longer had control. The company (re-named the Sierra Leone Company) was a commercial venture, founded to fulfil Clarkson's dream of establishing a profitable produce-trading centre in defiance of the slave trade. It could no longer be Sharp's self-governing "province". Clarkson and William Wilberforce were among the directors, but it was largely controlled by Henry Thornton, a wealthy London banker and close associate of Wilberforce. To its commercial aims were added "the Honourable Office of introducing to a Vast Country long detained in Barbarism the Blessings of Industry and Civilization".[11]

One of the Company's first tasks was to recruit someone to go out and reassemble the scattered settlers, and persuade the Temne authorities to allow the settlement to continue. Clarkson turned to his loyal associate Falconbridge. He abandoned his medical practice, and in January 1791 he and his wife set out for Sierra Leone.

* * *

Anna Maria Falconbridge described her experiences in a series of letters written to a friend in Bristol, but as she "candidly confesses" in her Preface, from the start, she had the idea of publishing them as a book. Though she was not the first white Englishwoman to visit Sierra Leone, hers is the first Englishwoman's narrative of a visit to West Africa[12] – possibly to Africa.[13]

But she must be allowed to tell her story herself in her own way. Her editor is not going not spoil it by letting it all out in an introduction. Inevitably her letters require contextual annotation to make them accessible to present-day readers. But I want to spare her the indignity of treating her narrative as if it were no more than a historical document illustrating the history of Sierra Leone (though it is that too). Nor do I feel it is my place to make judgments about her and her work. I have therefore tried to keep editorial comment to a minimum.

As she indicates in her Preface, the form of the letters changes. The first seem to have been written merely to interest and entertain the recipient.

---

[10] Braidwood, *Black Poor,* pp. 182–209.

[11] Fyfe, *A History,* pp. 25–31.

[12] "A List of the Living and Dead", 1702–14, in the papers of the Royal African Company shows a wife at York Island, and the York Island accounts for 1713–14 show living expenses for twelve white men and one white woman (Public Record Office [hereafter PRO], T70/1445, 18 July 1707; T70/591, 22 June 1713, 16 August 1714).

[13] Lady Anne Barnard's book, *Letters written from the Cape of Good Hope, 1797–1801,* appeared later (and was anyway only published in 1901). But I will leave "possibly", in case someone can supply an earlier narrative.

They certainly read as if they were spontaneous productions. But in the second half of the book the tone changes and another motive begins to emerge. Sometimes unobtrusively, sometimes clamorously, the narrative becomes blended with polemic as she exposes the failings of the Sierra Leone Company, and denounces its directors and employees. The book ends with an angry tirade addressed to Henry Thornton.

In reproducing her text I have decided not to follow slavishly the inaccuracies inflicted on her by a not very competent printer, whose vagaries she complained of in the Appendix at the end of the book. I have therefore corrected what seem to me printer's errors. Her footnotes have been marked with an asterisk and inserted in the text. I have also sometimes altered the punctuation to make the narrative more accessible to today's readers. But I have left idiosyncrasies of grammar and expression which I believe to be her own, as they help us to hear her story in her own voice.

My thanks to Mrs McGregor of the Bristol Record Office, and Michael Browning of the Bristol and Avon Family History Society, for helping me find biographical information, to Terry Barringer for letting me use the Royal Commonwealth Society Library during its last dark days in London, to Joe Opala for information on the present state of Bunce Island, to Ellen Wilson for help with copyrights and to Adam Jones for useful advice and a valuable reference. Finally I must thank Paul Hair for his help, and especially for his suggestion that I add the reprint of Alexander Falconbridge's *Account* as a supplement to his wife's *Narrative*.

Anna Maria Falconbridge
*Narrative of Two Voyages
to the River Sierra Leone
During the Years 1791–1792–1793*

DEDICATION

Inhabitants of Bristol

After revolving in my mind a length of time whose protection I might solicit for the subsequent pages, it strikes me I may look up with more confidence to the City I proudly boast to be a native of, than to any other quarter.

Permit me, therefore, to trespass on your patience for a short space, by entreating your Countenance, and Patronage, to a faithful and just account of two voyages to the inhospitable Coast of Africa – chequered throughout with such a complication of disasters as I may venture to affirm have never yet attended any of my *dear Country Women*, and such as I sincerely hope they never may experience.

I will not undertake to promise you either elegant or modish diction; and all I shall advance in my favour, is a rigid adherence to truth, which (without embellishment) I am persuaded will meet its just reward from the Inhabitants of Bristol, whom I trust will have the goodness to keep in mind the infancy of my pen, that the recollection may serve for an apology, should they at any time catch me giving too much scope to its reins.

May every description of happiness attend the Inhabitants of Bristol, is the earnest prayer

> Of their Townswoman,
> and most devoted,
> and obedient Humble Servant,
> ANNA MARIA –[14]

BRISTOL, *August* 1794.

[14] It will appear later why she signs herself in this way.

PREFACE

The Authoress will not imitate a threadbare prevailing custom, viz. assure the Public, the following letters were written without any design or intention of sending them into the world; on the contrary, she candidly confesses having some idea of the kind when writing them, though her mind was not fully made up on the business until towards the beginning of April – nay, for some time before then (from a consciousness of the inability of her pen) she had actually relinquished all thoughts of publishing them, which determination she would certainly have adhered to, if her *will* had not been overruled by the importunities of her friends.

In her first Voyage, she has given her reasons for going to Africa, described the incidents and occurrences she met with and (from ocular observations) the manners, customs, &c. of the people inhabiting those places she visited – she has also made an humble attempt to delineate their situations and qualities, with a superficial History, of the Peninsula of Sierra Leone and its environs, which she certainly would have enlarged upon during her second Voyage, had not *Lieutenant Matthews*, previous to her returning to England in 1791, taken a start of her, by publishing his voyage to that Country[15] – that being the case, it would not only have been superfluous, but discovering more vanity than she could wish the World to suppose her possessed of, had she offered to tread in a path already travelled over by such an ingenious and masterly pen, to which she begs to refer the inquisitive reader.

This consideration, and this alone, induced the Authoress to confine the letters of her last Voyage principally to the transactions and progress of a Colony, whose success or *downfall* she is persuaded the Inhabitants, at least the thinking part, of almost every civilized Country, must feel more or less interested about, and she is *sorely afflicted* to warn the reader, of an uncompromising account which could not be otherwise, unless she

---

[15] John Matthews, *A Voyage to the River Sierra Leone*, London 1789; Matthews, a former naval lieutenant who had lived on the Sierra Leone peninsula, trading in slaves, gave his readers a well-informed description of the country and its people, still of use to historians and anthropologists. His book, too, is styled as a series of letters.

had done *violence to veracity*. – she is well aware Truth is often unwelcome, and foresees many facts produced to the World in the course of those letters will not be acceptable to the ears of numbers – therefore, in vindication of herself, she refers the Public to the whole *Court of Directors of the Sierra Leone Company*, and hopes, if it be in their power, either severally or collectively, to contradict *one tittle* she has advanced, they will do so in the most candid manner – for the Authoress is open to conviction, and if convicted on this occasion, she will, with all due deference, *kiss the rod of correction.*

LETTER I

My Dear Friend,

The time draws nigh when I must bid adieu to my native land, perhaps for ever ! The thoughts of it damps my spirits more than you can imagine, but I am resolved to summon all the fortitude I can, being conscious of meriting the reproaches of my friends and relations, for having hastily married as I did, contrary to their wishes, and am determined rather than be an incumbrance on them, to accompany my husband even to the wilds of *Africa,* whither he is now bound, and meet such fate as awaits me, in preference to any possible comfort I could receive from them.

Mr Falconbridge is employed by the St George's Bay Company to carry out some relief for a number of unfortunate people, both blacks and whites, whom Government sent to the river Sierra Leone, a few years since, and who in consequence of having had some dispute with the natives, are scattered through the country, and are just now as I have been told, in the most deplorable condition.

He (Mr Falconbridge) is likewise to make some arrangements for collecting those poor creatures again, and forming a settlement which the company have in mind to establish, not only to serve them, but to be generally useful to the natives.

Mr Falconbridge, his brother Mr W. Falconbridge and myself, are to embark on board the *Duke of Buccleuch,* Captain McLean, a ship belonging to Messrs John and Alexander Anderson, of Philpot Lane; these gentlemen I understand, have a considerable factory at a place called Bance Island, some distance up the river Sierra Leone, to which island the ship is bound.[16]

---

[16] A "factory" was a trading post. The *Duke of Buccleuch* was a slave ship which was to take on board 358 slaves at Bance Island, six of whom died on the passage to Jamaica (House of Lords Record Office [hereafter HLRO], L5/J/11/2, "Return of Ships employed in the Slave Trade from 1791 to 1797" – I am grateful to Adam Jones who gave me this reference).

The company have either sent, or are to send out, a small cutter called the *Lapwing*, to meet Mr F—, on the coast, she carries the stores for relieving the people, &c.

This is all the information I can give you at present, respecting my intended voyage, but as it is an unusual enterprise for an English woman to visit the coast of Africa; and as I have ever flattered myself with possessing your friendship, you will no doubt like to hear from me, and I therefore intend giving you a full and circumstantial account of every thing that does not escape my notice, till I return to this land, if it pleases him who determines all things, that should be the case again.

I have this instant learnt that we set off tomorrow for Gravesend, where the ship is laying, ready to sail; should we put into any port in the channel, I may probably write you if I am able, but must now bid you adieu.

LETTER II

SPITHEAD, *Jan.* 12, 1791.

My dear Friend,

Contrary winds prevented us from proceeding directly out of the channel, and made it necessary to put into this place. We have been here two days, but I am told there is an appearance of the wind changing, and that it is probable we shall make the attempt to get away some time this day; therefore I shall think it best not to defer performing my promise of writing to you, lest we sail, and I am disappointed.

We embarked at Gravesend between eleven and twelve o'clock, the night after I wrote you. Every thing seemed in dreadful confusion; but this I understand is commonly the case on board ships when on the eve of sailing: besides the captain had several friends who came from London to bid him farewell.

You may guess that my mind, in spite of all the resolution a young girl is capable of mustering, could not be undisturbed; but I would not give way to any melancholy reflections, and endeavoured to smother them as often as they intruded; although I must confess they sometimes caught me off my guard, and my heart for the moment was ready to burst with the thoughts of what I had to encounter, which was pictured to me by almost every one in the worst of colours.

However I went to bed, and being much fatigued, was in hopes every care would be buried for the night in delightful sleep; but in this I was disappointed, for although my eyes were closed as soon as I got my head on the pillow, yet it was not of long continuance.

I had slept perhaps two hours, when the shocking cries of murder awoke me: I did not at the instant recollect where I was, but the first thoughts which occurred upon remembering myself on ship-board were, that a gang of pirates had attacked the ship, and would put us all to death.

All the cabin was by this time alarmed; the cries of murder still continuing while the captain and others were loudly calling for lights;

and so great was the confusion, that it was a long while before any could be procured: at length the light came, and I found myself somewhat collected, and had courage enough to ask what was the matter.

My fears were removed, by being informed it was a Mr B—, a passenger, whose intellects were a little deranged: he continued his disagreeable hideous cries the whole night, and prevented every one from sleeping; for my part I scarcely closed my eyes again.

At breakfast Mr B— apologised, by telling us that his wife had murdered his only child, for which reason he had left her. "And", said he, "the horrid act! has made such an impression on my mind, that I frequently think I see her all besmeared with blood, with a dagger in her hand, determined to take away my life also: it preys upon my spirits, for I want strength of mind to conquer the weakness".*

* I am inclined to think that this was only the imagination of a frantic
  brain, for we were not able to learn any thing more of the story.

Mr Alexander Anderson came on board, and dined: he politely enquired if I was comfortable; assured me, that every thing had been put on board to render us as much so as possible.

In the evening he returned to town, and we got under weigh.

Nothing occurred on our passage here except such frequent returns of Mr B's delirium, as has induced Captain McLean to put him on shore, from the opinion of his being an unfit subject to go to the coast of Africa.

I did not experience any of those fears peculiar to my sex upon the water; and the only inconvenience I found was a little sea- sickness, which I had a right to expect, for you know this is my first voyage.

There is one circumstance, which I forebode will make the remainder of our voyage unpleasant.

The gentlemen whom Mr Falconbridge is employed by are for abolishing the slave trade: the owners of this vessel are of that trade, and consequently the Captain and Mr Falconbridge must be very opposite in their sentiments.

They are always arguing, and both are warm in their tempers, which makes me uneasy, and induces me to form the conjectures I do; but perhaps that may not be the case.

I have not been on shore at Portsmouth, indeed it is not a desirable place to visit: I was once there, and few people have a wish to see it a second time.

The only thing that has attracted my notice in the harbour, is the fleet with the convicts for Botany Bay, which are wind bound, as well as ourselves.

The destiny of such numbers of my fellow creatures has made what I expect to encounter, set lighter upon my mind than it ever did before; nay, nothing could have operated a reconciliation so effectually; for as the human heart is more susceptible of distress conveyed by the eye, than when represented by language, however ingenuously pictured with misery, so the sight of those unfortunate beings, and the thoughts of what they are to endure, have worked more forcibly on my feelings than all the accounts I ever read or heard of wretchedness before.

I must close this which is the last, in all probability, you will receive from me till my arrival in Africa; when, if an opportunity offers, I shall make a point of writing to you.

Pray do not let distance or absence blot out the recollection of her,

Who is truly yours.

LETTER III

My Dear Friend,

We sailed the very day I wrote you from Portsmouth, and our passage was unusually quick, being only eighteen days from thence to this place.

The novelty of a ship ploughing the trackless ocean, in a few days became quite familiar to me; and there was such a sameness in every thing (for some birds were all we saw the whole way) that I found the voyage tiresome, notwithstanding the shortness of it.

You will readily believe my heart was gladdened at the sight of the mountains of Sierra Leone, which was the land we first made.

Those mountains appear to rise gradually from the sea to a stupendous height, richly wooded and beautifully ornamented by the hand of nature, with a variety of delightful prospects.

I was vastly pleased while sailing up the river, for the rapidity of the ship through the water afforded a course of new scenery almost every moment, till we cast anchor here. Now and then I saw the glimpse of a native town, but from the distance and new objects hastily catching my eye, was not able to form a judgment or idea of any of them; but this will be no loss, as I may have frequent opportunities of visiting some of them hereafter.

As soon as our anchor was dropped, Captain McLean saluted Bance Island with seven guns, which not being returned I enquired the cause, and was told that the last time the *Duke of Buccleuch* came out, she, as

---

[17] Bence Island, as it was first named, had been leased from the neighbouring African rulers in the 1670s by the Royal African Company. Substantial fortified premises were built, and it became the main trading centre in the river. After various vicissitudes the lease of what was by then known as Bance Island was taken over in 1785 by the Andersons. When the slave trade from the area ceased it lost its importance, and by the 1860s the buildings on what was by then called Bunce Island were in ruins. David Hancock in his *Citizens of the World*, Cambridge, 1995, gives an impressive account of the Brtish Atlantic trading economy of which Bance Island formed a part; his description of the island is however strangely fanciful.

is customary, saluted, and on the fort returning the compliment, a wad was drove by the force of the sea breeze upon the roof of one of the houses (which was then of thatch), set fire to the building, and consumed not only the house but goods to a large amount.

When the ceremony of saluting was over, Captain McLean and Mr W. Falconbridge went on shore; but it being late in the evening, I continued on board till next day.

Here we met the *Lapwing* cutter. She sailed some time before us from Europe, and had been arrived two or three weeks.

The master of her, and several of the people to whose assistance Mr Falconbridge is come, and who had taken refuge here, came to visit us.

They represented their sufferings to have been very great; that they had been treacherously dealt with by one *King* Jemmy, who had drove them away from the ground they occupied, and otherwise divested them of every comfort and necessary of life; they also threw out some reflections against the Agent of this island; said he had sold several of their fellow sufferers to a Frenchman, who had taken them to the West Indies.

Mr Falconbridge, however, was not the least inclined to give entire confidence to what they told us; but prudently suspended his opinion until he had made further enquiries.

Those visitors being gone, we retired to bed – I cannnot say to rest; the heat was so excessive I scarcely slept at all.

The following day we received a polite invitation to dine on shore, which I did not object to, although harassed for want of sleep the night before.

At dinner the conversation turned upon the slave trade: Mr Falconbridge, zealous for the cause in which he is engaged, strenuously opposed every argument his opponents advanced in favour of the *abominable* trade: the glass went briskly round, and the gentlemen growing warm, I retired immediately as the cloth was removed.

The people on the island crowded to see me; they gazed with apparent astonishment – I suppose at my dress, for white women could not be a novelty to them, as there were several among the unhappy people sent out here by government, one of whom is now upon the island.

Seeing so many of my own sex, though of different complexions from myself, attired in their native garbs, was a scene equally new to me, and my delicacy, I must confess, was not a little hurt at times.

Many of them appeared of superior rank, at least I concluded so from the preferable way in which they were clad; nor was I wrong in my conjecture, for upon enquiring who they were, was informed one was the *woman* or *mistress* of Mr—, another of Mr B—,[18] and so on: I then understood that every gentleman on the island had his *lady*.

While I was thus entertaining myself with my new acquaintances, two or three of the gentlemen left their wine and joined me; among them was Mr. B—, the agent; he in a very friendly manner begged I would take a bed on shore.

I thanked him, and said, if agreeable to Mr Falconbridge, I would have no objection; however Falconbridge objected, and gave me for reason that he had been unhandsomely treated, and was determined to go on board the *Lapwing*, for he would not subject himself to any obligation to men possessing such *diabolical* sentiments.

It was not proper for me to contradict him at this moment, as the heat of argument and the influence of an over portion of wine had *quickened* and *disconcerted* his temper; I therefore submitted without making any objection to come on board this tub of a vessel, which in point of size and cleanliness, comes nigher a hog-trough than any thing else you can imagine.

Though I resolved to remonstrate the first seasonable opportunity, and to point out the likelihood of endangering my health, should he persist to keep me in so confined a place.

This remonstrance I made the next morning, after passing a night of torment, but to no purpose; the only consolation I got was – as soon as the settlers could be collected, he would have a house built on shore, where they were to be fixed.

I honestly own my original resolutions of firmness was now warped at what I foresaw I was doomed to suffer, by being imprisoned, for God knows how long, in a place so disgusting, as this was, in my opinion, at that time.

Conceive yourself pent up in a floating cage, without room either to

[18] Ballingall.

walk about, stand erect, or even to lay at length; exposed to the inclemency of the weather, having your eyes and ears momently offended by acts of indecency, and language too horrible to relate – add to this a complication of filth, the stench from which was continually assailing your nose, and then you will have some faint notion of the *Lapwing* Cutter.

However, upon collecting myself, and recollecting there was no remedy but to make the best of my situation, I begged the master (who slept upon deck in consequence of my coming on board) to have the cabin thoroughly cleaned and washed with vinegar; entreated Falconbridge to let me go on shore while it was doing, and hinted at the indecencies I saw and heard, and was promised they would be prevented in future.

With these assurances I went on shore, not a little elated at the reprieve I was to enjoy for a few hours.

The gentlemen received me with every mark of attention and civility; indeed I must be wanting in sensibility, if my heart did not warm with gratitude to Messrs Ballingall and Tilly, for their kindnesses to me: the latter gentleman I am informed will succeed to the agency of the island; he is a genteel young man, and, I am told, very deservedly a favourite with his employers.

Mr Falconbridge this day sent a message to Elliote Griffiths, the secretary of Naimbana, who is the King of Sierra Leone, acquainting him with the purport of his mission, and begging to know when he may be honoured with an audience of his *Majesty*.[19]

In the evening he received an answer, of which the following is a copy:

ROBANA TOWN.

KING Naimbana's compliments to Mr Falconbridge, and will be glad to see him tomorrow.

(Signed)

A. E. GRIFFITHS, Sec.

---

[19] Naimbana, styled King by the Europeans, was in fact regent, not king, over the Koya Temne, who peopled the southern shore of the estuary; only after his death in 1793 was the royal title revived. He ruled from Robana, on the south shore. Griffiths, his secretary, was one of the Granville Sharp settlers (Fyfe, *A History*, pp. 19, 54).

Such an immediate answer from a *King*, I considered a favourable omen, and a mark of condescension in his Majesty, but the result you shall hear by and by; in the mean while, I must tell you what passed the remainder of the day at Bance Island, and give, as far as my ideas will allow me, a description of this factory.

We sat down to dinner with the same party as the first day, consisting of about fifteen in number; this necessary ceremony ended, and towards the cool of the afternoon, I proposed walking for a while: Mr Tilly and a Mr Barber offered to accompany and show me the island, which not being objected to, we set out.

Adam's Town was the first place they took me to; it is so called from a native of that name, who has the management of all the gramattos, or the free black servants, but under the control of the Agent.[20]

The whole town consists of a street with about twenty-five houses on each side – on the right of all is Adam's house.

This building does not differ from the rest, except in size, being much more spacious than any other, and being barricaded with a mud wall; all of them are composed of thatch, wood, and clay, something resembling our poor cottages in many parts of England.

I went into several of them – saw nothing that did not discover the occupiers to be very clean and neat; in some was a block or two of wood, which served for chairs; a few wooden bowls or trenchers, and perhaps a pewter bason, and an iron pot, completed the whole of their furniture.

In every house I was accosted by whoever we found at home, in the Timmany language *Currea Yaa*, which signifies – How do you do, mother? – the most respectful way they can address any person.

Leaving the town, we proceeded first to the burying ground for Europeans, and then to that for the blacks; the only distinction between them was a few orange trees, that shaded two grave-stones at the former – one in memory of a Mr. Knight, who had died here after residing fifteen years as Agent – the other on the supposed grave of a

[20] Adam's gravestone, inscribed "Placed Over His Remains By The Proprietors Of This Island As A Tribute Of Gratitude For His Faithful Services" survives on the island, though now broken. There is still a chief on the mainland with the hereditary title "Bai Adam" who goes every year with his family to offer a sacrifice on the grave (information from Joe Opala).

Captain Tittle,[21] who was murdered by one Signior Domingo, a native chief, for (as Domingo asserts) being the cause of his son's death.[22]

The circumstance leading to the murder, and of the murder itself, has been represented to me nearly in the following words :

"One day while the son of Domingo was employed by Captain Tittle, as a gramatto, or pull away boy (African term for an Oar-man), Tittle's hat by accident blew overboard, and he insisted that the boy should jump into the water and swim after it, as the only means of saving his hat.

"The boy obstinately refused, saying he could not swim, and he should either be drowned, or the sharks would catch him; upon which Tittle pushed him into the water, and the poor boy was lost; but whether devoured by sharks, or suffocated by water, is immaterial, as he was never heard of, or seen, after.

"The father, though sorely grieved for his son's death, was willing to consider it accidental, and requested Tittle would supply him with a small quantity of rum to make a cry or lamentation in their country custom.

"The Captain, by promise, acquiesced to the demand, and sent him a cask; but, instead of Spirit, filled with emptyings from the *tubs* of his slaves.

"As soon as Domingo discovered this insult and imposition, he informed Tittle he must either submit to the decision of a Palaver, or he would put him to death if ever opportunity offered; but Tittle laughed at these threats, and disregarded them, vauntingly threw himself into the way of Domingo – while the trick played upon him, and the loss of his son were fresh in his memory.

"The African, however, instead of being daunted at the sight of this headstrong man, soon convinced him he was serious: he had Tittle seized, and after confining him some time in irons, without food, ordered him to be broken to death, which was executed under the inspection of the

---

[21] Knight's gravestone (but not Tittle's) survives. The inscription records his having resided "eighteen" years on the island (information from Joe Opala).

[22] Domingo, who was of Afro-Portuguese descent and a Roman Catholic, ruled from Royema, a town on the south shore of the estuary (Fyfe, *A History*, p. 44). In the various British records his name always appears in the Italian form "Signior", rather than the more appropriate Portuguese "Senhor".

injured father, and to the great joy and satisfaction of a multitude of spectators."

Not a sentence or hint of the affair is mentioned on the tombstone; the reason assigned for the omission, was a wish to obliterate the melancholy catastrophe, and a fear lest the record might be the means of kindling animosities at a future day.

Now, although I cannot without horror contemplate on the untimely end of this man, yet he assuredly in some degree merited it, if the account I have heard, and just now related to you, be true, which I have no reason to question; for he who unprovoked can wantonly rob a fellow creature of his life, deserves not life himself!

From the catacombs which lay at the south east end, we walked to the opposite point of the island; it is no great distance, for the whole island is very little more than a fourth of a mile in length, and scarcely a mile and a half in circumference.

Several rocks lay at a small distance from the shore at this end; they are by the natives called the Devil's Rocks – from a superstitious opinion that the *old Gentleman* resides either there or in the neighbourhood.[23]

Sammo, King of the Bulloms, comes to this place once a year to make a sacrifice and peace-offering to his Infernal Majesty.[24]

From this King, Messrs Anderson hold all their possessions here, and I understand they pay him an annual tribute – but to what amount I cannot say.

The King comes in person to receive his dues, which are paid him in his canoe, for he never ventures to put his foot on shore, as his *Gree Greemen,* or fortune-tellers, have persuaded him the island will sink under him, if ever he lands.

I am told at one time he suffered himself to be dragged up to the Factory House in his boat, but no argument was strong enough to seduce

[23] Temne fishermen still associate the rocks, and the island itself, with a "devil" or spirit (information from Joe Opala).

[24] As explained in the Introduction, the trading forts occupied by Europeans on the West African coast were always leased to the occupiers, not sold, so that the land they were built on remained in the ownership of an African landlord. The ruler on the adjacent Bulom Shore, the north bank of the estuary, who bore the title Bai Sama, received the annual rent for Bance Island. The present Paramount Chief of Loko Massama still lays claim to it (information from Joe Opala).

him to disembark, for he did not consider he incurred the penalty his prophets denounced while he continued in his canoe; though he could not avoid showing evident tokens of uneasiness, till he was safe afloat again.[25]

We now returned to the Factory, or as it is otherwise called, Bance Island House.

This building at a distance has a respectable and formidable appearance; nor has it much less upon a nearer investigation: I suppose it is about one hundred feet in length, and thirty in breadth, and contains nine rooms, on one floor, under which are commodious large cellars and store rooms; to the right is the kitchen, forge, &c, and to the left other necessary buildings, all of country stone, and surrounded with a prodigious thick lofty wall.

There was formerly a fortification in front of these houses, which was destroyed by a French frigate during the last war; at present several pieces of cannon are planted in the same place, but without embrasures or breast-work; behind the great house is the slave yard, and houses for accommodating the slaves.[26]

Delicacy, perhaps, prevented the gentlemen from taking me to see them; but the room where we dined looks directly into the yard.

Involuntarily I strolled to one of the windows a little before dinner, without the smallest suspicion of what I was to see – judge then what my astonishment and feelings were, at the sight of between two and three hundred victims, chained and parcelled out in circles, just satisfying the cravings of nature from a tub of rice placed in the centre of each circle.

Offended modesty rebuked me with a blush for not hurrying my eyes from such disgusting scenes; but whether fascinated by female curiosity, or whatever else, I could not withdraw myself for several minutes – while I remarked some whose hair was withering with age, reluctantly tasting

---

[25] A not uncommon stratagem used by African rulers to avoid putting themselves under European control.

[26] Despite its fortifications, it never resisted an enemy successfully, having been taken by French warships in 1704, by pirates in 1719 and 1720, by the armed retainers of a neighbouring Afro-Portuguese in 1728, and by the French again in 1779 (Fyfe, A History, pp. 4–5,7). It was to be taken yet again by the French in 1794 when the buildings Mrs Falconbridge described were destroyed. They were subsequently rebuilt, the ruins of this final structure being those that survive today.

their food – and others thoughtless from their youth, greedily devouring all before them; be assured I avoided the prospects from this side of the house ever after.

Having prolonged the time until nine at night, we returned to our floating prison, and what with the assiduity of the master in removing many inconveniences, my mind being more at ease, want of rest for two nights, and somewhat fatigued with the exercise of the day, I, thank God, slept charmingly, and the next morning we set sail for Robana, where we arrived about ten o'clock: I think it is called nine miles from Bance Island.

We went on shore, and rather caught his *Majesty* by surprise, for he was quite in *dishabille*; and at our approach retired in great haste.

I observed a person pass me in a loose white frock and trowsers, *whom I would not have suspected for a King!* if he had not been pointed out to me.

Mr Elliote and the *Queen* met us; and after introducing her Majesty and himself, we were then conducted to her house.

She behaved with much indifference, – told me, in broken English, the *King* would come presently – he was gone to *peginee* woman house to dress himself.[27]

After setting nigh half an hour, Naimbana made his appearance, and received us with seeming good will: he was dressed in a purple embroidered coat, white satin waistcoat and breeches, *thread stockings,* and his left side emblazoned with a flaming star; his legs to be sure were *harliquined,* by a number of holes in the stockings, through which his black skin appeared.

Compliments ended, Mr Falconbridge acquainted him with his errand, by a repetition of what he wrote the day before: and complained much of King Jemmy's injustice, in driving the settlers away, and burning their town.

The King answered through Elliote, (for he speaks but little English)

---

[27] By this period a distinctive form of English was already spoken, as a *lingua franca*, in coastal West Africa (see David Dalby, "The Place of Africa and Afro-America in the History of the English Language", in *African Language Review*, 9 (1970–71), pp. 287–9; Ian Hancock, "An Account of Anglophone Creole Origins", in P. Muysken and N. Smith (eds), *Substrata vs. Universals in Creole Genesis*, Amsterdam, 1986, pp. 71–103. It was influenced by the Portuguese-influenced speech previously current there for centuries. "*Peginee*" is a variant of Portuguese *pequeno/a* (small), which across the Atlantic became "pickaninny".

that Jemmy was partly right – the people had brought it on themselves; they had taken part with some Americans, with whom Jemmy had a dispute, and through that means drew the ill will of this man upon them, who had behaved, considering their conduct, as well as they merited; for he gave them three days notice before he burned their town, that they might remove themselves and all their effects away; that he (Naimbana) could not prudently re-establish them, except by consent of all the Chiefs – for which purpose he must call a court or palaver; but it would be seven or eight days before they could be collected; however he would send a summons to the different parties directly, and give Falconbridge timely advice when they were to meet.[28]

Falconbridge perceived clearly nothing was to be effected without a palaver, and unless the King's interest was secured his views would be frustrated, and his endeavours ineffectual; but how this was to be done, or what expedient to adopt, he was at a loss for.

He considered it impolitic to purchase his patronage by heavy presents, lest the other great men might expect the same; and he had it not in his power to purchase them all in the same way, as the scanty cargo of the *Lapwing* would not admit of it.

At length, trusting that the praise-worthy purposes he was aiming at insured him the assistance of the King of Kings, he resolved to try what good words would do.

Having prefaced his arguments with a small donation of rum, wine, cheese, and a gold laced hat (which Naimbana seemed much pleased with), Falconbridge began by explaining what advantages would accrue to his *Majesty*, and to all the inhabitants round about, by such an establishment as the St George's Bay Company were desirous of making – the good they wished to do – *their disinterestedness in point of obtaining wealth*,[29] and concluded by expostulating on the injustice and imposition of dispossessing the late settlers of the grounds and houses they occupied, which had been honestly purchased by Captain Thompson of the Navy, in the name of our gracious Sovereign, his Britannic Majesty.[30]

[28] An account of this episode, which confirms Naimbana's version, can be found in Fyfe, *A History*, pp. 24–5.

[29] As we shall see, she had her own reasons for putting these words in italics.

[30] Captain Thomas Boulden Thompson, RN, had been in charge of the expedition taking the "Black Poor" to Sierra Leone, and had made a treaty on their behalf with King Tom and other chiefs. The treaty is printed in Christopher Fyfe, *Sierra Leone Inheritance*, London, 1964, pp. 112–13.

That it was unusual for Englishmen to forgo fulfilling any engagements they made; and they held in detestation every person so disposed.

He then entreated the King would use all his might to prevent any unfavourable prejudices which a refusal to reinstate the Settlers, or to confirm the bargain made with Captain Thompson, might operate against him in the minds of his good friends the King of England and the St George's Bay Company.

The King said he liked the English in preference to all white men, tho' he considered every white man as a *rogue,* and consequently saw them with a jealous eye; yet, he believed the English were by far the honestest, and for that reason, notwithstanding he had received more favours from the French than the English, he liked the latter much best.

He was decidedly of opinion, that all contracts or agreements between man and man however disadvantageous to either party should be binding; but observed he was *hastily drawn in* to dispose of land to Captain Thompson, *which in fact he had not a right to sell,* because says he, "this is a great country, and belongs to many people – where I live belongs to myself – and I can live where I like; nay, can appropriate any unin-habited land within my dominions to what use I please; but it is necessary for me to obtain the consent of my people, or rather the head man of every town, before I sell any land to a white man, or allow strangers to come and live among us.

"*I should have done this you will say at first* – Granted – but as I disobliged my subjects by suffering your people to take possession of the land without their approbation, from which cause I was not able to protect them, unless I hazarded civil commotions in my country; and as they have been *turned away* – it is best now – they should be replaced by the unanimous voice of all interested.

"I am bound from what I have heretofore done, to give my utmost support; and if my people do not acquiesce, it shall not be my fault."

Here Falconbridge, interrupting the King, said – "The King of the English will not blame your people, but load yourself with the stigma; it is King *Naimbana* who is ostensible to King *George* – and I hope King, you will not fall out with your good friend".

This being explained by *Mr Secretary Elliotte,* his Majesty was for some moments silent – when clasping Falconbridge in his arms, told him –

"*I believe you and King George* are my good friends – do not fear, have a good heart, I will do as much as I can for you".

They then shook hands heartily, and Naimbana retired, I suppose to his *Peginee woman's house,* but presently returned dressed in a suit of black velvet, except the stockings, which were the same as before.

I often had an inclination to offer my services to close the holes: but was fearful lest my needle might blunder into his *Majesty's* leg, and start the blood, for drawing the blood of an African King, I am informed, whether occasioned by accident or otherwise, is punished with death; the dread of this only prevented me.

We were now invited to walk and see the town, while dinner was preparing.

It consists of about twenty houses irregularly placed, built of the same materials, but in a superior way to those of Adam's town – the whole of them are either occupied by the King's wives and servants, or appropriated as warehouses.

I saw several of his wives, but his *Peginee* woman is a most beautiful girl of about fourteen.

None of them are titled with the appellation of *Queen* but the oldest, who I was introduced to, and by whom the King has several children; one of the daughters, named Clara, is wife to Elliotte, and a son named Bartholomew, is now in France for his education.

In different parts of the town I observed some rags stuck on poles; at the foot of each were placed – perhaps a rusty cutlass, some pieces of broken glass, and a pewter bason, containing liquid of some sort; these are called *Gree Grees,* and considered as antidotes against the Devil's vengeance.

I was thoughtlessly offering to examine one of them, when Mr Elliotte requested me to desist, or I should give offence, they being held in a very sacred point of view.

We were now led to the garden, which was only furnished with African plants, such as pines, melons, pumpkins, cucumbers, &c. &c.

The King cut two beautiful pines and presented to me: he then showed us a large new house, at present building for him, which is after the same form, and of much the same materials, with the rest of his town, but much larger.

In our walk we saw many of the King's slaves employed in preparing the palm-nuts, to make oil from them: It may not be amiss here to give you some description of the tree which produces these nuts.

It is remarkably strait and of gigantic height; the trunk is quite naked, having neither limb or bark, for the only branches grow immediately from the top, and incline their points somewhat towards the ground.

This is a valuable tree, the nut not only produces a quantity of oil, but is esteemed excellent food by the natives, who also extract a liquor from the tree, which they call palm wine.

This I am told is done by means of an incision in the upper part of the trunk, in which a pipe is entered to convey the liquor into bottles placed beneath.

I have tasted some of this wine, and do not think it unpleasant when fresh made; it has a sweetish taste, and much the look of whey, but ferments in a few days, and grows sour – however I really think this liquor distilled would make a decent kind of spirit.

Having seen all the raree-shows of Robana town, we returned to the Queen's house to dinner, which was shortly after put on a table covered with a plain calico cloth, and consisted of boiled and broiled fowls, rice, and some greens resembling our spinage.

But I should tell you, before dinner Naimbana again changed his dress for a scarlet robe embroidered with gold.

Naimbana, Elliotte, Falconbridge and myself only set down; the Queen stood behind the King eating an onion I gave her, a bite of which she now and then indulged her *Royal Consort* with: silver forks were placed on the King's plate, and mine, but nowhere else.

The King is rather above common height, but meagre withal; the features of his face resemble a European more than any black I have seen; his teeth are mostly decayed, and his hair, or rather wool, bespeaks old age, which I judge to be about eighty; he was seldom without a smile on his countenance, but I think his smiles were suspicious.

He gave great attention while Falconbridge was speaking, for though he does not speak our language, he understands a good deal of it; his answers were slow, and on the whole tolerably reasonable. The Queen is of a middle stature, plump and jolly; her temper seems placid and accommodating; her teeth are bad, but I dare say she has been a good looking woman in her youthful days.

I suppose her now to be about forty-five or six, at which age women are considered old here.

She sat on the King's right hand while he and Falconbridge were in conversation; and now and then would clap her hands, and cry out *Ya hoo,* which signifies, that's well or proper.

She was dressed in the country manner, but in a dignified style, having several yards of striped taffety wrapped round her waist, which served as a petticoat; another piece of the same was carelessly thrown over her shoulders in form of a scarf; her head was decorated with two silk handkerchiefs; her ears with rich gold ear-rings, and her neck with gaudy necklaces; *but she had neither shoes nor stockings on.*

Clara was dressed after the same way, but her apparel was not quite of such good materials as the Queen's: Mr Elliotte apologised after dinner, that for want of *sugar* they could not offer tea or coffee.

The tide serving, and approaching night, obliged us to re-embark and return to this place.

On the whole I was much pleased with the occurrences of the day; indeed, methinks, I hear you saying, "Why the weak mind of this giddy girl will be quite intoxicated with the courtesy and attention paid her by such great folks"; but believe me, to whatever height of self-consequence I may have been lifted by aerial fancies, overpowering sleep prevailed, and clouding all my greatness – I awoke next morning without the slightest remains of fancied importance.

The news of our arrival having by this time circulated through different parts of the country, we found several, who either excited by curiosity or some other cause, had come here to pay their obeisance, or as the Africans term it, *make service* to us; but there was none of note or quality worth naming among those visitors, except an elderly man called *Pa, or Father, Boson,* who is the head man of a considerable town about fifty miles up the river, and who, guided by the impulse of a good heart, invited the wretched exiles in the hour of distress to refuge at his place, which was accepted by the greater part, who have been fostered and protected ever since by the almsdeeds of this good old man; he was habited in a white linen surplice, and a cap of the same, and made, I assure you a reverential appearance.

I am told this is the dress of a nation in the interior country, called Mundingoes; but Pa Boson is not a Mundingo himself.[31]

He respectfully accosted me in broken English, and bending his knee, offered me his right hand supported under the elbow by his left.

I held out my hand which he slightly touched, and then repeated the same to Falconbridge: he was now invited to be seated under the awning we had erected over the *Lapwing's* deck – when he detailed a most pitiable account of sufferings and hardships which the unfortunate people had undergone; but he said there were many bad people among them, who had abused his kindness by ingratitude.

Falconbridge and myself endeavoured what we could to convince him we were highly pleased with his behaviour; but as words are not sufficient to convey thankful acknowledgments in this country, Falconbridge confirmed the assurances we made by a present of a quantity of rum, and some hard ware, and a promise to represent his conduct to the St George's Bay Company in a proper light, which he was certain would induce them to make a more ample recompense at a future time.

Well pleased with his reception, and somewhat inebriated with the effects of repeated glasses of spirits he had taken, Pa Boson left us; but first promising faithfully he would befriend us all in his power at the Palaver.

He travelled with much seeming consequence: his canoe was longer than our cutter, and manned by fourteen people, viz. ten oarsmen, a cockswain, two poignard bearers, and another who beat time on a flat sounding drum to a song given out by the coxswain, and re-echoed by the oarsmen; the song I am told was expressive of praises to their Chief, and of their satisfaction for the treatment they had received from us.

The following day we visited a small island named Tasso, opposite Bance Island, at about one mile and a half distance. This is a well wooded island and I should suppose if cultivated would be a fruitful one.*

* A small part of this island is now planted with cotton, coffee, and sugar cane, for account of Messrs Anderson.

[31] Many of the inland "Mundingo" (Mandinka) people, who traded regularly with the coastal peoples, were Muslims, and wore the customary Muslim white robe.

It supplies Bance Island with water, which is remarkably fine, and the present holders of the latter claim a right to this also, but upon what grounds I cannot say.

Approaching the shore I saw many monkeys playing on the beach and catching small fish at the edge of the water, but they all ran away as we drew near; being informed there was no danger to be apprehended from wild beasts of prey, we penetrated some distance into the woods.

In our walk we saw many pine apples and lime trees, the spontaneous production of the country, and a variety of birds beautifully plumed, but none that sung.

We were also treated with the perfumes of fragrant aromatic plants, and indeed were vastly delighted, and entertained, though I felt fatigued, with our perambulation.

The next day, we went up the river, about twelve miles, to see a secret or reserved factory belonging to Bance Island, at a place called Marre Bump, but our curiosity had nearly led us into a serious scrape.

Falconbridge neglected to obtain permission, and consequently had no sanction, from the Proprietors.

After landing we walked, at least half a mile on a narrow path, through amazing thick woods before we reached the houses; as soon as the inhabitants perceived us, the women took to their heels and ran to the woods, the men flew to arms, and in a moment we were met by more than twenty huge fellows armed with guns, pistols and cutlasses.

We were four in number, viz. Falconbridge, the master of the cutter, a Black man and myself; our Black spoke to them in their own language – they would not listen to him; but said, if we did not return immediately, they would put us all to death.

It is easier for you to imagine what horrors those threats occasioned, than for me to point them out.

Finding argument fruitless, we put to the right about, and hastened to our boat; they, following, flanked us on each side of the road, watchfully observing our motions till they saw us clear off, when, as a mark of exultation, they discharged their muskets over our heads, and made the woods ring with peals of triumphant clamour.

Recovering from my fright a little, I could not help, you may suppose, exulting (though in a different way) as well as the savages.

My heart overflowed with gratitude, to the Author of its animation, for our providential escape.

Returning down the river, we observed numbers of orange trees; a cluster of them, overloaded with fruit, invited us on shore, and after gathering what we chose, made the best of our way, and arrived here before night.

Three days are now elapsed since our expedition to Marre Bump, during which time I have confined myself mostly on board, occupied in writing this letter.

It has been, really, a fatiguing job, being obliged to sit in bed with a book placed on my knee, which serves for a writing desk; but I was determined whatever the inconveniences might be, not to let slip an opportunity, as I find they but seldom offer.

I lament the Palaver is not over, that I might give you an account of an African Court, but my next will remedy this loss.

Mr Elliotte has informed us the Chiefs will be at Robana the day after tomorrow, when Falconbridge is desired to attend; I shall accompany him, and long to know the result.

Adieu, Heaven bless you, &c. &c.

LETTER III [*sic*]

My dear Friend,

Occasional visits to Bance Island, unattended by any important Occurrence worth troubling you with, and a continual concourse of strangers making their African compliments, engrossed two days interval between the date of my last letter, and our second expedition to Robana, when we set out in a boat and four hands, taking with us plenty of spirits for the common people, and a little wine for the King and his associates.

When we came in sight of the Town, multitudes of people thronged the Beach.

Mr Elliotte met us at the boat, and the crowd formed an avenue, through which he conducted us to the Queen's house, amidst such thundering acclamations, that it was almost impossible to hear one or other speak.

The King and Queen met us at the door, and seemed to give us a hearty welcome.

We were then ushered in, and introduced in general terms to the company, consisting of the parties who were to compose the Court, and a multiplicity of women, their wives, daughters, and attendants.

Having seated ourselves, and wasted almost an hour in receiving the civilities of shaking hands with every individual in the room, the members of the Court then took their seats, round the large table we dined off, when first there, which was now covered with a green cloth.

The King sat at the head of the table in an old arm chair: on his right was his secretary, and on his left his Palaver man; or, as his office is termed in England, his Attorney general: the other Chiefs appeared to seat themselves by seniority; the oldest next the *Throne,* if I may so term the *old chair.*

The King wore his hat, which was the gold laced one Falconbridge gave him.

On the table was placed wine and rum, of which every one helped himself plentifully.

I was astonished to see, not only the men, but women drink rum in half pints at a time, as deliberately as I would water.

After amusing themselves some time in this way, Mr Palaver Man got up, bending his right knee, presented his *Majesty* with some Cola* from the crown of his hat, then retired to the opposite end of the table, when he opened the business of the day, by a speech of at least an hour and a half long; it being in their own language, I, of course, did not understand a word, but during the time he spoke, there was the greatest silence and attention observed.

* A fruit much esteemed in Africa, not unlike a horse chestnut, but somewhat larger. It is an excellent bitter.

The next spokesman, was King Jemmy, who previously went through the same ceremony his predecessor had done: whether this man's language was eloquent or not, I cannot judge, but his vociferation was enough to deafen one; though I had reason to think what he said gave great satisfaction to the by-standers, who frequently interrupted him by clapping of hands and shouts of, *Ya Hoo! Ya Hoo! Ya Hoo!* and other tokens of applause.

My heart quivered with fear lest they might be forming some treacherous contrivance: I could not conceal the uneasiness it felt: My countenance betrayed me, a shower of tears burst from my eyes, and I swooned into hystericks.

Recovering in a short time, I observed every one around treating me with the utmost kindness, and endeavouring to convince me that neither insult or injury would be offered to us: but my fears were not to be removed, or even checked hastily, for I had scarcely got the better of my fright at Marre Bump; however I struggled to awaken my resolution, and collected enough, after a while, to affect composure; but believe me it was mere affectation. Night was drawing nigh, and I solicited Falconbridge to return as soon as possible. He argued the Court had been impeded by the awkward situation my fears had thrown me into: but he would set out time enough to reach *Bance Island* before dark.

The Assembly now resumed their business.

Falconbridge told Naimbana, he would be very glad to take his son to England, where he was sure the Company would have him educated and treated kindly without considering him a hostage.

This pleased the old man vastly, and it was agreed, John Frederic shall accompany us, when we leave Africa.

The following, or sixth day, Falconbridge had engaged to carry down to Robana the stipulated goods for repurchasing the land, and by his importunities I was prevailed on to accompany him. We arrived early in the morning, and having soon made a delivery of the goods, which was all the business of the day, I was just about expressing a desire to see some salt works I learned were upon the Island, when the King, as though he had anticipated my wishes, enquired if we liked to see them? If so, he would walk there with us. We accordingly went, passing in our way a hamlet or two, inhabited by the King's slaves.

These works lay near a mile from the town, and are a parcel of small holes, or basons formed in a low muddy place; they are supplied with seawater, which the burning sun quickly exhales, leaving the saline particles, and by frequent repetition, a quantity of salt is thus accumulated, which the King conveys into, and disposes of, in the interior country, for slaves.[35]

Making this salt is attended with a very trifling expense, for none but *old, refuse, female* slaves are employed in the work, and the profit is considerable.

Early in the afternoon we returned to Bance Island, taking Clara, the wife of Elliotte, with us. She remained with me several days, during which I had the opportunities (for I made a point of it) to try her disposition; I found it impetuous, litigious and implacable. I endeavoured to persuade her to dress in the European way, but to no purpose; she would tear the clothes off her back immediately after I put them on.

(see *footnote* 24). The treaty however declared the land to be permanently alienated to the settlers. This misunderstanding, which persistently confused and embittered relations between the Colony government and its Temne neighbours, was to lead to wars in 1801 and 1802, and ultimately to the expulsion of the Temne from the whole northern shore of the peninsula and to its annexation in 1807 (Fyfe, *A History*, pp. 96–7).

[35] Matthews (see *footnote* 16) described how the local salt industry was protected from foreign competition : " ... the natives of the sea-coast will not permit the import of it in European vessels, because it would interfere with the only article of their own manufacture which they have for inland trade" (Matthews, *A Voyage*, p. 146).

Finding no credit could be gained by trying to new fashion this *Ethiopian* Princess, I got rid of her as soon as possible.

Falconbridge now had effected the grand object; he was next to collect and settle the miserable refugees. No time was to be lost in accomplishing this; the month of February was nearly spent, only three months of dry weather remained for them to clear their land, build their houses, and prepare their ground for a crop to support them the ensuing year. He therefore dispatched a Greek, who came out in the *Lapwing*,[36] with some of the blacks, up to Pa Boson's, to gather and bring down the people, while we went in the Cutter, taking a few who were at Bance Island, to locate an eligible place, for the settlement.

The spot they were driven from was to be preferred to any other part; but by treaty it was agreed they should not settle there. There were other situations nearly as good, and better considerably than the one fixed on, but immediate convenience was a powerful inducement.

Here was a small village, with seventeen pretty good huts, which the natives had evacuated from a persuasion they were infected by some evil spirits; but as they made no objection to our occupying them, we gladly took possession, considering it a fortunate circumstance to have such temporary shelter for the whole of our people.

When those from Pa Boson's had joined us, Falconbridge called them all together, making forty-six, including men and women; and after representing the charitable intentions of his coming to Africa, and issuing to them such clothing as were sent out in the *Lapwing*, he exhorted in the most pathetic language, that they might merit by their industry and good behaviour the notice now taken of them, endeavour to remove the unfavourable prejudices that had gone abroad, and thereby deserve further favours from their friends in England; who, besides the clothes they had already received, had sent them tools of all kinds, for cultivating their land, also arms and ammunition to defend themselves, if necessary; that these articles would be brought on shore when they got a storehouse built, where they would be lodged for the common good and occasional use; he then concluded by saying – he named the place GRANVILLE TOWN, after their friend and

---

[36] Theodore Kalingee — he was Falconbridge's servant (Fyfe, *A History*, p. 30).

benefactor, GRANVILLE SHARP, Esq. at whose instance they were
provided with the relief now afforded them.[37]

I never did, and God grant I never may again, witness so much misery
as I was forced to be a spectator of here: Among the outcasts were
seven of our countrywomen, decrepid with disease, and so disguised
with filth and dirt, that I should never have supposed they were born
white; add to this, almost naked from head to foot; in short, their
appearance was such as I think would extort compassion from the most
callous heart; but I declare they seemed insensible to shame, or the
wretchedness of their situation themselves. I begged they would get
washed, and gave them what clothes I could conveniently spare. Falconbridge had a hut appropriated as a hospital, where they were kept
separate from the other settlers, and by his attention and care, they
recovered in a few weeks.

I had always supposed these people had been transported as convicts,
but some conversation I lately had with one of the women, has partly
undeceived me: She said the women were mostly of that description of
persons who walk the streets of London, and support themselves by the
earnings of prostitution; that men were employed to collect and conduct
them to Wapping, where they were intoxicated with liquor, then inveigled
on board of ship, and married to *Black men*, whom they had never seen
before; that the morning after she was married, she really did not
remember a syllable of what had happened over the night, and when
informed, was obliged to inquire *who was her husband?* After this, to
the time of their sailing, they were amused and buoyed up by a prodigality
of fair promises, and great expectations which awaited them in the
country they were going to. "Thus", in her own words, "to the disgrace
of my mother country, upwards of one hundred unfortunate women,
were seduced from England to practise their iniquities more brutishly
in this horrid country".

Good heaven! How the relation of this tale made me shudder – I
questioned its veracity, and enquired of the other women who exactly
corroborated what I had heard; nevertheless, I cannot altogether reconcile
myself to believe it; for it is scarcely possible that the British Government,
at this advanced and enlightened age, envied and admired as it is by the

[37] This name had originally been given to the settlement burnt down by King Jemmy,
a couple of miles to the west — the site on which Freetown was subsequently built.

universe, could be capable of exercising or countenancing such a Gothic infringement on human Liberty.[38]

Immediately after we had fixed on this Place for the settlement, I singled out one of the best huts for my own residence, where I remained nigh a month, though I did not sleep on shore the whole time. About a fortnight I continued to go on board the Cutter at night; when it was necessary to send her to Bance Island, I then had a kind of bedstead, not unlike an hospital cradle, erected in my hovel; but the want of a door was some inconvenience, and as no deal, or other boards could be procured for the purpose, I made a country mat supply the place – for I now find 'tis necessary to accommodate myself to whatever I meet with, there being but few conveniences or accommodating things in this part of Africa.

The river abounds with fine fish, and we get abundance of them; which, with rice, wild deer, and some poultry, forms my common food since I came to Granville Town.

In something less than four weeks we got a large store house and several additional huts for the settlers built, and had the goods landed from the *Lapwing* – they consist chiefly of ironmongery, such as black-smiths and plantation tools, a prodigious number of children's trifling *half-penny knives,* and some few dozen scissors of the same *description.*

[38] The story of this "Gothic infringement on human Liberty" has been repeated again and again. But the details are dubious. The very comprehensive official papers dealing with the embarkation of the "Black Poor", and listing the white women passengers, give no hint of their having been abducted (PRO, series T1, in bundles 630–38, 641–43). More significantly, the London newspapers, most of which were extremely hostile to the scheme, and gave it a lot of adverse publicity, did not mention something that would have been ready-made to discredit it, if it had been authentic. Such "marriages" were not valid under the then English law, and as several months elapsed between the period when the women embarked, and their final sailing for Sierra Leone, anyone who had wanted to, could have gone ashore. So even if brought on board in a drunken state, they must have agreed to stay — indeed at least a dozen of them signed the agreement signed by the other settlers contracting themselves to be bound by the rules of the settlement. Moreover, on 28 November 1786, while they were waiting to embark, John Lettsom, a friend of Sharp's, wrote in a letter, "As there are more black men than women the girls of Wapping are petitioning to marry the black men, in order to accompany them on board this expedition" (C. M. Morris (ed.), *Papers of William Thornton*, Charlotteville, 1995, vol. I, pp. 36–7 – I am grateful to Marika Sherwood who supplied me with this reference). Nor were there "upwards of one hundred". The sailing lists show sixty-three "White Women married to Black Men", and another seven "White Women waiting to be married" (PRO, T1/643.487).

I am *charitable enough* to think the *benevolent gentleman,* who purchased those goods, had a double purpose in view, viz. to serve his sister from whom he bought them [39] – and the persons to whom they are sent; but certainly he was unacquainted with the quality of the latter articles, or he must have known they were very improper gifts of charity.

A part of the store-house being partitioned off for us, we took up our abode there whenever it was ready for our reception – it is rather larger, and consequently more cool, which is the only preference I can give it to the last habitation.

The men all do duty as militia, and we have constant guard kept during the night; but the natives seem to dread this spot so much, that we see very few, and I really think we have less to fear from them than from our own people, who are extremely turbulent, and so unruly at times, that with difficulty Falconbridge can assuage them, or preserve the least decorum.

He was desired by the Company to build a fort, and they sent out six pieces of cannon, which are now on board the *Lapwing* – but omitted to *send carriages,* and consequently the guns are useless; though if they were complete, Falconbridge thinks it would not be prudent to trust them with the present settlers, from a belief that they might apply them improperly.

He is also requested by his instructions to collect as many samples of country productions as he can, and wished to employ some of the people in that way, but none of them would give their services for less than half a guinea a day, which price he has been forced to pay them; this is the greatest instance of ingratitude I ever met with.

We were alarmed a little while since by dreadful shouts, in the vicinity of our town, and supposed the natives meant to attack us; immediately Falconbridge armed his militia, and marched out towards where the noise was heard; they had not gone far when they met three or four *Panyarers,*[40] or man thieves, just in the act of ironing a poor victim they had caught hunting, and the shouts we heard proved to be the rejoicings of the banditti.

---

[39] Granville Sharp's brother James was a London ironmonger. When he died, Sharp managed the business for his widow (P. Hoare, *Memoirs of Granville Sharp,* London, 1820, p. 383); in eighteenth century usage "sister" could include sister-in-law. These two paragraphs, reflecting unfavourably on Sharp, may well have been added later.

[40] Another word from Portuguese, *apanhar,* to catch.

Falconbridge did not think it advisable to rescue the prisoner by force, or to interfere further than what words would do; and as some of the *Panyarers* spoke English, he remonstrated against the devilish deed they were committing, but to little effect.

They said somebody belonging to the prisoner's town had injured them, and it was the custom of the country to retaliate on any person living in the same place with an offender, if they could not get himself, which the present case was an example of.[41]

They then carried him away, and in all probability this man will be deprived of his liberty while he lives, by the barbarous customs of his country, for the imaginary offences of another.

I omitted mentioning in my last letter, that the day after we arrived at Bance Island, Mr William Falconbridge, in consequence of a trifling dispute with his brother, separated from us, and went into the service of Messrs Anderson's, but his constitution was not adapted for this unhospitable climate.

He went down the coast to York Island, in the river Sherbro, about twenty leagues distance, where he was unavoidably exposed to the severity of the weather, from which he got a fever; and although he immediately returned to Bance Island, and had every assistance administered, yet, I am sorry to say, the irresistible conqueror, *Death*, made all endeavours fruitless, and hurried him to eternity yesterday, after a short illness of four days.

The tornados, or thunder squalls, which set in at this season of the year, preceding the continued rains, have commenced some time, the vivid intense lightning from dismal black clouds, make them awfully beautiful; they are accompanied with violent winds and heavy rains, succeeded by an abominable stench from the earth, and disagreeable hissings and noises from frogs, crickets, and many other insects which the rains draw out.

Musquettos also are growing so troublesome, as to oblige us to keep continued smokes in and about the house.

---

[41] The custom was also sometimes practised against Europeans. If a white ship's captain kidnapped someone, the people might retaliate on the next ship that came from his port of origin (John Newton, *Thoughts upon the African Slave Trade*, London, 1788, p. 22).

I have not seen any serpents, but am told there are abundance, and some very venemous.

Here are a vast quantity of beautiful lizards constantly about the door catching flies: and I have often seen the changeable chameleon.

We have not yet been troubled by any of the ferocious wild beasts which inhabit the mountains of Sierra Leone; but I understand there are numbers, both tygers and lions, besides divers other kinds.

I have now in spirits an uncommon insect, which was caught here a day or two ago, in the act of stinging a *Lascar* (one of the settlers);[42] it is rather larger than a locust, covered with a tortoise coloured shell, has forceps like a lobster, and thin transparent wings like a fly; the bite has thrown the poor Lascar into a dreadful fever, which I fear will carry him off.

I have three monkeys, one a very handsome Capuchin, with a sulphur coloured beard of great length.

Nature seems to have been astonishingly sportive in taste and prodigality here, both of vegetable and animal productions, for I cannot stir out without admiring the beauties or deformities of her creation.

Every thing I see is entirely new to me, and notwithstanding the eye quickly becomes familiarized, and even satiated, with views which we are daily accustomed to; yet there is such a variety here as to afford a continual zest to the sight.

To be frank, if I had a little agreeable society, a few comforts, and could ensure the same good health I have hitherto enjoyed, I should not be against spending some years of my life in Africa; but wanting those sweetners of life, I certainly wish to return to where they may be had.

When that will be, it is not in my power at present to tell; but if I have a chance of writing to you again, I then may be able; in the interim accept an honest farewell from

Your affectionate, &c.

---

[42] The "Black Poor" included a few Lascar seamen stranded in London (for whom see Rozina Visram, *A Long Presence: Asians in Britain, a History, 1600–1947*, London, forthcoming).

LETTER IV

My dear Madam,

Since my last visit I have been to the French Factory, visited several neighbouring towns, and made myself a little intimate with the history, manners, customs, &c. of the inhabitants of this part of Africa, which, it seems, was first discovered by the Portuguese, who named it *Sierra de Leone,* or *Mountain of Lions.*

The tract of country now called Sierra Leone, is a Peninsula one half of the year, and an island the other – that is, during the rains the Isthmus is overflowed.

The river, which was formerly called *Tagrin,* now takes its name from the country; at its entrance it is about ten miles from one Promontory to the other, but here, it is scarcely half that distance across, and a few miles higher up it becomes very narrow indeed.

It is not navigable for large vessels any higher than Bance Island, but small craft may go a great distance up.

Besides the islands I have mentioned, there are several others, uninhabited, between this and Bance Island.

Granville Town is situated in a pretty deep bay, on the south side of the river, about nine miles above Cape Sierra Leone* fifteen below Bance Island, and six from Robana.

* The Cape lies in 8.28. N. Lat. – 12.30. W. Long.

Half a mile below us is the town of one *Pa Duffee,* two miles lower down is *King Jemmy's,* and beyond him is *Queen Yamacubba's,* and two or three small places; a mile above us *Signior Domingo* lives, and a little higher one *Pa Will.*

I have been at all these places, and find a great similitude in the appearance of the people, their behaviour, mode of living, building, amusements, &c.

The men are tall and stout, and was it not that their legs are generally small in proportion to their bodies, and somewhat crooked, I should call them well limbed.

The mode of treating infants till they are able to walk, accounts for their being bandy legged.

A few days after a woman is delivered, she takes her child on her back to wherever her vocation leads her, with both its legs buckled round her waist, and the calves pressed to her sides, by which means the tender bones are forced from their natural shape, and get a curve that never after grows out; and thus, the infant is exposed either to the scorching sun, or any change of weather that happens.

The women are not nigh so well shaped as the men; being employed in all hard labour, makes them robust and clumsy; they are very prolific, and keep their breasts always suspended, which, after bearing a child or two, stretches out to an enormous length, disgusting to Europeans, though considered *beautiful* and ornamental here.

They are not only obliged to till the ground, and do all laborious work, but are kept at a great distance by the men, who seldom suffer a woman to sit down or eat with them.

The day I dined at King Naimbana's, he told me I was the first woman that ever eat at the same table with him.

Great respect and reverence is shown to old age, by all ranks of people.

Polygamy likewise is considered honourable, and creates consequence.

When an African speaks of a great man, he or she will say, "Oh! he be fine man, rich too much, he got too much woman".

The higher class of people hereabouts mostly speak broken English, which they have acquired from frequent intercourse with vessels that come to purchase slaves.

They seem desirous to give education to their children or in their own way of expressing it, "Read book, and learn to be *rogue* so well as white man"; for they say that if white men could not read or wanted education, they would be no better rogues than *black gentlemen.*

I was treated with the utmost hospitality at every town I visited.

Their common food is rice, pepper pot, or palaver sauce, palm nuts, and palm oil; with the latter both sexes anoint their bodies and limbs daily, though it does not prevent them from smelling vastly strong.

Wherever I went, there was commonly a fowl boiled or broiled for me: I liked the pepper pot, it is a kind of soup made with a mixture of vegetables highly seasoned with salt and red pepper.

Their houses are much like those I have heretofore described, but very low, they are irregularly placed, and built either in a square or circular form; and as this part of the country is thinly inhabited, each town contains very few houses.

The inhabitants are chiefly Pagans, though they credit the existence of a God, but consider him so good that he cannot do them an injury; they therefore pay homage to the Devil, from a belief that he is the only Supernatural Being they have to fear; and I am informed they have consecrated places in different parts of the woods, where they make annual sacrifices to him.

Cleanliness is universally observed; their simple furniture, consisting generally of a few mats, wooden trenchers and spoons made by themselves, are always tidy, and their homely habitations constantly clean swept, and free from filth of any kind: nor do I think nature has been so unkind to endow those people with capacities less susceptible of improvement and cultivation than any other part of the human race.

I am led to this conjecture, from the quickness with which even those who cannot understand English, comprehend my meanings by gestures or signs, and the aptness they have imitated many things after me.

Their time is calculated by plantations, moons, and days; the reason of the first is, they clear a new field once a year, and if asked the age of a child, or any thing else, they will answer, so many plantations, in place of years: they register their moons by notches on a piece of wood which is carefully hanged up in some particular part of the house.

Their chief amusement is dancing: in the evening men and women assemble in the most open part of the town, where they form a circle, which one at a time enters, and shows his skill and agility, by a number of wild comical motions.

Their music is made by clapping of hands, and a harsh sounding drum or two, made out of hollowed wood covered with the skin of a goat.

Sometimes I have seen an instrument resembling our guitar, the country name of which is *bangeon*.[43]

The company frequently applaud or upbraid the performer, with bursts of laughter, or some odd disagreeable noise; if it is moonshine, and they have spirits to drink, these dances probably continue until the moon goes down, or until day light.

The *Timmany* dialect is commonly spoke here, though the nation so called is some distance to the northward.

The natives account for this in the following way.

Many years ago the Burees, a tribe of people formerly living upon the banks of the river Sierra Leone, were conquered and drove away to other parts of the country by the Timmanys, who having possessed themselves of the land, invited many strangers to come and live among them.

The Timmanys being again engaged in war, which the inhabitants of Sierra Leone did not choose to join in, they therefore alienated the connection, and declared themselves a distinct nation, and have been considered as such ever since.[44]

Every chief or head man of a town is authorized from the King to settle local disputes – but when disagreements arise between people of separate places, then a Palaver is summoned to the residence of the complainant, when the King attends or not as suits him; but if inconvenient to go in person, he sends his Palaver-man, who carries the King's sword, or hat, as a signal of inauguration to his office.

When all the parties are met, they enquire into the business of their meeting, and a majority of voices determine who has *reason* of his or her side.

If the crime is fornication, the punishment is slavery, unless the offender can ransom him or herself, by paying another slave, or the equivalent in goods.

It is customary when the *Judges* cannot procure sufficient proof, to

---

[43] Though the *Oxford English Dictionary* (2nd edition, 1989) declares the word *banjo* a "corruption of *bandore*", a musical instrument of impeccably Greek and Roman origin, it seems more plausible to imagine that it passed into Anglo-Caribbean and Anglo-American speech via Temne.

[44] She was given a version of the standard Temne tradition which represents them as originally an inland people who conquered the coastal region.

oblige the party accused to take a poisonous draught, called Red Water; this potion is prepared by the *Judges* themselves, who make it strong or weak, as they are inclined by circumstances – if strong, and the stomach does not reject it instantaneously, death soon ensues – but if weak, it seldom has any other effect than a common emetic.

At the last town I visited, the head man's favourite woman, had a beautiful *mulatto* child, and seeing me take much notice of it, he said, "God amity sen me dat peginine, true, suppose he no black like me, nutting for dat, my woman drinkee red water, and suppose peginine no for me, he dead".[45]

I could not help smiling at the old fool's credulity, and thinking how happy many of my own countrywomen would be to rid themselves of a similar stigma so easily.

Crimes of larger magnitude, such as *witchcraft*, murder, &c are punished in the same way, i.e. the criminal is obliged to drink of this liquor, unless there be evidence sufficiently strong to acquit or condemn him: when that is the case, if convicted, he either suffers death, or is sold as a slave.

On the opposite shore lives a populous nation called the Bulloms, whose King I had occasion to mention in a former letter.[46] I have been at only one of their settlements, a place directly over against us, belonging to a man called Dean.

The people appear more inclined to industry than the Sierra Leoneans, which a stranger may readily discern, by a superior way their houses are furnished in.

I am told it is a fertile country, and the inhabitants make so much rice, that they are able to sell a quantity annually.

In the neighbourhood of Dean's Town, at a place called Tagrin Point, was formerly an English factory, belonging to one Marshall; but he unluckily got into a dispute with the natives, who drove him away, and pillaged his goods; they are a barbarous, implacable sort of people.

[45] In the coastal *lingua franca* (*footnote* 27) "he" included "she".
[46] See *footnote* 24. At that period the northern shore was still controlled and inhabited by the Bulom (Sherbro) people, who also occupied the country to the south of the peninsula. Today they have been largely replaced on the northern shore by Temne and Susu.

This is all the history I have learnt of the Bulloms, therefore I shall return to my own side of the water.

We have had heavy tornados and falls of rain for several weeks, and I yet enjoy my health as well, if not better, than I did for several years past in Europe.

Deaths are not frequent among the natives; indeed I have not heard of one since we arrived.

Their national diseases are few; probably anointing themselves as they do with palm oil, makes them less liable to evil consequences from the unhealthy putrid vapour that almost constantly hovers about these mountains, the poisonous effects of which carries off numbers of foreigners.

About ten days ago the master of the cutter went to Bance Island, where he drank too freely, and returning a little indisposed, signified a wish of going to the French factory for medical assistance.

Falconbridge, having had some difference with this man, therefore, lest he might wrong construe any offers to serve him, without hesitation complied with his desire, and he immediately set out in the cutter to Gambia, Falconbridge and myself accompanying him.

The distance being but six miles, and a fresh sea breeze, we soon ran up.

Mr Rennieu not only received us with the politeness of a Frenchman, but with kindness and friendship.

When he saw the master of the *Lapwing*, he said to me, "Madam, Captain Kennedy (for that was his name) will never leave Africa, but in two or three days time he will come under my *big tree*".

I did not instantly comprehend him, which the Frenchman perceived, and explained himself by saying, "under the large tree I saw a little distance off was the burying ground", and, added he, "there is something in the countenance of Kennedy denoting his dissolution to be near at hand; and I am persuaded the man cannot live more than two or three days".

I took care not to mention or hint to Kennedy what Mr Rennieu said to me, lest the force of imagination might kill him – however, in spite of all our endeavours, the prophecy was fulfilled; a severe fever came on the same night, and the second day he was a corpse.

There was no accommodation for sleeping on shore at the factory, which Mr Rennieu could offer us – we were, consequently, obliged to sleep on board.

I could not think of allowing the poor sick man to be exposed to the inclemency of the night air, and insisted on his taking a berth in the cabin – nor could I think of continuing in the cabin while he was ill, lest his disorder might be infectious; and the only alternative was to lay upon deck, or in the hold.

The former being most preferable, our mattresses were spread at night under the awning, where we lay; but I took the precaution to wrap myself up in a flannel gown, and covered my head with a cap of the same – was it not for that, in all probability, I must have added to the number under Mr Rennieu's big tree.

For two nights we lay on deck, and each of them, we were unlucky enough to have violent tornadoes; during the storm I threw large blankets over me, and though the rain penetrated through both, yet my flannel gown and cap intercepted it and prevented me from getting wet, except my feet, which I bathed in spirits when the tornado was over, and thus, I believe, escaped any bad consequences; but being under the necessity of staying another night at Gambia, I did not choose to experience the good effects of my blankets a third time, and accepted an invitation which the Captain of an American had made us – to take a bed on board his ship.

Immediately after the corpse was removed, we had the *Lapwing* scoured, washed with vinegar, and smoked with tobacco and brimstone, to free her from every suspicion of dangerous infection.

I must avail myself of the present moment to give you some description of Gambia Island.

It is small and low, not two miles in circumference, situated in the midst of swamps and marshes, from whence a continual stench comes sufficient to choke a carrion crow – 'tis wonderful how any human beings could pitch on such a place to live in.

The Europeans there have all complexions as if they were fed on madder and saffron.

Their manner of living is slovenly and hoggish, though they seem to have plenty of fresh stock, and provisions of almost every kind – they are very inactive and indolent, which I am not astonished at, for such must ensue from the lassitude produced by the unhealthiness of the place.

The buildings are of mean and disrespectable appearance, being a pile of grass and sticks clumsily put together.

They have a factory ship, and few goods are kept on shore, from a fear of being surprised and robbed by the natives. Formerly the Island was protected by a company of French soldiers, but the vast and rapid mortality deterred their government from sending fresh supplies.

Rennieu, however, preserves a kind of consequence, and keeps his neighbours in awe by a number of strange legerdemain tricks he has learnt, some of which he shows whenever he has visitors.

After seeing Gambia, I consider Granville Town a delightful spot, where we have none of those swampy low grounds, but a reviving sea breeze that cheers us every day, which is almost spent before it reaches them; I suppose this must be owing to the heavy dense atmosphere that opposes its progress, for distance cannot be the cause.

Since the rains commenced, the nights grew alternately cooler, indeed I find a blanket very comfortable; even during the dry weather (when I had room to breathe), I found night many degrees colder than day; but it is now, at times, so cold, that I am glad to find a fire.

This sudden transition from heat to cold, and from cold to heat, I am rather disposed to think, accounts for the turpitude of the climate, at all events it is certainly one of the most considerable causes.

From a fear my inadequateness to give historical delineations, will expose me to your criticism, I have to beg you will look over any rhapsodies with lenity; *this* is all I can hope for – *that* all I dread.

Falconbridge thinks of leaving Africa the middle of this month; the loss of Kennedy, want of provisions fit for taking to sea, and the late Mate (now Master) of the cutter, and several of our people, being sick, disconcerts us a good deal; but we are told the rains will be considerably worse, and every day will render it more dangerous and difficult to get off the coast: Falconbridge is determined to do his best, and get away as quick as possible.

Oh my friend! what happiness shall I feel on seeing Old England again; and if it pleases God for us to arrive safe, the difficulties, dangers

and inconveniences I have surmounted, and have yet to encounter, will
only serve me to laugh at.

Yours, &c. &.

LETTER V

My dear Friend,

I have many apologies to make for not giving you earlier intelligence of our arrival; but my excuses are good ones, and no doubt will convince you my silence cannot be attributed to the slightest shadow of negligence or forgetfulness.

We arrived at Penzance, in Cornwall, the 2d instant, when (not being able to walk), I was carried in an arm chair by two men to the house of *Mrs Dennis,* who friendly invited us to shelter under her hospitable roof while we remained there.

The hurry and fatigue of moving, with the restraint one customarily feels more or less of, upon going to a strange house, prevented me writing you the first day; but the day subsequent I wrote as follows:

My dearest Madam,

"I am returned to this blessed land; join with me in fervent prayer and thanksgiving to the Author of all good works, for his miraculous protection and goodness during a circuitous passage of nigh three months, replete with hardships unprecedented, I believe, in any voyages heretofore related, the particulars of which I must take some opportunity to furnish you with".

Here I made a full pause; and, after thinking and re-thinking for near half an hour, whether I should subscribe my name and send it to the post, a thought struck me – "Why! I shall be in London in eight or ten days, when it will be in my power to send a narration of what has happened since I last wrote Mrs—; and if I write now, I shall only excite curiosity, and keep her in unpleasant suspense for some time; so it is best to postpone writing till I can do it fully".

Now, in place of ten days, it was almost three weeks before we reached the metropolis; and since I arrived, my time has been wholly occupied in receiving inquisitive visitors, and answering a few pertinent, and a number of ridiculous questions.

I could make many other reasonable pleas in behalf of my silence, but trust what is already said will be amply satisfactory; shall therefore forbear making any further apologies, and proceed with an account of myself since I last wrote to you.

The 16th of June we went to Robana to take leave of the *Royal Family*, and to receive the young Prince John Frederic on board; all this we accomplished, and sailed the same day.

Naimbana seemed unconcerned at parting with his son, but the old Queen cried, and appeared much affected.

The Prince was decorated in an old blue cloak, bound with broad gold lace: which, with a black velvet coat, pair of white satin breeches, a couple of shirts, and two or three pair of trowsers, form a complete inventory of his stock of clothes, when he left Africa.

The old man gave John all the cash he had, amounting to the *enormous sum* of eight Spanish dollars (about thirty-five shillings); and just when we were getting under way, saluted us with twelve guns, from some rusty pieces of cannon, laying on the beach without carriages.

The *Lapwing* was badly equipped for sea; the crew and the passengers amounted to nine: four of the former were confined with fevers, consequently there were only four (and but one a sailor) to do the ship's duty.

Mr Rennieu gave me a goat and half a dozen of fowls: King Naimbana put a couple of goats, and a dozen of fowls on board with his son.

Besides these, I purchased some poultry, and when we sailed, considered ourselves possessed of a pretty good stock, consisting of three goats, four dozen of fowls, a barrel of flour, half a barrel of pork, and a barrel of beef.

We had not been at sea a week, when all our live stock were washed or blown overboard, by repeated and impetuous tornadoes – so that we had not a thing left but the flour and salt provisions; however we were in hopes of getting in a few days to Saint Jago, one of the Cape De Verd Islands, where the loss of our stock might be replaced.[47]

In this we were disappointed, for instead of a few days, a continuous interruption of calms and boisterous weather, made it six weeks before

---

[47] Santiago, the largest of the Cape Verde Islands.

we reached that Island; during the whole of which time I was confined to my cabin, and mostly to my bed, for it rained incessantly.

After being about three weeks at sea, our sick got clear of their fevers, but were so emaciated as to be unfit for any duty, *except eating,* and though there was no food fit for convalescent persons on board, yet the coarse victuals we had stood no chance with them, and made it necessary to put all hands to an allowance.

Upon enquiring into the state of our provisions, we found they had been lavishly dealt with; there was not more than one week's full allowance of meat, and scarcely four days of flour remaining.

These were alarming circumstances, for we had two thirds further to go, than we had then come, toward Saint Jago.

I did not selfishly care for the want of beef or pork, as I had not tasted either since we sailed from Sierra Leone, but I lamented it for the others.

All hands were restricted to a quarter of a pound of beef or pork, and a small tea-cup full (rather better than a gill) of flour per day.

What would have been more dreadful, we should have wanted water, was it not for the rains; the worms having imperceptibly penetrated our water casks, all the water leaked out, except a small cask, which would not allow us more than a pint each, for three weeks.

My tea-cup full of flour, mixed with a little rain water and salt, boiled to a kind of pap, when the weather would admit a fire, otherwise raw, was, believe me, all my nourishment for ten days, except once or twice, when some cruel unconscionable wretch robbed me of the homely morsel, I was forced to taste the beef.

The week before we arrived at St Jago, our Carpenter, who had been very ill, and was on the recovery, relapsed, and died in twenty-four hours; which circumstance terrified me exceedingly, lest our afflictions were to be increased with some pestilential disease; however, no similar misfortunes attended us afterwards.

We arrived at Porto Praya in St Jago, I think, the 25th of July, when Falconbridge immediately went on shore to obtain sufferance to remain there a few days, while he re-victualled and watered.

An officer met him as he landed, and conducted him to the chief magistrate of the Port, who lives in a Fort on top of a hill which commands the harbour.

Falconbridge was well received, his request granted, and he and myself were invited to dine at the Fort next day – but he was informed provisions were not to be had for any price – a fleet of European ships had just sailed from thence, and drained the country of almost every kind of eatable.[48]

After being six weeks confined in the narrow bounds of the *Lapwing's* cabin, and most of the time in bed, fed as I was on scanty wretched food, notwithstanding the benignity of heaven had preserved me from disease of any kind, you will not question my energy of mind and body being considerably enervated; indeed, so enfeebled did I see myself, that it was with much difficulty I accompanied Falconbridge to dinner at the Consul's, for so the Chief Officer of Porto Praya is termed; but the distance I had to walk was short, and with the help of a Portuguese officer on one side, and my husband on the other, I accomplished it tolerably well.

The company consisted of the Portuguese and French Consuls, five Portuguese and two French gentlemen, two Portuguese ladies, Falconbridge, and myself.

None of the foreigners spoke English, so you will readily guess we but poorly amused or entertained each other; through the medium of a linguist who attended, any compliments, questions or answers, &c. &c. were conveyed to and fro.

Our dinner was very good, and I had prudence enough to be temperate, having often heard of fatal consequences from indulgencies in similar cases.

During dinner we had excellent claret and madeira, but no wine was drunk after; directly as the cloth was removed, tea was introduced in the most uncommon way I ever saw or heard of before; it was brought in china mugs, containing three pints each, and every person was presented with one of those huge goblets.

I had not tasted tea for several weeks, nevertheless, one third of this quantity was more than I chose to swallow – but with astonishment I beheld others make a rapid finish of their allowance.

[48] The economy of the Cape Verde islands was in any case precarious, with regular periods of devastating famine (see António Carreira, *The People of the Cape Verde Islands: Exploitation and Emigration*, London, 1982).

Having thus inundated their stomachs, every one arose, and our host desired the linguist to acquaint me they were going to repose themselves for a while, and if I was inclined to follow their example, a sofa, or bed, was at my service; being bed sickened, I declined the offer, and chose, in preference, to stretch my feeble limbs with gentle walking in a pleasant portico, fronting the sea; for I had gathered strength enough in the few hours I was on shore to walk alone.

The company having indulged about an hour in their habitual sloth-fulness, re-assembled; we were invited to take a bed on shore, but Falconbridge learnt, the generality of people were thievishly disposed, and for that reason did not choose to sleep from the cutter; and you know it would have been very uncomfortable for me to remain without him, among a parcel of strangers, when we could not understand what one or other said; besides, I had other prudential objections for not remaining without Falconbridge, which the horror of our loathsome bark could not conquer.

After this, we remained four days in Porto Praya Road, during which I went ashore frequently.

The town is situated on the same height with the fort.

They have a Romish chapel (for the inhabitants are all Roman Catholics), market place and jail, and covered with slate in the European way – the other buildings are mostly of wood and thatch, after the African manner.

The French Consul has his house within the fort, which is a decent good looking building, as is the Portuguese Consul's; but this is of stone, and that of wood.

The people of most countries have their peculiar modes of habiting themselves, but surely the custom of Porto Praya is more odious than any other; in meeting a hundred men, two are not to be seen dressed alike – perhaps one will have a coat thrown over his shoulders without occupying the sleeves; another a woman's petticoat drawn round his neck, with his arms through the pocket holes, and so on, except the higher ranks.

The women dress rather more uniformly; they wear very short petti-coats, and tight jackets, of a coarse linen, like Osnaburg, but no *shifts*; I mean the lower class, or natives, who are mostly black, or of mixed complexions; for the few European ladies there, are genteely habited with fine India muslins, and their hair neatly plaited, and put up in silk nets.

A narrow, handsome kind of cotton cloth is manufactured at St Jago; I went to one of the manufactories, and purchased several pieces; they are in great estimation, and sell for a high price – I paid five and six dollars a piece (about two yards and a half) for those I bought. The loom they are wove in resembles our garter loom.[49]

I understand the inhabitants raise their own cotton and have several small sugar works, which makes a sufficiency of sugar for the consumption of those islands, but no quantity for exportation.

The Governor resides at a town named St Jago, a considerable distance from Porto Praya, and on the opposite side of the island, which put it out of our power to visit it.

The Consul at Porto Praya is his Vice-gerent, but has his authority from Portugal; there appeared to me a great want of government among the people, notwithstanding a strong military force is kept there.

We got a superabundance of fine fish while we remained at St Jago, which was a fortunate circumstance – for our intelligence respecting the scarcity of provisions was perfectly true.

With our utmost endeavours we could not procure but two goats and two dozen fowls to take with us to sea; and those I was obliged to purchase with some of my wearing apparel, which was preferred to money; or, I should say, they were not to be had for money.

Bread and salt provisions were not to be had in the smallest quantity, for any price; however, we purchased a number of cocoa nuts, which they have in plenty, as a substitute for bread.

With these trifling and ordinary sea-stores we departed from Porto Praya, the 30th of July, trusting by oeconomical management to make them serve till we reached some other port.

I recovered my strength and spirits considerably during the short time we were at that place, as did all our sick; indeed it was necessary and lucky, for it enabled us to contend against misfortune, and conquer the hardships and inconveniencies which afterwards attended us.

[49] For the famous Cape Verdean cloths, see António Carreira, *Panaria Cabo-Verdiano-Guineense*, Porto, 1969.

We had fine moderate weather the first twenty-four hours, and got the length of St Vincent, one of the same islands, where, falling calm, we came to anchor.[50]

Some of the people went on shore, thinking to kill a few birds, and supposing the islands uninhabited, it being a small barren place, without a tree or shrub of any sort, a kind of fern excepted, so that no houses could be there and escape our notice.

The boat's crew had scarcely landed, when were were greatly astonished and alarmed to behold from the cutter (for we lay at no distance off the shore) five *naked human beings*, who had just started up from behind a hillock, running towards them – however, our fears were quickly abated, by seeing the boat returning.

The master was one that went on shore, and he understood a little Portuguese, in which language these victims to barbarity addressed, and told, him, they had several months past, been banished from an adjacent island called Mayo, and landed where they then were in the deplorable condition he beheld them.

The *Lapwing* was the first vessel that had anchored there since their exilement, and they begged and prayed we would take them off – they did not care where!

This we could not do with any kind of discreetness, from the danger of starving them and ourselves.

They consisted of three men and two women, and we mustered two petticoats and three pair of trowsers for them.

I was curious to know something more of the poor wretches, and went with Falconbridge and the Master on shore.

Before we landed, they had retired behind the hillock, and we sent forward their clothing, that they might be dressed by the time we came up.

We found them in the act of broiling fish over a fire made of dry fern, which was the only fuel they could possible have.

Our Skipper asked if they had any houses, but was answered in the negative, and pointing to the heaven and the earth, signifying *this* was

[50] São Vicente, still deserted at this period, became an important naval coaling station, used by the British navy, in the nineteenth century.

their bed, and *that* their covering; he then enquired how they subsisted and for what they were banished?

To the second, no further answer could be obtained, than their having offended the Governor of Mayo, who was a *Black* man.

They were miserably emaciated, and a hapless melancholy overhang'd their countenances. When we first came up, joyful smiles beamed through the cloud, which soon darkened when they learnt there was no prospect of being relieved.

They followed us to the boat, and I readily believe, if they had been armed, they would have taken her from us; as it was, our men were obliged to use violence, and turn them out, for all hands had jumped in, and attempted to get off.

We offered to take any one of them, but not one would consent to separate or share any good fortune the whole could not partake of.

When we got clear from the shore, they pursued us up to their necks in water, crying and howling so hideously, that I would have given the world ! (were it at my disposal) if it was either in our power to bring them away, or that I had not seen them.

Here we remained all night, and till three o'clock the day following, when a light favourable breeze enabled us to sail; before our departure, we sent the convicts an iron pot, for cooking, and a few fishing utensils, which was all we could possibly spare them.

To the northward of St Vincent's, about eight or nine miles, is St Anthony, another of the Cape de Verd Islands, which we had to pass close by.

The wind was very weak, but every one imagined there was enough of it to take us clear off that Island before morning; whether that was not the case, or whether things were badly managed, I shall not decidedly say, though I have a decided opinion on the subject; for towards four o'clock in the morning, being uncommonly restless, I thought, as the vessel appeared very quiet, and the moon shone beautifully bright, I would get up and set upon deck for a while.

Perhaps merciful Providence directed this – for the like I never did before or since; and had I not, in all probability we must have been driven against the rude rocks of St Anthony, and God only knows what would have been the consequence, as I was the only person awake.

The first thing I saw, upon lifting my head out of the cabin, was those lofty perpendicular rocks pending almost directly over us, and not a man upon deck but King Naimbana's son, and him fast asleep.

"Good God!" cried I, "Falconbridge, we are on shore!"

He instantly sprung up, and called all hands, who got the boat out, and with the utmost exertion towed us off a small distance.

When day light came on, our danger appeared more forcibly, for, notwithstanding the oars had been diligently employed an hour and a half, we were not two hundred yards from the Island.

Some said it was the current; others, it was the land which induced or attracted us; but what the real reasons were I know not; this only I can tell you – after trying every possible means to no purpose, till four o'clock in the afternoon, when the men complaining their strength was exhausted, and they could do no more, it was agreed to abandon the *Lapwing*, and look out for a place where we might land before night, and thereby secure safety for our lives, if the vessel could not be preserved.

Accordingly every one was desired to get into the boat, but we found she was too small to carry us all at once; and two of the sailors consented to stay till she could make a second trip.

Falconbridge and myself got in, taking with us a few shiftings of clothes and our bedding; we then rowed to the land, and after pulling to and fro for near two hours, could not discover a single spot where there was a possibility of landing; during which time we observed the Cutter drifting fast toward the shore, and expecting every moment to see her strike.

Despondency was visibly pictured in every face! – "What shall we do, or what is best to be done?", was the universal cry.

Conscious of a woman's insignificance in such matters, I was silent till then, when, finding a general vacancy of opinion among the men, I ventured to say – "Let us return to the *Lapwing*, and put our trust in him who is all sufficient, and whose dispensations are always unquestionably just".

To this forlorn proposition every one assented; but said it was only deferring the evil moment a few hours, for we should certainly have to trust to our boat very shortly again, unless a breeze came off the land.

After getting on board it was settled – one person should watch while the rest refreshed themselves with sleep, that they might be somewhat able to encounter the looked-for fatigues of the night.

For my part, I did not in the least incline to sleep, but with watchful eyes and aching heart, awaited the expected moment when eight of us were to commit ourselves, in a small open boat, to the mercy of the ungovernable ocean.

Many reflections pressed upon me, but one more powerful than any – "that our dilemma was probably a mark of divine vengeance, for not relieving the distressed people at St Vincent's".

I often asked the watch, if we neared the rocks; sometimes he answered in the affirmative, and sometimes doubtfully – but said we seemed to drift coastways withall, and he believed there was a strong current setting to the southward.

About twelve o'clock Falconbridge came on deck, when I mentioned this information to him: he then took notice himself, and found it really so.

All hands were immediately turned out, and the boat again manned to tow our bark with the current, for though it had not been observed, we were doubtless working against it all the preceding day.

This proved to be a propitious speculation; in about four hours we could see the south-west end of the Island, and at the same time had got near a mile off the land.

What a change of countenance was now on board: I felt my bosom fill with gratitude at hearing the glad tidings!

General tokens of joy and congratulations passed from one ship-mate to another; and when daylight appeared, instead of gloom and sorrow, every cheek blush'd cheerfulness.

We then found ourselves clear of the Island, and having a fine moderate breeze, bid adieu to the African coast; nevertheless our troubles did not end here.

After running to the Westward eight and forty hours, a tremendous storm came on, and continued to increase in violence for five days.

This had scarcely abated, when it was succeeded by another, nearly as bad – which however ran us as far as Fayal, one of the Azores, or Western Islands, where we arrived the 18th of August.

I do not mean to take up your time with a description of those storms, or the detail of our sufferings since we left St Anthony till our arrival at Fayal, though I must not pass over them wholly unnoticed.

Every horror the most fertile ideas can picture a sea storm with, aggravated the former; and, consequently augmenting the miseries of the latter, rendered them almost unbearable and past representation.

God knows they would have been bad enough without; for the day we reached Fayal, about two pounds of salt beef and half a dozen cocoa nuts, were all the provisions we had left.

We remained there a week, and were hospitably entertained by Mr Graham, the English Consul, who had the goodness to insist on our taking a bed at his house, directly as our arrival was announced to him.

Being much bruised and indisposed by our boisterous rough passage, and eating food I had not been accustomed to, prevented me from walking abroad for two or three days; while thus confined, I was highly delighted and amused with admiring Mr Graham's beautiful garden adjoining the house, where are almost all the fruits of the torrid, frigid and temperate zones, in the greatest perfection; peaches, apples, pears, oranges, pine apples, limes, lemons, citron, grapes, &c. &c. the finest I ever saw.

Mrs Graham treated me with motherly kindness; by her attention, and the wholesomeness of the climate, I gained so much strength and spirits, that before I came away, I was able frequently to walk about the town, and once took an excursion into the country, with her and a party of her friends, to the seat of a Mr Perkins, an English gentleman.

We all rode on asses, for carriages (if they have any) could not pass the way we went.

I was pleased with the reception this gentleman gave us, as well as his polite and generous behaviour.

In our way thither we passed a number of vineyards; and, as far as I could judge, the country seemed fruitful.

Besides this excursion, Mr and Mrs Perkins persuaded me to take one with them, to the Island of Pico, about eight miles from Fayal, where they have a valuable vineyard; and where they assured me, I should see the most wonderful natural curiosity, in the Azore Islands, viz. two springs of water within eighteen feet of each other – one nearly as cold as ice, the other boiling with heat.

When we arrived there, several washerwomen were employed in their vocation; they told me the water was soft, and well adapted for washing; that they made it of what temperature they pleased, by mixing a proportion of each, and declared they had frequently boiled fish in the hot well: I had a mind to try the heat by putting my finger in, but found the steam powerful enough to convince me I should be *scalded.*

There are public baths at those Wells well attended by the inhabitants of Fayal and the adjacent Islands; they lay somewhat to the eastward, at the foot of the mountain, which gives its name to this Island.

This is the highest mountain I ever saw, very thickly wooded towards its base, but picturesque, with many gentlemen's seats, and on the whole vastly gratifying to the eye.

It produces a particular and favourite kind of wood, called *Teixa,* or *Teixo,* which, from its valuable qualities, no one is allowed to sell for private use, it being reserved for the Queen of Portugal, after the custom of her predecessors, solely for the use of the Portuguese government.

I was but a few hours at Pico, and this was all the information I collected.

There are two nunneries, and a magnificent Romish church at Fayal, which I visited.

The former were crowded with nuns, and many of them beautiful women.

I saw two who spoke English, with whom I conversed for some time, and purchased several artificial flowers, and a few sweetmeats from them.

One of them had all the traces of beauty yet unblemished but to a certainty somewhat singed by ruinous time; for by her own account she must be far advanced in years.

Upon asking her opinion of monastic life, she said, "Madam, I have been within the walls of this convent forty-three years, and had I to travel my life anew, I would prefer the same path to all others".

But a charming buxom young girl thought otherwise. She said, "Can you suppose an animated creature, like me, full of youthful fire, was designed by nature to spend her days within these dismal walls? No! nor can I figure to myself, that any one (in spite of what many will tell you) can find pleasure in burying herself alive, and thwarting the purposes of her creation, for such is certainly the case with all nuns"; and, continued she: "My parents placed me here at a time when I was not capable of judging for myself; nor do I scruple to say that my ideas and fancies are fluttering among the amusements and gaieties of the world, and had I my will, my person would be there also".

I attended the church at mass time; after service was ended, I observed several men bringing in a large sail of a ship, which had a curious appearance to a stranger, as I was; but a gentleman present said, "Those people have been in the same storm with yourselves, and they are giving that sail to the church as a thanks offering for their deliverance"; he then showed me part of the boat which Captain Inglefield had been saved in, and which was kept here as a record of divine favour to that gentleman.[51]

This circumstance refreshed my memory with the notorious sufferings and wonderful escape of Captain Inglefield and his boat's crew; and, after mentally weighing our misfortunes with his, I summ'd them both up as follows.

"Captain Inglefield experienced all the miseries of hunger, fatigue and oppression of spirits, which sixteen days in an open boat, exposed to the furious untameable wind and sea, without provision, in momentary ex-pectation of being hurried into eternity, could inflict, besides the additional horrors produced by ruminating on the hapless condition of such members of his fellow creatures, in the same situation as himself.

"We have been fifty-eight days in a deck'd boat, not twice the size of Captain Inglefield's – continued rains almost all the while – three weeks a quarter of a pound of beef, and about half the quantity of flour our allowance – eighteen days more baffled by calms and contrary winds, or beat about by merciless storms, fed upon mean disagreeable food, and scarcely enough of that to keep soul and body together; and what was worse than all, the apprehension of being left morselless of any kind of

[51] Captain Inglefield had been shipwrecked in the Atlantic in 1782, and after sixteen days in an open boat he and eleven others landed up, as the Falconbridges did, at Fayal. Like them he was kindly received by Mr Graham "whose humane attention made very ample amends for the formality of the Portuguese" (*Shipwrecks and Disasters at Sea*, Edinburgh, 1812, vol. III, pp. 40–58).

nourishment; which certainly must have been the case, had we not arrived at Fayal when we did."

Having done this, I compared them with one another – and though it is unfair to give my decision, we being too often apt to magnify our own misfortunes, and always supposing them greater than those of others; yet I shall hazard making you acquainted with the conclusion I drew, which, however, was very laconic.

I said to myself, "Captain Inglefield's sufferings are matchless, and were it not for the duration and repetition of mine, they could have but little semblance to one another".

The small pox was committing prodigious ravages among all ranks of people when we left Fayal, and, I suppose, continues still to do so.

A child of the French Consul's lay dangerously ill with that disease, and he requested Falconbridge would visit it; he did so, and found the infant confined in a small close room, where every means were taken to shut out the least breath of air.

Falconbridge directly recommended the child be brought into a large open hall, which was done against the absurd remonstrances of the Portuguese Physician, who pronounced immediate death to it; however, before our departure we had the pleasure of seeing this innocent babe (who would in all probability have otherwise fallen a victim to those ridiculous notions of treating the small pox) quite out of danger; and I trust the precedent will be generally attended to, and may prove equally efficacious.[52]

Many of our countrymen reside there, who are Roman Catholics, and married to Portuguese ladies, with few exceptions.

I saw two or three English women – perhaps all on the island; they seem to have preserved their native manners and customs in high perfection, which the Portuguese ladies emulously try to copy, more especially in the article of dress, than in any thing else; but in this they are much hinder'd by the jealousy and narrow ideas of their husbands, who never suffer their wives to go abroad, or appear in company with other men, whether single or married, without a deep black or white satin veil that hides not only the face but the body.

[52] Exposing smallpox patients to fresh air, recommended by Thomas Sydenham in the mid-seventeenth century, had become the standard English method of treatment.

In conversation with one of these ladies, she said to me, "The women of your country must surely be very happy: they have so much more liberty than we have, or, I believe, than the women of any other country, I wish I was an English woman!" I thanked her in behalf of my country-women, for her good opinion, but assured her they had their share of thorns and thistles, as well as those of other countries.

How deeply do I regret our short stay at Saint Jago and Fayal disables me from giving you a more historical and intelligent account of those islands; but I was long enough at each place to form this summary opinion: The latter is, without exception, the most desirable spot I ever saw; and the former as far opposite as it is possible for you to conceive.

Having repaired such damage as our vessel had received coming from St Anthony, and supplied ourselves with abundance of stores to bring us to this country, we set sail from Fayal the 25th of last month, and arrived at the time and place before mentioned.

Our passage was short and unattended with such boisterous weather as we had experienced, yet it was so stormy that I was obliged to keep my bed the whole time, which circumstance, and a cold I caught, threw me into an indisposition that I have not yet recovered from.

The day after landing at Penzance, Falconbridge wrote to Mr Granville Sharp, and by return of Post received his answer, a copy of which I herewith enclose.

"LEADENHALL STREET, 7th *Sept.* 1791

"Dear Sir,

"The agreeable account of the safe arrival of the *Lapwing* at Penzance, which I received this morning, gives me very particular satisfaction.

"I have communicated your letter to Henry Thornton, Esq., Chairman of the *Sierra Leone Company* (for under this title the late St George's Bay Company is now established, by an act of the last Session of Parliament) and to some of the Directors, and they desire you to come by land as expeditiously as you can, bringing with you in a postchaise, Mrs Falconbridge and the Black Prince, and also any such specimens of the country as will not be liable to injury by land carriage.

"I enclose (from the Directors) a note from Mr. Thornton's house for thirty pounds, for which you may easily procure cash for your journey, and if more should be wanting for use of the people of the *Lapwing*, I have no doubt but Mrs Dennis (to whose care I send this Letter) will have the goodness to advance it, as she will be reimbursed by return of the Post, when I receive advice of your draft.

"The *Lapwing* may be left to the care of any proper person whom you may think capable of taking due care of her, until the Directors give further orders respecting her.

> "I remain with great esteem,
> > "*Dear Sir,*
> > > "Your affectionate Friend
> > > "And humble Servant
> > > GRANVILLE SHARP"

Mr Alexander Falconbridge

In the interim Falconbridge went to Falmouth to procure money for our journey to London.

There he met the Rev. Thomas Clarkson, that unwearied stickler for human liberty, with whom (or at whose instimulation) the abolition of the slave trade originated, and at whose instance Falconbridge quitted his comfortable situation at Lodway, to enlist in the present (though I fear chimerical) cause of freedom and humanity.

Mr Clarkson is also a Director of the Sierra Leone Company, under which title, you find by Mr. Sharp's letter, the late St George's Bay Company is now called.

He informed Falconbridge that his brother, Lieutenant Clarkson of the navy, was gone to Nova Scotia, authorised by the government to collect several hundred free Blacks and take them to Sierra Leone, where they are (under the care and patronage of the Directors of our new Company) to form a Colony.[53]

---

[53] The settlers whom Lieutenant John Clarkson had gone to recruit were black loyalists who had liberated themselves from slavery during the War of American Independence, and found shelter with the British forces. They were sent to settle in Nova Scotia, but were dissatisfied there, since they were denied the grants of land they had been promised, and were fearful of being again reduced to slavery. One of them, Thomas Peters, made his way to England to present their grievances. He contacted the directors of the newly-formed company, and returned with an offer of land in Sierra Leone. Clarkson followed, to explain to them the terms the company was offering, and to arrange embarkation. On 15 January 1792, 1190 of them sailed from Halifax for Sierra Leone (Fyfe, *A History*, pp. 31–5).

It was surely a premature, hair-brained, and ill-digested scheme, to think of sending such a number of people all at once, to a rude, barbarous and unhealthy country, before they were certain of possessing an acre of land; and I very much fear will terminate in disappointment, if not disgrace to the authors; though at the same time, I am persuaded the motives sprung from minds unsullied with evil meaning.[54]

We set out from Penzance the 12th, taking with us the Black Prince, and the following day arrived at Plymouth, where by appointment we met Mr. Clarkson; after staying there four days, we went on towards London, stopped at Exeter three days, and arrived here on the 24th.

As soon as our arrival was known, Mr Thornton (the Chairman), Mr Sharp, and several others of the Directors came to see us, and after many compliments expressive with condolence for our misfortunes, and con-gratulations for our deliverance and safe arrival, a number of enquiries, &c. &c., Mr Thornton requested Falconbridge and the Prince would dine with him, at the same time gave the latter to understand he was to consider his (Mr Thornton's) house as his home.[55]

I could not help secretly smiling to see the servile courtesy which those gentlemen paid this young man, merely from his being the son of a nominal King.

It has slip'd my notice till now to describe him to you: – His person is rather below the ordinary, inclining to grossness, his skin nearly jet black, eyes keenly intelligent, nose flat, teeth unconnected, and filed sharp after the custom of his country, his legs a little bandied, and his deportment easy, manly and confident withal. In his disposition he is surly, but has cunning enough to smother it where he thinks his interest is concerned; he is pettish and implacable, but I think grateful and attached to those he considers his friends; nature has been bountiful in giving him sound intellects, very capable of improvement, and he also possesses a great thirst for knowledge.

[54] Possibly this paragraph, which smacks of wisdom after the event, was added to the letter later.

[55] Henry Thornton was a wealthy banker and Member of Parliament. He was an intimate friend of William Wilberforce, and was associated with him in the campaign against the slave trade, and also as a member of what was later to be called the "Clapham Sect", an Evangelical pressure group which sought to remodel British society on religious principles. As chairman of the board of directors of the Sierra Leone Company he was largely responsible for making and carrying out policy (Fyfe, *A History*, p. 28).

While with me, although it was seldom in my power, now and then I amused myself teaching him the alphabet, which he quickly learned, and before we parted, he could read any common print surprisingly well.

He is not wanting in discernment, and has already discovered the weak side of his patrons, which he strives to turn to good account, and I dare say, by his natural subtlety, will in time advantage himself considerably by it. *

    * This young man returned to Sierra Leone in July 1793, and died the day after his arrival.[56]

The Directors seem much pleased with Falconbridge's exertions, have appointed him Commercial Agent to the Company, and he is shortly to return to Sierra Leone. They are very pressing for me to accompany him, but my late misfortunes are yet too fresh in remembrance to consent hastily. Indeed, you may suppose, I cannot but painfully remember them while the bruises and chafes produced by the voyage on different parts of my body continue unhealed. However, it is probable, whether with or against my will, I must tacitly assent to hazard a repetition of what I have already undergone.

When matters are wholly fixed you will hear from me, and perhaps I may shortly have the happiness of assuring you in person how I am,

Yours, &c.

[56] A little tract, *The African Prince, A Sketch of the Life of John Henry Naimbana, An African King's Son* (London, n.d.) was published after his death. It has a woodcut frontispiece in which he is depicted spurning an improper book.

LETTER VI

My dear Madam,

The Directors have acted so honourable and handsome it was not possible for me to hold out in refusing to return to Sierra Leone; besides increasing Falconbridge's salary near three times what it was, they have voted us a sum of money as an equivalent for the extraordinary services they consider he has rendered them, and as a compensation for our private losses of clothes, &c.

But surely mortal never was more harassed than I have been by their importunities.

They used every flattering and enticing argument the ingenious brain of man is capable of to no purpose – however, though all their rhetoric could not persuade me to revisit Africa, their *noble, generous* actions have effected it.

Mr Thornton is a good creature, one of the worthiest men I ever met, he has assured me, should any action happen to Falconbridge, I shall be well provided for by the Company; he has also, as well as many others of the Directors, made me a profusion of friendly promises and professions, so extravagant that if they came from any other set of men I should look upon them either as chicanery or without meaning.

The Court has granted £50 to be laid out in presents for King Naimbana and his old Queen, and have particularly desired, I shall purchase those for the latter, and present them as from myself, by way of enhancing my consequence.

They have likewise granted another sum for me to lay out in such private stores as I may choose to take with me for our use after we get to Africa, besides ordering a very handsome supply for the voyage.

A few days ago I only hinted an inclination to visit my friends at Bristol, before we left England, and Mr Thornton said I should have a

Chaise when I liked, and the expense should be defrayed by the Company. Do you not think these are pretty marks of attention? [57]

We have thoughts of setting out for Bristol in the course of next week, where I figure to myself much of that undescriptionable pleasure which lively affectionate minds involuntarily feel upon meeting the bosom friends and sportive companions of their youthful days, grown to maturity with hearts and countenances neither altered by absence, or rusted by corroding time.

But I lament to say this happiness will be of short duration, being obliged quickly to proceed to Falmouth, where we are to embark on board the Company's ship *Amy*, for Sierra Leone.

Adieu.

[57] These paragraphs are plainly to be read in the context of her later denunciations of Thornton and the other directors.

TWO VOYAGES

TO

SIERRA LEONE,

DURING THE

YEARS 1791—2—3,

In a Series of Letters,

BY

ANNA MARIA FALCONBRIDGE.

To which is added,

A LETTER FROM THE AUTHOR,

TO

Henry Thornton, Esq. M. P.

And CHAIRMAN of the Court of DIRECTORS

OF THE

SIERRA LEONE COMPANY.

If I can hold a Torch to others,
'Tis all I want———

The Second Edition.

LONDON:

PRINTED FOR THE AUTHOR, AND SOLD BY
DIFFERENT BOOKSELLERS THROUGHOUT
THE KINGDOM.

1794.

1 Title-page from the 1794 edition of Anna Maria Falconbridge's
Two Voyages to Sierra Leone.

NARRATIVE

O F

TWO VOYAGES

TO THE RIVER

SIERRA LEONE,

DURING THE

YEARS 1791---2---3,

PERFORMED BY

A. M. FALCONBRIDGE.

WITH A

Succinct account of the Distresses and proceedings
of that Settlement; a description of the
Manners, Diversions, Arts, Commerce, Cultivation, Custom,
Punishments, &c.

And Every interesting Particular relating to the

SIERRA LEONE COMPANY.

ALSO

The present State of the SLAVE TRADE in the
West Indies, and the improbability of
its total Abolition.

THE SECOND EDITION.

LONDON.

Printed for L. I. Higham, N° 6, Chiswell Street.

MDCCCII.

PRICE 3s. 6d.

2 Title-page from the 1802 edition of Anna Maria Falconbridge's
Narrative of Two Voyages to the River Sierra Leone.

AN

ACCOUNT

OF THE

SLAVE TRADE

ON THE

COAST OF AFRICA,

BY

ALEXANDER FALCONBRIDGE,

LATE SURGEON IN THE AFRICAN TRADE.

THE SECOND EDITION.

LONDON:

PRINTED AND SOLD BY JAMES PHILLIPS, GEORGE-
YARD, LOMBARD-STREET. 1788.

3 Title-page from the 1788 edition of Alexander Falconbridge's
Account of the Slave Trade on the Coast of Africa.

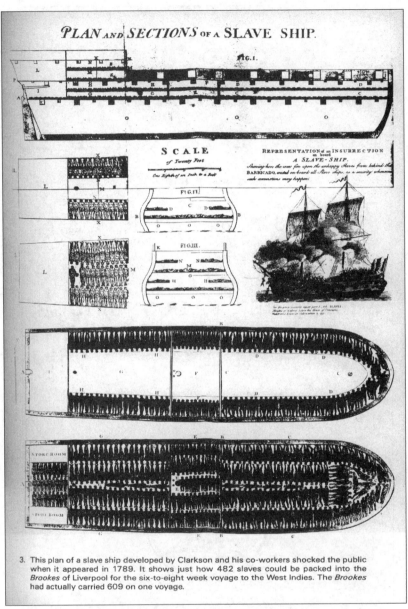

PLAN AND SECTIONS OF A SLAVE SHIP.

3. This plan of a slave ship developed by Clarkson and his co-workers shocked the public when it appeared in 1789. It shows just how 482 slaves could be packed into the *Brookes* of Liverpool for the six-to-eight week voyage to the West Indies. The *Brookes* had actually carried 609 on one voyage.

4 Plan and sections of the slave ship, *Brooks*, 1789.

5 Bance Island, watercolour by John Beckett, 1792.

THE

AFRICAN PRINCE,

A SKETCH

OF THE

LIFE

OF

JOHN HENRY NAIMBANNA,

AN AFRICAN KING'S SON.

LONDON:

Printed by W. Nicholson, Warner Street,

FOR WILLIAMS & SMITH, 10, STATIONERS' COURT,

LUDGATE STREET.

No. XXIV.

6 Title-page from *The African Prince.*

LETTER VII

FREE TOWN, SIERRA LEONE,
10th April, 1792

My dear Madam,

Here I am, once more exposed to the influence of a Torrid sun, near three thousand miles apart from my dearest friends, experiencing not only the inevitable hardships of Colonization, but wallowing in a multiplicity of trouble and confusion, very unnecessarily attached to the infant Colony.[58]

We sailed from Falmouth the 19th of December, and arrived at this place the 16th of February, when we found the *Harpy*, Wilson, a Company ship, that left England some time after us; but our voyage was prolonged, in consequence of being obliged to stop at Teneriffe for a few pipes of Wine.[59]

Immediately on entering the river we were visited by Captain Wilson, and after the customary civilities, he told us several Colonial Officers, a few soldiers, and some independent Settlers came passengers with him, who were greatly rejoiced at seeing the *Amy*, for, being all strangers, they were at a loss what to do, and wholly relied on Falconbridge to make good their landing.

In the course of conversation many sentences escaped Captain Wilson, importing a very unfavourable account of his passengers, but imagining they proceeded from some misunderstanding between them and him,

---

[58] The story of the foundation of the Sierra Leone Colony has been told in detail by Ellen Gibson Wilson in her *The Loyal Blacks*, New York, 1976, and her *John Clarkson and the African Venture,* London, 1980, also by James Walker in his *The Black Loyalists,* London, 1976. The letters written by the Nova Scotian settlers have been published in Christopher Fyfe (ed.), "*Our Children Free and Happy*", Edinburgh, 1991.

[59] Pipes were large casks. While they were there, Falconbridge consumed a great deal of Teneriffe wine, and became publicly drunk, an episode which, as we shall see, was reported to his employers in London (British Library [hereafter BL], Clarkson Papers, Add. MS 41262A, Thomas Clarkson, 17 July 1792).

neither Falconbridge or myself allowed what he said to bias or prejudice us in any shape.

Captain Wilson having directed the most eligible spot for us to bring up, waited until our anchor was gone, and then returned to his ship: Falconbridge accompanied him, to make his obeisance to the Ladies and Gentlemen on board.

In a short time, he was confirmed our surmise with regard to dis-agreements subsisting between the parties was well grounded, for they were constantly snarling at each other; but it required very little pene-tration to arrive at the true source of their animosities, and before I proceed further I must acquaint you, the Directors have appointed eight persons to represent them, and conduct the management of their Colony, under *the dignified appellation of Superintendent and Council.*

It is a pity, when making those appointments, they had not probed for characters of worth and respectability, as success in any enterprise greatly hinges on skilful, prudent conduct; qualities more especially req-uisite in an undertaking like this, labouring under a load of enemies, who will, no doubt, take advantage to blow the smallest spark of mal-conduct into a flame of error.

Perhaps the Directors imagine they were particularly circumspect in their choice of representatives; if so, they are grossly deceived, for never were characters worse adapted to manage any purpose of magnitude than some whom they have nominated.

Are men of little worth and much insignificance fit to be guardians and stewards of the immense property required for erecting the fabric of a new Colony? [60] Are men, whose heads are too shallow to support a little vicissitude and unexpected *imaginary* aggrandizement, whose weak minds delude them with wrong notions of their nominal rank, and whose whole time is occupied with contemplating their fancied consequence, in place of attending to the real and interesting designs of their mission, calculated for the executors of a theory, which can only be put into practice by wise and judicious methods ?

Certainly not; yet of this description are the greater part who guide and direct our Colony, a majority of whom came passengers in the

[60] The Sierra Leone Company was well financed, with subscribed capital of £235,840. £30,000 was estimated for the expenses of the first year, for subsequent years, £7,000 annually (Fyfe, *A History*, p. 30).

Harpy, and who, intoxicated with false ideas of their authority, wished to assume the prerogatives of controlling Captain Wilson in managing and governing his ship; but the latter treated their arrogance with contempt, and consequently grew the dissensions alluded to, which have since been the cause of many disagreeable, unpleasant consequences.

Falconbridge soon returned with Captain and Mrs Wilson, whom we had invited to dine with us; four Honourable members of the Council, dressed *cap a pie*,[61] in a uniform given them by the Directors to distinguish their rank, came with them, to make their bows to your humble servant, as the wife of their *superior*, Falconbridge being the eldest member of this *supreme* body.

A message was then sent to King Jemmy (opposite whose town the *Amy* lay) to announce our arrival to him and King Naimbana (who was there at the time) requesting they would come on board.

Naimbana, accompanied by Mr. Elliotte and a number of attendants, soon complied with our request, but Jemmy would not be prevailed upon.

The old King was overjoyed at seeing me; being seated, Falconbridge showed him the portrait of his son,* a present from the Directors.

  * The first of his family transferred on canvas.

The picture is an admirable likeness, and the poor Father burst into tears when he saw it.

He stayed with us five days; and, notwithstanding every courteous art was used to persuade King Jemmy to honour us with a visit, we could not effect it. He once consented on condition I remained in his town a hostage till he returned; this I agreed to, and went on shore for the intention; but his people dissuaded him just as he was going off.

You may remember I mentioned in a former letter, the ground where the *first Settlers* were driven from by King Jemmy being the most desirable situation hereabouts for a settlement, but by the Palaver it was objected to; however, with coaxing, and the irresistibility of presents, King Naimbana was prevailed upon to remove whatever objections there were, and on the 28th of February put us in quiet possession of the very spot,

[61] From head to foot.

which is named *Free Town,* from the *principles* that gave rise to the establishment.* [62]

> * It is situated on a rising ground, fronting the sea; six miles above Cape Sierra Leone, and eighteen from Bance Island; separated from King Jemmy's town by a rivulet and thick wood, near half a mile through: before the town, is pretty good anchorage for shipping, but the landing places are generally bad, in consequence of the shore being bound with iron rocks, and an ugly surge most commonly breaking on them.

The second day after our arrival, there was a grand Council held on board the *Amy* when their Secretary delivered Mr Falconbridge new instructions from the Directors, directly counter to those he received from London; subjecting him, in his commercial capacity, to the control of the Superintendent and Council, and acquainting him, Lieutenant Clarkson was appointed Superintendent.

This has disconcerted Falconbridge vastly, and inclines him to construe their conduct to us in England as juggle and chicane, for the mere purpose of enticing him here, knowing he was the fittest, nay only, person to secure a footing for the Nova Scotia Emigrants; but I cannot think so harshly.

After being here a fortnight, Mr Clarkson arrived, with the Blacks from America, a part of whom came some days before him.

When he left Nova Scotia, they amounted to between eleven and twelve hundred, but during the voyage a malignant fever infested the Ships, and carried off great numbers.[63]

Mr Clarkson caught the fever, and miraculously escaped death, which would have been an irreparable loss to the Colony, being the only man calculated to govern the people who came with him, for by his winning manners, and mild, benign treatment, he has so gained their affections and attachments, that he can, by lifting up his finger (as he expresses it), do what he pleases with them.

They are, in general, a religious, temperate, good set of people; at

[62] This was the site occupied by the original "Black Poor" settlers (see *footnote* 10). She consistently writes "Free Town", though it was normally written as one word, "Free-town".

[63] Sixty-seven of the Nova Scotian settlers died on board, and another thirty-eight during the first weeks on shore (Fyfe, *A History*, p. 38).

present they are employed in building huts for their temporary residence, till the lands promised them can be surveyed; when that will be God only knows; the surveyor,[64] being a *Counsellor*, and *Captain* of our *veteran host*, is of too much consequence to attend to the servile duty of surveying, notwithstanding he is paid for it.

Few of the Settlers have yet got huts erected, they are mostly encamped under tents made with sails from the different ships, and are very badly off for fresh provisions; indeed such is the case with us all, and what's worse, we have but half allowance of very indifferent salt provision, and bad worm eaten bread. *

> * The *James*, of Bristol, being unfit to proceed her voyage, was con-
> demned and sold at Bance Island about this time; from her a quantity
> of beans and other provisions were purchased which was a fortunate
> circumstance for the Colony, then in a starving state.

Painfully do I say, nothing promises well. – Mr Clarkson, as Super-intendent, is so tied up, that he cannot do any thing without the approbation of his Council, and those opinionated upstarts thwart him in all his attempts.

He is an amiable man, void of pomp or ostentation, which his senatorial associates disapprove of exceedingly, from the ridiculous idea that their *dignity* is lessened by his frankness.

How truly contemptible it is to see men stickle in this way after foolish unbecoming consequence, blind to the interests of their employers, whereby they must, without question, rise or fall.

Their absurd behaviour* make them the laughing stocks of the neigh-bouring Factories, and such masters of slave ships as have witnessed their conduct, who must certainly be highly gratified with the anarchy and chagrin that prevails through the Colony.[65]

> * Few days escaped without a quarrel, which sometimes came to the
> length of blows: Members of Council were daily ordering goods from

64 James Cocks.
65 Her account of the "anarchy and chagrin" was matched by John Clarkson in a ten
  page letter to Thornton demanding that the form of government be changed (BL,
  Add. MS 41262A, Clarkson, 18 April 1792). He subsequently recalled, "in short,
  nothing but Pride Arrogance Self-sufficiency Meanness Drunkenness Atheism and
  Idleness were dayly [sic] practised by those who were sent out to assist me" (*ibid.*,
  Clarkson, 4 April 1793).

the ships, not wanted, and inevitably to be destroyed, merely for the purpose of showing their authority.

The Blacks are displeased that they have not their promised lands; and so little do they relish the obnoxious arrogance of their rulers, that I really believe, was it not for the influence of Mr Clarkson, they would be apt to drive some of them into the sea.

The independent European Settlers are vastly disappointed, and heartily wish themselves back in their own country.[66]

This is not to be wondered at when, in addition to the calamity of being now in a new Colony, over-run with confusion, jealousy, and discordant sentiments, they are exposed to the oppression of wanting almost every necessary of life, having no shops where they might purchase, or any other medium of procuring them.

I have only one piece of pleasing intelligence to give you. – The Colony just now is tolerably healthy; very few deaths have occurred among the Blacks since their arrival, and but two among the Whites; the latter were Doctor B—,[67] (our Physician) and the *Harpy*'s gunner.

The gunner's death was occasioned by that of the former, who brought on his dissolution by inebriety and imprudence; being a member of the Magisterial body, he was buried with all the pomp and ceremony circumstances would admit of.

While the corpse moved on in a solemn pace, attended by Members of Council and others in procession, minute guns were fired from the *Harpy*; in executing this, the gunner lost his arm, of which he died very shortly.

I yet live on ship board, for though the Directors had the goodness to send out a canvas house purposely for me, I have not the satisfaction

---

[66] The European population included ten who had come out as settlers, at their own expense, as well as about a hundred, some with wives and children, employed by the Company (Fyfe, *A History*, p. 35).

[67] Dr John Bell. Thornton had already written to John Clarkson, "I am sorry to have to hint to you that I have heard some things of an unpleasant nature said concerning him particularly that he has been observed to be in liquor once or twice". He went on to explain that he had been appointed, and paid a high salary, because of "his abilities and experience of diseases of warm climates" (BL, Add. MS 41262A, Thornton, 30 December 1792).

of occupying it, our *men of might* having thought proper to appropriate it in another way.

Mr Gilbert, our clergyman, returns to England in the vessel I write by, a fast sailing schooner Mr Clarkson has purchased for the painful but indispensable intention of sending the Directors information of our distracted, deplorable situation; at the same time exhorting them in their *wisdom* to make some immediate, efficacious change in our government, without which their Colony will, irrevocably, be stifled in its infancy.

Mr Gilbert is a man of mild, agreeable manners, truly religious, without the hypocritical show of it; he is universally liked in the Colony, and I am sure his absence will be greatly regretted; but Mr Clarkson's indisposition, rendering him unable to write so fully as he wishes, or necessity demands, has prevailed on him (Mr Gilbert) to return to England, and represent to the Directors, by word of mouth, whatever he may neglect to do in writing.

A party of us will accompany him to the Banana Islands, about ten leagues from hence, where he is in hopes of procuring fresh stock, and other necessary sea stores, which are not to be had here for love or money.

I do not think it will be in my power to write you from the Banana's; shall, therefore, close this letter with sincere hopes my next may give you a more favourable account of things.

Farewell, &c. &c.

LETTER VIII

FREE TOWN, *July* 1, 1792.

My Dear Friend,

We accompanied Mr Gilbert to the Island Banana's, where he succeeded in getting some fresh stock, and after staying there two days departed for your quarter of the globe, and I hope is safe arrived in London long ere now.

The Banana's derives its name from the fruit so called, which grows there spontaneously, and in great abundance, as do most tropical fruits.

It is a small Island, but a wonderfully productive, healthful spot, throngly inhabited by clean, tidy, sociable, and obliging people.

They have a town much larger and more regularly built than any other native town I have yet seen; the inhabitants are mostly vassals to one Mr Cleavland, a Black man, who claims the sovereignty of the Island from hereditary right.[68]

The houses are chiefly constructed in a circular form, but of the same kind of stuff with those I formerly noticed.

In the centre of the town is a Palaver, or Court House; here we observed a bed neatly made up, a wash hand bason, clean napkin, and every apparatus of a bed chamber.

This had a very curious appearance; but we were told, the late Mr Cleavland used to indulge himself with the luxury of sleeping in this airy place, and the inhabitants superstitiously thinking (though he has been dead more than a year) he yet invisibly continues the practice, they would not, on any account, forgo the daily ceremony of making up his bed, placing fresh water, &c. as was the custom in his life time.

The idolatry shown the memory of this man, I make no doubt is

---

[68] James Cleveland (or Clevland) was the grandson of an English slave trader, member of a prominent Devonshire landowning family, who had settled on the island early in the eighteenth century, and married into a prominent Sherbro ruling family (Fyfe, *A History*, p. 10).

greatly encouraged by his son, as it secures consequence and popularity to him.

He was from home, I therefore did not see him, but understand he is clever, and (being educated in England) rather polished in his manners.

We sailed from the Banana's in company with Mr. Gilbert, consequently my time was so short, that I am not able to give you but a superficial account of that island; but shall refer you to Lieutenant Matthews's *Voyage to Sierra Leone*, where you will find it amply described.[69] While there, we dined on board an Irishman, who has since been here entertaining himself at the expense of our *Senators*.

He invited them all to dine with him, which being accepted (by every one but Mr Clarkson and Falconbridge), they were treated with true Hibernian hospitality, and made beastly drunk.

Our illegitimate son of Mars was of the number,[70] who the master of the ship cull'd out for his butt; he not only played upon him during dinner, but afterwards, finding him lull'd into the arms of Morpheus, in consequence of too much wine, had the ship's cook, a slave, dressed in the noble Captain's dashing coat, hat, sword, &c. and stationed immediately before him with a *mop-stick* on his shoulder, when the master, himself, fired two pistols, very heavily charged, within an inch of his ear, and having thus roused him from his lethargy, the sable cook was desired to show with what expertise he could perform the Manual Exercise, which he went through, our *Hero* giving the word of command, to the ridicule of himself, and the great amusement of his colleagues and the ship's crew.

Since this, I have taught a large overgrown female Monkey of mine to go thro' several manoeuvres of the same, and have made her exhibit when the Captain came to see me, who, not seeing the diversion I was making of him, would sometimes take the pains of instructing her himself; but poor fellow ! he has been sadly galled lately by the arrival of a gentleman from England, who supersedes him in his military capacity.

When I last wrote to you, I was in hopes my next would atone by a more favourable and pleasing account, for the hapless description I then gave of our new Colony, but alas! alas! in place of growing better, we seem daily advancing towards destruction, which certainly awaits us at no great distance, unless some speedy change takes place.

[69] See *footnote* 15.

[70] She means James Cocks (see *footnote* 64). When he left in July, Clarkson wrote that he had done no surveying, and had caused only confusion and expense.

There is about twelve hundred souls, including all ranks of people, in the Colony, seven hundred, or upwards, of whom are at this moment suffering under the affliction of burning fevers, I suppose two hundred scarce able to crawl about, and am certain not more, if so many, able to nurse the sick or attend to domestic or Colonial concerns; five, six, and seven are dying daily,* and buried with as little ceremony as so many dogs or cats.

* About three-fourths of all the Europeans who went out in 1792, died in the course of the first nine or ten months.

It is quite customary of a morning to ask, "how many died last night?" Death is viewed with the same indifference as if people were only taking a short journey, to return in a few days; those who are well, hourly expect to be laid up, and the sick look momentarily for the surly Tyrant to finish their afflictions, nay seem not to care for life!

After reading this, methinks I hear you invectively exclaim against the country, and charging those ravages to its unhealthiness; but suspend your judgment for a moment, and give me time to paint the true state of things, when I am of opinion you will think otherwise, or at least allow the climate has not a fair trial.

This is the depth of the rainy season, our inhabitants were not covered in before it commenced, and the huts they have been able to make, are neither wind or water tight; few of them have bedsteads, but are obliged to lie on the wet ground without medical assistance, wanting almost every comfort of life, and exposed to nauseous putrid stenches, produced by stinking provision, scattered about the town.[71]

Would you, under such circumstances, expect to keep your health, or even live a month in the healthiest part of the world ? I fancy not; then pray do not attribute our mortality altogether to baseness of climate.

I cannot imagine what kind of stuff I am made of, for though daily in the midst of so much sickness and so many deaths, I feel myself much better than when in England.

I am surprised our boasted Philanthropists, the Directors of the

[71] She however had a house to live in. Clarkson complained in his journal (27 April 1792) that Falconbridge, aided by his brother-in-law, was spending his time building a house instead of going off, as Commercial Agent, on a trading expedition. She nowhere mentions in her letters that her brother, Charles Horwood, was with them in Sierra Leone. (For the location of the various manuscript versions of John Clarkson's journal, see Wilson, *John Clarkson*, pp. 206–9.)

Company, should have subjected themselves to the censure they must meet for sporting with the lives of such numbers of their fellow creatures – I mean by sending so many here at once, before houses, materials for building, or other conveniences were prepared to receive them, and for not hurrying a supply after they had been guilty of this oversight.

But I really believe their error has proceeded from want of information, and listening, with too much credulity, to a pack of designing, puritanical parasites, whom they employ to transact business; I cannot help thinking so, nay, am convinced of it, from the cargoes they have sent out, composed of goods no better adapted for an infant Colony than a cargo of slaves would be for the London market.

Two vessels arrived from England last month, viz the *Sierra Leone Packet* belonging to the Company; and the *Trusty* of Bristol, a large ship they chartered from that port; several passengers came in each of them; in the former were a Member of Council, a worthy discreet man;[72] a Botanist, who I can say nothing of, having seen but little of him;[73] a sugar planter, who is since gone to the West Indies in disgust, and the Gentleman who has superseded our *gallant* Captain, and who, I understand, is also a cotton planter; but it is not likely that he will have much to do in either of these departments for some time, his fellow soldiers being mostly dead, and agriculture not thought on.[74]

[72] John Wakerell. After a few months his health broke down and he had to return to England where he died (Clarkson, journal, 22 September 1793).

[73] Adam Afzelius, a Swedish botanist, who did the first systematic botanical work in West Africa (see A. P. Kup (ed.), *Adam Afzelius: Sierra Leone Journals, 1795–96*, Uppsala, 1967). The mineralist (geologist) mentioned in the next paragraph, Augustus Nordenskiöld, was also Swedish.

[74] This was Isaac DuBois, whom we shall hear more of later. He was a white American loyalist from a wealthy family in Wilmington, North Carolina, born about 1764. In 1776 he and his widowed mother and her two younger children were banished from Wilmington, and their property confiscated. After serving with the British army as a lieutenant in the New York Volunteers, he went to London at the end of the war to claim compensation for his losses, but was told by the Commissioners for Loyalist Claims that, as he had been under age when his property was taken, he was protected from loss under the Peace Treaty, and should return home and claim it. But on return to Wilmington he was at once put in prison for ten months, and on release banished from the state for life as a traitor. By the time he he got back to London, he found the Claims Office had closed down (*House of Commons Journals*, vol. lxii, pp. 277–8, 845, 954–5). In his penniless state, he took up employment with the Sierra Leone Company. Practical and versatile, he turned doctor during this period of severe illness in Freetown, saving many lives. Then he turned to building houses. He was liked by the Nova Scotian settlers, some of whom had already known him in North Carolina (BL, Add. MS 41263, Clarkson to Hartshorne, September 1793).

In the latter came the Store-keeper, with his wife, mother-in-law, and a large family of children; a mineralist, and several clerks and tradesmen, in all twenty-three. *

* Six returned to England, one left the Colony, and went into the employ of Bance Island, and the remainder died in the course of three or four months.

Those vessels brought so little provisions (with which they should have been wholly loaded) that we have not a sufficiency in the Colony to serve us three weeks. The goods brought out in the *Trusty*, and quantities by other ships, amounting to several thousand pounds value, at this moment line the shore, exposed to the destructive weather and *mercy* of our neighbours, who cannot, I am sure, withstand such temptation. Those remaining on ship board, I have heard Falconbridge say, are perishing by heat of the hold, and damage received at sea. Notwithstanding the Company's property is thus suffering, and our people dying from absolute want of nourishment, Mr Falconbridge has been refused the *Sierra Leone Packet* to go in quest of cattle, and otherwise prosecute the duties of his office as Commercial Agent. She is the only vessel fit for the business, but it is thought necessary to send her to England; yet, if things were ordered judiciously, she might have made one serviceable trip in the mean while, and answered three desirable purposes by it: relieve the Colony, bartered away goods that are spoiling, and please the Directors by an early remittance of African productions; in place of this she has only been used as a *Pleasure Boat*, to give a week's airing at sea to *Gentlemen* in perfect health.

Mr. Falconbridge has had no other opportunity but this to do any thing in the commercial way; the Directors, no doubt, will be displeased, but they should not blame him; he is placed altogether under the control of the Superintendent and Council, who throw cold water on every proposal of the kind he makes. His time is at present employed in attending the sick, particularly those of scrophulous habits, while our military gentleman, who has acquired by experience some medical knowledge, attends those afflicted with fevers, &c. This is the only physical help at present in the Colony, for though we have two surgeons they are both so ill, as to disable them from helping either themselves, or others; one of them returns to England in the *Packet*, as does our *mortified soldier*.

I am, &c.

LETTER IX

SIERRA LEONE, *Aug.* 25, 1792.

My Dear Friend,

You must not promise yourself either instruction or entertainment from this letter, for my strength of body and mind are so debilitated by a severe fit of illness, that with much ado I could summon resolution enough to take up my pen, or prevail on myself to write you a syllable by this opportunity, but having made a beginning (which is equal to half the task), I shall now endeavour to spin out what I can.

I was confined three weeks with a violent fever, stoneblind four days, and expecting every moment to be my last; indeed I most miraculously escaped the jaws of death: fortunately, just as I was taken sick, a Physician arrived, to whose attention and skill I consider myself principally indebted for my recovery.[75] I am yet a poor object, and being under the necessity of having my head shaved, tends to increase my ghastly figure. You will readily guess it was very humbling and provoking for me to lose my fine head of hair, which I always took so much pride in, but I cannot help it, and thank God my life is preserved.

A few weeks since arrived the *Calypso,* from Bulam, with a number of disappointed adventurers who went to that Island;[76] they came here in expectation of finding accommodation for a part of them during the rainy season, who meant afterwards to return to Bulam: but they entertained wrong notions of our Colony, when they supposed we had it in our power to accommodate them, for most of our own gentlemen are obliged to sleep on ship board, for want of houses or lodgings on shore.

[75] This was Dr Thomas Winterbottom, who was to stay in Sierra Leone until 1796. He published a comprehensive two-volume account of the country, including the first systematic work on African medicine (Thomas Winterbottom, *An Account of the Native Africans in the Neighbourhood of Sierra Leone,* London, 1803, reprinted London, 1969). Not only did he survive his stay in Sierra Leone, he lived to the age of ninety-four, and when he died was said to be the oldest doctor in Europe.

[76] "Bulam" was the island of Bulama about 250 miles north of Sierra Leone. Lieutenant Philip Beaver, whom she mentions at the end of her "laconic" narrative of this disastrous venture, eventually published a full account of it: *African Memoranda,* London, 1805.

The adventurers seem vexed at being thus defeated in their expectations, and intend to return to England in the *Calypso* when she sails, which will be shortly.

Perhaps you have not heard of the Bulam expedition before, and I can give you but an imperfect account of it; however, I will laconically tell you what I know.

A Mr Dalrymple was engaged by the Directors of the Sierra Leone Company to come out as Governor of this Colony; but they disagreed from some trifling circumstance, and Mr Dalrymple, feeling himself offended, set on foot (towards the latter end of last year), a subscription for forming a settlement on the Island I am speaking of, in opposition to the Sierra Leone Company. A number of speculators soon associated, subscribed to Mr Dalrymple's plan, and, I fancy prematurely, set about the completion of its objects, before they had well digested the theory, or accumulated a sufficient fund to ensure success; be that as it may, they purchased a small sloop, chartered the *Calypso* and another ship, engaged numbers of needy persons, who, with many of the subscribers, personally embarked on the enterprise, and placing themselves under the direction of Mr Dalrymple, and a few others, sailed from England in April last, and arrived at Bulam in June.

I understand they were all novices in the arts and modes requisite for attaining their wished for possession, which was unfortunate, for their ignorance led them into an error, that proved fatal to several.

Although the island of Bulam was uninhabited, it was claimed by persons residing on the adjacent Islands, who, by some means or other, learned of the errand of the adventurers, and to prevent them from getting a footing without the consent of the proprietors, secretly landed a party of men on the Island, where they for several days watched the motions of Mr Dalrymple's people: between thirty or forty of whom having disembarked and landed (without any previous ceremony, according to the custom of the country), the natives took the first opportunity to catch them off their guard, fell upon them, killed five men and one woman, wounded two men, carried off three women and children, and obliged the remainder to return to their ship.

After this Mr Dalrymple went to the neighbouring Island of Bissao, belonging to the Portuguese, where he, through the medium of a merchant of that country, became acquainted with the measures he should have adopted at first, and having courted the friendship of the native chiefs, and made them sensible of his peaceable and honourable intentions, they restored the women and children uninjured and gave him possession of the Island, for some trifling acknowledgment I have not yet ascertained.

Mr Dalrymple had accomplished this but a short time when he fell sick, and many of the emigrants foreseeing frightful hardships which they were unwilling to encounter during the present rains, he and they resolved to return to England, but first to come hither for the purpose I before mentioned.

The Island is not altogether abandoned, a Lieutenant Beaver of the Navy, with a few people, remain upon it.

Since their arrival here many of them have died, and the ship is just now very sickly. – So much for Bulam.

Now I must say something of ourselves, which I have the heartfelt satisfaction of telling you before hand will be more cheerful and satisfactory than any thing I have heretofore said.

By the last ship, Mr Clarkson received instructions from the Directors, vesting him with more ample powers than he held before: this was much to be wished for, and its beneficial effects are already visible.

Directly after getting this enlargement of authority, Mr Clarkson invited all the gentlemen and ladies in the Colony to dine at a mess house, built for the gentlemen who came out in the *Sierra Leone Packet* ; every one who was well enough gladly attended to celebrate a meeting which was intended to give birth to pleasantness, unanimity and perpetual harmony; and to deface every thing to the contrary. that previously existed in the Colony. The day I am told (for being sick at the time, I could not be there) was spent, as it should be, with every demonstration of satisfaction, by all parties, and the house was named *Harmony Hall* , by which name it is now, and I suppose ever will be, known, while a stick of it stands.[77] This house, and the one I have, are all the buildings yet finished (I mean for the Whites), but several others are about.

The Colony is growing healthier every day; most of the Blacks are able to turn out to work. The men are employed in the Company's service, and receive two shillings per day wages, out of which they pay four shillings per week for their provisions.

---

[77] It was destroyed, with the Company's other buildings, when the French attacked Freetown in September 1794.

The women are occupied in attending their little gardens, and rearing poultry.

The natives daily grow more intimate with us, and are constantly bringing in fruits of different kinds, but seldom any live stock, unless now and then a few fowls, or perhaps a goat, which they barter away for cloth, soap or spirits.

Every moon-light night we hear the drums of King Jemmy's town, which is scarcely half a mile from hence. This music of our neighbours, for a long time after we arrived, used frequently to alarm the Colony; but by custom it has become familiar. For several months *King* Jemmy could not be persuaded to come into Free Town; but at last being prevailed upon, and relishing his reception, he now repeats his visits so often, as to be very troublesome. Whenever he comes, a boy attends him with a pair of horseman's pistols, loaded, and I will not be surprised, if he does mischief with them some day or other, for he never returns home until he has drank a sufficient quantity of rum or brandy, to kindle his savage nature for any manner of wickedness.

The last ship brought out a large house of one hundred feet in length, which is to be erected in the vicinity of the town as an hospital; but the people being mostly on the recovery, I think it would be more advisable to erect it as a store-house, and thereby not only save the Company's valuable property, which is just now perishing for want of shelter, but would serve as a repository for vending many goods that are wasting on board of ships, which would greatly contribute to our comfort, and which we are deprived of from not having a proper place where they might be exposed to sale; and again, I do not think our Blacks will submit to be sent to an hospital, therefore, the intention will be frustrated; however, the house is so constructed, that it can be put up or taken down in a few hours, consequently may, at any time hereafter, be removed; and we understand several houses of the same kind are expected in two large ships, which are hourly looked for.

Since the rains, we have been sadly infested by a variety of insects, but more particularly cockroaches and ants; the latter come from their nests in such formidable force, as to strike terror wherever they go. You will think it strange, that such an insignificant insect as the ant is in England, should be able in another country, to storm the habitations of people, and drive out the inhabitants; but I pledge my veracity to you, I have known them in one night, force twelve or fourteen families from their houses, who were obliged to make use of fire and boiling water to destroy them, which are the only weapons we can attack them with, that will effectually check their progress.

Musquettos are not so troublesome here as I have felt them elsewhere; but we have a perpetual croaking of frogs and buzzing of various vermin, very discordant and unpleasant to the ear of a person in perfect health, yet much more so to those who are sick.

There has been several large serpents killed in the Colony, but none of the overgrown size Lieutenant Matthews and other authors mention; the largest I have heard of measured nine feet in length. We have been twice visited by some ferocious wild beast, supposed to be a Tyger; the last time it was attacked by two mastiffs of ours, who were beat off and materially injured. One of my poor domestics, a very heavy Newfoundland dog, had his throat terribly lacerated: the other, I imagine, fought shy, as he came off with little damage.[78]

There are many good hunters among our Settlers, through whom we sometimes get wild deer or pork; the latter is a coarse, unpleasant food; I lately had a haunch, the hide of which was full an inch and an half thick; the former is meagre, dry meat, very unlike your English venison, but such as it is, we are glad when it comes in our way.

Some little time ago an accident happened to one of the most expert hunters we have, which has considerably lessened our supply of game; he was laying in ambush near where he knew a deer frequented; another person, in pursuit of the same, passing hard by, and hearing the rustling of leaves, immediately fired into the thicket from which the noise proceeded, and lodged the greater contents of his gun in the head and right shoulder of his unfortunate rival, but, not killing him, he brought him home, two miles through the wood, on his shoulder. Falconbridge extracted several of the shot, and thinks he may recover.

Our Botanist and Mineralist have, as yet, made little proficiency in those branches of natural philosophy; the confusion of the Colony has retarded them as well as others; they are both Swedes, and considered very eminent in their professions.[79] The Mineralist is about to make an

[78] Another account of this episode describes the animal more plausibly as a leopard (BL, Add. MS 41264, fol. 14). There are no indigenous tigers in Africa.

[79] They were both members of the Swedenborgian Church, and were hoping to discover, somewhere in the heart of Africa, the pure African Church which Emanuel Swedenborg believed was hidden there (see Fyfe, A History, pp. 42–3).

excursion into the interior country, and is very sanguine in his expectations. He has but slightly explored the country hereabouts, and been as slightly rewarded; the only fruits of his researches are a few pieces of iron ore, richly impregnated with magnetism, with which the mountains abound.

The Botanist is preparing a garden for experiments, and promises himself much amusement and satisfaction, when he can strictly attend to his business. His garden is now very forward, but it is attended with considerable expense; however, a mere nothing, when put into the great scale of Colonial charges, which, including shipping, Officers' salaries, wages of labourers, and provisions, does not amount to less than the enormous sum of one hundred and fifty pounds per day, without naming incidental charges, such as presents to natives, daily waste and destruction of property, &c. Those aggregated from the birth of the Company, to the present time, may at least be computed at £25,000.[80]

This is not a supposition of my own, for I have heard it from those who must certainly be informed on the business; but notwithstanding the Company's purse is so much weakened by folly and want of circumspection, if the harmony and good understanding at present existing in the Colony continues, it is yet sufficiently strong, by being applied with method, and proper exertions, not only to retrieve their losses, and answer their original laudable and magnanimous purposes, but amply requite any pecuniary motives they may have.

Mr Falconbridge has obtained permission from Mr Clarkson to commence his commercial career, and had selected goods for the purpose, but was checked by illness, and is dangerously ill at this moment. If he recovers, his first assay will be on the Gold Coast, where he anticipates success, and often says he hopes to cheer the despondent Directors, by a valuable and unexpected cargo.[81]

Mr Clarkson thinks it too early to meddle with trade, from the idea that it will procrastinate the regularity and comfort of the Colony which

[80] Clarkson was later to estimate the money wasted during the first year as "upwards of £40,000". (BL, Add. MS 41263, Clarkson to Hartshorne, September 1793).

[81] Clarkson's story was very different — that Falconbridge knew nothing about trade and had taken to drink instead. His health had broken down, and on 18th August, a week before she wrote this letter, Clarkson wrote in his journal, "Mr Falconbridge talks of going in the *Ocean* to fetch stock from the Sherbro country but it *is all talk*, he is very ill, and will never be better". He added on the 19th, "Dr Winterbottom ... has given up Mr Falconbridge as a lost case".

he is strenuously endeavouring to establish; but from my slender notion of things, I humbly beg leave to differ from him, and rather suppose it would greatly contribute to accelerate his wishes; at least it would not be the smallest hindrance, or by any means interfere with our police,[82] which to be sure will not yet bear a scrupulous investigation; however it is mending, and I dare say, in time, our able, zealous pilot, will steer us clear of the labyrinth which he found us entangled in.

May it be so, is the earnest wish of,

Yours, &c, &c.

---

[82] "Police" in the sense of "administration".

Editor's Comment

As the next letter shows, a decision about Falconbridge had already been taken. Henry Thornton, the Chairman of the Board of Directors, had written privately to Thomas Clarkson on 30 December 1791 with doubts about Falconbridge.

> We were at first considerably pleased with him and after a few weeks inquiry and deliberation were so far satisfied as to appoint him chief Commercial Agent at a salary of £250 p. a. adding £100 present also – We discovered in him however by degrees a great constitutional warmth of temper which has rather alarmed and made us fear, lest with power in his hands he should be carried to any sudden act of violence – want of punctuality and of regular commercial habit has also made us think him as unfit for the Leader in a commercial Factory, tho' notwithstanding both these points we are disposed to think favorably of him in general and we are grateful to him as I am sure we ought to be for the services he has rendered to the Company.

Clarkson however sent his brother, John, who was directing affairs in Sierra Leone, a more explicit account ("for your own privacy and conduct") of how the Company intended to treat John's erstwhile campaign comrade and bodyguard (letter dated January 1792).

After telling him that Falconbridge's salary had been raised to £250 a year, he went on, "The Directors however do not approve his conduct. They consider him hot, rash and impetuous; as likely to involve us in Wars; and as perhaps not over careful how he offends those united with him in office". They had only sent him back because he had made friends with Naimbana and Elliot, and it was now for John to try and supplant him in their affections:

> As your influence increases, that of Falconbridge will decline. This is in fact what the Company wish: for it would be a Pity that the noble Objects of our Institution should be hazarded by the Impetuosity and Warmth of Temper of an Individual, or that we, with so large a Capital, should be wholly at his Mercy.

> The above circumstances will not only render it necessary that you should *create the Interest* alluded to [i.e. make friends with Naimbana and Elliot], but that when you make up your mind how long you will stay at Sierra Leone (which you should do as soon as you can) you should give the Directors the earliest notice of it and not leave the Country till they send a Successor to you ... *This is actually necessary,* for Falconbridge is the next

in Precedence in the Council to you, and in Case of your leaving Sierra Leone without a Successor from England, he comes directly into the Office of Governor, a thing which of all things the Company would be most afraid. All their Hopes would be undone by such a Measure".

His next letter (3 May 1792) added a postscript asking to be remembered to Falconbridge and his wife, and an apology that he had been too busy to write to them.

Clarkson's next letter (17 July 1792) came with the news of Falconbridge's dismissal:

> You will be sorry to find, as I am, that poor Falconbridge is to be recalled. It was impossible for us to help him out of it. He is said to have given no account whatever of the *Lapwing*'s cargo; to have taken up without leave of the Company a person of the name of Coppinger at Falmouth; to have disregarded in every Instance his Instructions; to have acted such a drunken Scene at Teneriffe as to be disgraceful to a Company whose object is so amiable. These and a variety of other things are alleged against him, but particular [sic] the disregard to all the Instructions given him.

He went on to suggest that if Falconbridge could be persuaded to resign and come home immediately, his dismissal could be kept secret (though as his successor as Commercial Agent had already arrived, it is hard to see how it could have been).

Wilberforce, another director of the Company, also wrote to John Clarkson (17 July 1792) about Falconbridge:

> I regret very sincerely that in my public capacity I have been compelled to consent to the Measure of his Removal. But in these Cases we must be ready to sacrifice our private feelings no less than our personal Interests. What I wanted to add on this head is that I hope if Falcge. behaves well, the Directors will be prevailed on to make him some pecuniary Acknowledgment beyond what he has a Right to demand: of course no assurance of this Sort ought to be given him, but perhaps it might not be amiss for you to throw out the Idea as from yourself, and as what you would be willing to promote – All this is left to your Discretion.

However, Company sympathy for Falconbridge soon dissipated.

In a further letter (14 September 1792) Thornton made Falconbridge a general scapegoat for the early misfortunes of the settlement (a charge that, as we shall see, he was to repeat later publicly): "I think however much of the evils that have happened are to be laid at his door". He also absolved himself and the other directors from blame with the excuse that it was not in fact they who had originally appointed him – that he had been "rather continued than appointed by us". (The above letters are to be found in BL, Add. MS 41262A).

LETTER X

My dear Friend,

Within ten or twelve days after the date of my last, arrived the two ships that were expected. One is the *York,* a large vessel of a thousand tons (belonging to the Company), that is intended to end her days here in the character of a storeship, for which purpose she is admirably adapted; the other is the *Samuel and Jane,* likewise a vessel of great burden, chartered to remain here six months if wanted. This vessel arrived some days before the *York,* in her came a Mr Wallis, to supersede Falconbridge,[83] the Directors having thought proper to annul his appointment as Commercial Agent.

That they had a right to do so, I will not question; but methinks it develops treachery; and I now suspect their whole conduct to us in England, was only a complication of hypocritical snares, to answer selfish purposes, which having attained, they cared not any longer to wear the mask.

In their dismission they accuse Falconbridge of not extending their commercial views, and wanting commercial knowledge. The latter charge may be in some measure well founded, for Mr Falconbridge was bred to physic, and men of perspicuity would have known how unfit such a person must be for a merchant, indeed he was aware of it himself, but it being a place of much expected profit (a temptation not to be withstood), he was in hopes by application, soon to have improved the little knowledge he had, so as to benefit both his employers and himself; but

---

83 Wallis was a bankrupt slave trader who had spent twenty-five years in the slave trade, and (so Thomas Clarkson wrote to his brother) "has no objection to the trade at present" (BL, Add. MS 41262A, T. Clarkson, 17 July 1792). He too was addicted to drink. Clarkson wrote in his diary, "I am persuaded when he gets from the Colony with the entire charge of his vessel and cargo and no check upon his conduct, he will continually be in such a state as to be unfit for active and profitable business" (7 September 1792). His drunkenness and incompetence were to be confirmed by Clarkson's successors (Zachary Macaulay's journal, Huntington Library, San Marino, California, MY 418, 29 August 1793).

in this they disappointed him, and were actually the cause of choking the attempts he might have made.

They should recollect the deep deception played upon him. He left England with independent and unlimited powers, which were restrained immediately on our arrival here. Thus bridled, with the reins in possession of men who considered commerce only as a secondary view of the Company, and who negatived every proposition of the kind Falconbridge made, till a very short time before his appointment was annulled – What was he to do ?

Two days before his dismission came out, he crawled from his sick bed, and, at the moment it was delivered him, was in the act of arranging and preparing matters for the trading voyage I mentioned in my last. I am certain it proved a mortal stab to him; he was always addicted to drink more than he should; but after this, by way of meliorating his harrowed feelings, he kept himself constantly intoxicated; a poor, forlorn remedy you will say; however, it answered his wish, which I am convinced was to operate as poison, and thereby finish his existence; he spun out his life in anguish and misery till the 19th instant, when without a groan he gasp'd his last!!! [84]

I will not be guilty of such meanness as to tell a falsehood on this occasion, by saying I regret his death, no ! I really do not, his life had become burthensome to himself and all around him, and his conduct to me, for more than two years past, was so unkind (not to give a harsher term) as long since to wean every spark of affection or regard I ever had for him. This I am persuaded, was his greatest crime; he possessed many virtues, but an excellent dutiful son, and a truly honest man, were conspicuous traits in his character.

I shall now return to the arrival of the *York;* in this ship came out the Rev. Mr Horne and a Mr Dawes, who is a new appointed member of council. I must not proceed any further till I inform you, the Directors have wholly changed their original system of government, dismounted the old Council, and placed their political reins in the hands of Mr Clarkson, who is to be assisted by two Counsellors, one of whom is the gentleman I just mentioned, the other is not yet appointed.

[84] John Clarkson wrote in his journal, "He has been killing himself by slow degrees for the last three months, and for some days past his Bones have been through his skin in several parts of his Body. He died this eveng. at six o'clock a very happy release both to him and to those about him" (Journal, 19 December 1792, quoted in Wilson, *John Clarkson*, p. 117).

The new ministry is titled, "The Governor and Council", and are charged with the management of all civil, military, and commercial affairs, but have no authority whatever to interfere in ecclesiastical matters, which are left to the guidance of Mr Horne or any other Minister for the time being.

Time will show whether this alteration of politics proves propitious, as yet things have not fallen off, but rather mended.

We are and have been frequently much pestered by renegade seamen, quitting ships employed in the Slave Trade, and refuging here, to the great detriment of their employers and inconvenience of the Colony. This circumstance considerably perplexes Mr Clarkson, who, on the one hand, is not only threatened with lawsuits by the masters and owners of ships detained for want of their sailors, but is well convinced of the injury they sustain; on the other, his orders are to *protect every man,* which leaves him in an awkward situation, and at a loss what to do; however, by way of intimidation to practices of the kind, he had the following notification (which has not availed any thing) sent to some of the neighbouring factories and stuck up in the Colony:

FREE TOWN, SIERRA LEONE,

Sept. 3rd, 1792.

"This is to give Notice, that I will not on any account, permit Seamen, who may leave their respective Vessels, to take shelter in this Colony; and I shall give orders in future that the Constables seize every man who cannot give a good account of himself, or whom they may suspect to have deserted from their employ. At the same time I shall always be ready to listen to the complaints of every injured man, and shall transmit their affidavits home to England, provided they make application in a proper manner.

(signed)

JOHN CLARKSON"

It is much to be lamented, however desirable the abolition of the Slave Trade may be, while it is sanctioned by the English Government, property of individuals in that trade should be harassed and annoyed by want of order and regularity in this Colony, or by the fanatical prejudices of any set of men. One ship in particular has suffered most essentially, viz. the *Fisher,* Clark, of Liverpool, whose men deserted from her in July last, and though she has had her cargo engaged ever since, she is not yet able to quit the coast for want of seamen; some of whom died, and others are now here, *employed in the Company's service.*[85]

On the 26th, 27th, and 28th of September, there was an assembly of native Chieftains here, and a Palaver was held for the purpose of ascertaining the limits of the Company's territory. This was attended with considerable more expense than Falconbridge's palaver, and the consequence far less productive. They finished by curtailing the bounds, from twenty miles square (the quantity purchased by Captain Thompson, and afterwards confirmed to the St George's Bay Company), to about two miles and a quarter fronting the sea, and running in a direct line back, as far as the district of Sierra Leone may be, which is generally supposed not to exceed five or six miles, and three fourths of it a barren, rocky, mountainous country, where it will be impossible for men, who are to earn their bread by agriculture, even to support themselves; but admitting it was all good, there is not more than will enable the Company to comply with one-fifth part of their engagements to the Blacks brought from America, which proportion is now surveying for them.

This circumstance, I am persuaded, will hereafter lead to much discontent and uneasiness among the settlers, and, if I do not soothsay wrongly, will shackle those gentlemen who have been the instruments of removing them with such disgrace as they will not easily expunge.

When the Palaver was ended, and Naimbana (who presided at it on the part of the natives) was about to return to Robana, Mr Clarkson, by way of amusing and complimenting the King, took him in a boat with six oarsmen and a cockswain, who rowed them through the fleet in the harbour, consisting of six or seven sail; each vessel, as they passed, saluted them with several guns, till they came to the *Harpy*, when they were not noticed by the smallest token of respect, on the contrary, Captain Wilson called to Mr. Clarkson and told him he had a few words to say to him; Mr Clarkson replied, if they were not of much consequence he wished to be excused just then, but upon Wilson's assuring him they were of some importance, the Governor complied with his request and went on board: Captain Wilson then said, he was much offended that Mr Clarkson should take a boat's crew from his ship, and a cockswain

[85] The *Fisher* had arrived at the Isles de Los, north of Sierra Leone, at the end of June and was only able to sail in March 1793. Meanwhile fourteen of the 356 slaves purchased had died, and another nineteen died on the passage to Grenada (HLRO, L5/J/11/2).

from another; till that moment Mr. Clarkson had not observed such to be the case, and assured Captain Wilson it was done inadvertently, without the slightest intention of giving offence. This acknowledgment was not enough for Captain Wilson, and his temper being irritated, he used some very indiscreet expressions to Mr Clarkson, such as telling him: "Damn me, Sir, if ever you shall have another boat's crew from my ship, unless you have a cockswain also", &c. &c. The Governor was hurt at such language and returned to his boat; King Naimbana enquired of him why that ship did not fire? He answered, "Mrs. Wilson is sick, and the Captain does not like to disturb her with the noise".[86]

The King then embarked on board the *Lapwing* Cutter and went home. When he was gone, and the Colony clear of all the Chiefs, Mr Clarkson sent a message to Captain Wilson, desiring him to make an apology for his unhandsome behaviour, or he (Mr Clarkson) would be under the necessity of taking steps very repugnant to his inclination. Wilson positively refused, and continuing obstinate two days (wholly engrossed with messages and answers, to and fro), Mr Clarkson, although a man of humility and condescension, unwilling to brook so gross an insult, summoned every gentleman in the Colony to meet him on board the *Amy;* and when they were collected, wrote a letter, summoning Captain Wilson: which summons being disobeyed, he appealed to the assembly, who unanimously determined the delinquent should be dismissed from command of the *Harpy;* in consequence whereof, his dismission, signed by the Governor and Mr Dawes, was sent immediately.

When the boat that carried it came under the *Harpy's* stern (being a little after eight at night), she was hailed, and asked whither she was

---

[86] Here is Clarkson's own account in his journal (28 September 1792):

> When I arrived on the quarter deck, he accosted me with much haughtiness, asked me why I had a coxswain from another vessel to steer his boat, and added with an oath that he would not suffer any coxswain but his own to steer a boat of his while his people were rowing me. I was ignorant of this circumstance, but, as I saw that the man had worked himself up to great irritation, and not wishing the King to notice any dispute between Captain Wilson and myself, I took no notice of his conduct, but asked him how Mrs Wilson did, as I knew she had been ill. He replied in the same tone as before, "she is dying, Sir", upon which I wished him a good afternoon and walked out of the ship. The insult in so far as it related to myself, I did not in the least regard, but I thought more of the impression it might make upon the King who partly noticed it and asked me why the ship did not cheer. Fortunately for me, from Captain Wilson's reply about his wife, I instantly had an answer and said, "woman too much sick, King".

bound? "To the *Harpy*, with a letter for Captain Wilson", answered the bearer. "I am desired to inform you, no boat will be permitted to come along side at such an improper hour; and if you proceed a boat's length further, Captain Wilson's orders are to fire on you", replied a voice from the *Harpy*: these threats not intimidating the boat's crew, two muskets were actually fired on them, but did no mischief; and reaching the ship before another fire, the undaunted messenger attempted to ascend the gangway, but was prevented by the ship's company, who cut away the gangway ropes, and beat him off with cutlasses, sticks, &c.

Captain Wilson having learned the purport of this letter, from some person who afterwards went on board, declared he would not be removed from his ship with life, and he would blow out that man's brains, who dared attempt to enforce him! This boisterous disposition subsided by the following day, when his dismission, with minutes of every gentleman's opinion who had been at the meeting over night, were sent him. He then persisted that he would not *tamely* leave his ship, but if any person, authorised, forcibly attempted to take him out, he would make no unlawful resistance. Mr Dawes volunteered this duty, went on board, and after, in vain, persuading Wilson not to put him to the unpleasant task of using violence, he took him by the collar, and *gently* led him over the ship's side. When descending into the boat, he called to his Officers and men, "Observe ! I am forced out of my ship". He was then conducted to the *York*, where he was informed his residence would be until an opportunity offered to send him to England.

This fracas being thus quieted, perfect harmony otherwise subsisting among us, Mr Clarkson, having some idea of returning to Europe, wished before hand, to furnish Mr Dawes with a trial of his influence among the Blacks, and individual management of the Colony; and judging a trip to sea, for a few weeks, would be the best means of affording such an opportunity, he sailed in the *Amy* on the 2nd of October, in company with a small brig of the Sierra Leone Company's, then bound home to England; but in which Mr and Mrs Wilson could not take their passage, the accommodations being previously disposed of.

When Mr Clarkson sailed, he desired Captain Wilson might be informed, he was not to consider himself a prisoner, but at liberty to conduct himself as he pleased, and visit any where he liked, except the *Harpy,* which ship he was strictly prohibited from putting his foot on board.

In about three weeks Mr Clarkson returned; a multiplicity of complaints were then poured into him by the Settlers, against Mr Dawes, whose austere, reserved conduct (so reverse to the sweet manners of the other) they could not possibly relish, and consequently all hopes or expectations of the latter gaining popularity, proved abortive. It may not be *mal-a-propos* to mention here, that Mr Dawes is a subaltern of Marines; that the prejudices of a rigid military education have been heightened by his having served some time at Botany Bay, where, no doubt, it is necessary for gentlemen to observe an awful severity in their looks and actions;[87] but such behaviour, however suitable for a Colony formed wholly of Convicts, and governed by the iron rod of despotism, should be scrupulously guarded against in one like this, whose *basis is Liberty and Equality*, and whose Police is dependent, in great measure, if not altogether, on the whimsical disposition of an ignorant populace, which can only be advantageously tempered by placidness and moderation.

The Directors having ordered home the *Harpy*, when she could be spared from the Colony, Mr Clarkson, on his return, desired she might be expeditiously fitted for sea, and on the 28th of last month, being Sunday, and most of the Colony piously engaged, Captain Wilson, knowing she was nearly ready, availed himself of the chance, and through the means of her boat, that came under pretence of giving him an airing, replaced himself, by consent of his Officers and crew, in command of his ship, and immediately after divine service Mr Clarkson received the following letter from him.

November 18, 1792.

SIR,

I apprehend it is needless to inform you I have taken possession of the *Harpy*, and mean, in defiance of all opposition, to carry her to England.

As I should be very sorry to be exceeded in politeness on this occasion,* I write this to ask your commands for London, intending to sail immediately; nevertheless, Sir, if within an hour I receive an answer, assuring

---

[87] William Dawes had served for several years at Botany Bay, but was dismissed from the service by the governor, because he objected to being made to take part in an attack on some Aborigines (M. B. Eldershaw, *Phillip of Australia*, London, 1938, pp. 201–2, 314).

me of your pacific intentions, signed by *yourself* and *Mr Dawes,* I will wait your orders.

Take care, Sir, how you attempt any thing like force; if blood is shed, be it upon your head. Wishing you more prudence, and better advisers,

I remain, Sir,
Your most humble Servant,
T. H. WILSON.

John Clarkson, Esq. &c. &c.

* Mr. Clarkson had wrote a day or two before this to Mrs Wilson, offering *her* a passage in the *Harpy,* and at the same time informing Captain Wilson she was to sail in a few days, if he wished to write.

This was a step so unlooked for, that it puzzled the Governor and Council how to conduct themselves: after some deliberation, they determined not to answer Captain Wilson's letter, and the time he limited having elapsed, we saw the *Harpy* under the guns of the *York,* and under the guns of the Battery, get under way, and triumphantly sail off.

Various opinions prevailed respecting the propriety of Captain Wilson's repossessing himself of the *Harpy:* some said it was an act of piracy, and they were certain he would never take her to England; but others judged less harshly, with whom I join; and, from my knowledge of Captain Wilson, feel myself authorised to say, he possesses too great a share of pride, and too high a sense of honour, to shipwreck his character on the rock of infamy – but at the same time will not aver him inerrable; on the contrary, think his behaviour to Mr Clarkson monstrous disrespectful and inconsistent, which, without doubt, he was betrayed into by warmth of temper, and too lofty, but wrong, notions of punctilios.

I have been particularly obliged to Captain Wilson, therefore it would be truly ungenerous, nay, the blackest ingratitude in me, mischievously, to hint at any thing prejudicial to him, and must beg you not to suppose I have touched upon the subject by way of assailing his character; considering it a circumstance of importance, I could not pass over it in silence*.

* Should this Narrative meet the eye of Captain Wilson, I trust he will do me the justice to say, I have not wandered from the broadway of truth.

On the 2nd instant arrived the *Felicity* from England. I mention the arrival of this vessel, because she was expected to bring a number of useful stores for the Colony, in place of which her cargo consisted principally of *garden watering pots*. [88]

In her way out she stopped at Gambia, and took in several head of cattle, whereby we are now and then indulged with roast beef, the first we have had since our arrival, for the inhabitants, here-abouts, are too indolent to attend to rearing domestic quadrupeds of any kind. – King Naimbana has two or three very fat beeves; and I think there may be as many more at Bance Island; but before the *Felicity* arrived, I can venture to say, those were all in this part of the country, unless I include a couple of milch cows and a bull brought out from England by the *York,* which from the inimical climate, died in a very short time. These brought from Gambia are thin, the flesh dark and coarse, and only the name of beef as a recommendation. Mutton and goat's flesh are the most preferable in their kinds; indeed, the former, though not overloaded with fat, I think nearly as sweet as our English mutton, but the little we get of them come chiefly from the interior country.

About the latter end of October, the rains began to diminish; and for a month past have entirely ceased: they are succeeded by dense, disagree- able, and unwholesome fogs, which are supposed will continue near a month longer. These are termed smokes, [89] and considered more unhealthy than the first rains, but we cannot say so from experience, for the Colony is healthier just now, than it has been since the beginning of May; yet a few deaths happen now and then. Among those who lately died was Mr. Nordenschold, the Mineralist, who was taken ill on the expedition I noticed in my last he was then about to make, and forced to return without acquiring any satisfaction for his journey, which was attended not only with innumerable disadvantages from the time of year, but with many other impediments he did not foresee or expect.

The loss of him is much to be regretted, for he was an enterprising, clever man, and no doubt, had he lived, would have procured a vast deal of useful information.

The Governor and Council have at last thought it advisable to embark

---

[88] Clarkson commented in his diary, 21st (not "2d") November 1792, "The *Felicity's* cargo does not appear to be well selected considering our wants; she has brought out an immense number of *garden watering pots,* which seem to occasion a smile from every one".

[89] The *harmattan* season.

in Agriculture, and have purchased a small track of land on the opposite (Bullom) shore. This new undertaking is placed under the management of a man who was some time an overseer in Dominica, and who was a *Member of the first Council:*[90] it is called *Clarkson's Plantation,* and from the richness and apparent fertility of the soil, much advantage may be looked for, provided no disagreement arises with the natives, and a sufficient number of steady labourers can be obtained; but being in its infancy, all we can do at present is to wish it success, which time must determine.

Three or four new houses are now erected, and most of the gentlemen are comfortably lodged; there is a retail shop opened in the Colony, from whence we are furnished with such goods as the Directors have sent out, most of which are not only badly adapted for a warm climate, but wretchedly bad in their kind.

We have little gold or silver among us; that want is substituted by paper notes, from five dollars down to six-pence, signed by the Governor or Mr Dawes. – The credit of this medium is established by giving bills of exchange to the holders, upon the Directors, at a trifle more than eleven per cent. discount, which is only the difference between sterling and currency, a guinea being nominally twenty-three shillings and four-pence here; it is taken in payment for goods at the Company's store, and its reputation is now so good, that the neighbouring Factories and casual Traders receive it for what our Settlers purchase from them.

Mr Clarkson is so convinced the Company have been sadly imposed upon, that a few weeks ago he wrote a circular letter to the gentlemen of the Colony, acquainting them of his intention of sailing for England very quickly – requesting their opinion of the various goods that came under their notice – their general ideas as to the wants of the Colony, and their advice how to prevent abuses being practised on the Company in future.

I saw part of a letter from one gentleman in answer, wherein he says – "You have done me the honour of asking my advice, how to prevent abuses being practised on the Company in future? In answer to this I shall only say, it would be the height of presumption in me to offer an opinion on the subject, being persuaded your own penetration and discernment is sufficient to discover a remedy, without the assistance of any one; and if the Directors will attend to your advice upon this, as

[90] James Watt, who remained in Sierra Leone until his death in 1795.

well as every other circumstance respecting the Colony, I am sure they will find their advantage in it".

Had my opinion been asked, I should have said, "Let the Directors shake off a parcel of hypocritical puritans they have about them, who, under the cloak of religion, are sucking out the very vitals of the Company; let them employ men conversant in trade, acquainted with the coast of Africa, and whose *religious tenets have never been noticed;* under this description they will find persons of sound morals, fit to be entrusted, but they will ever be subject to impositions, while they employ a pack of canting parasites, who have just cunning enough to deceive them".[91]

We are in great tribulation about Mr Clarkson's going away, for Mr Dawes is almost universally disliked, and more than probably, anarchy and discord will again return in full force among us, when the management of things are left to him alone; however, it is wrong to anticipate misfortunes, and our Governor has made every arrangement in his power to prevent intruders of this kind.

The Surveyor has assured him, the Blacks shall have the proportion of land now surveying for them, in a fortnight at farthest.[92] Every one has pledged himself to use his utmost efforts to preserve harmony and order during Mr Clarkson's absence, which we expect will be five or six months; and to insure Mr Dawes the good will of King Naimbana, he has been allowed to make the King a very considerable present *out of the Company's Property.*

Adieu,

Your's, &c.

---

[91] As this is not a theme she has hitherto mentioned in her letters, but will bring up subsequently, this paragraph may well have been inserted later.

[92] Richard Pepys had now succeeded James Cocks as surveyor.

JOURNAL

Two days ago Mr Clarkson sailed; his departure operated more power-fully and generally upon people's feelings, than all the deaths we have had in the Colony; several gentlemen accompanied him two or three leagues to sea, and returned the same night.

Jan. 2nd. The Surveyor has stopped surveying the lots of land for the Settlers, although he assured Mr Clarkson, they should have them in a fortnight. His attention is now taken up with fortification, which seems to be the hobby-horse of Mr Dawes, and a large Fort is planed out upon a hill, about half a mile from the water side.

King Jemmy came to see me this day; he asked what was the reason Mr Clarkson did not call on him before he sailed, and said he did not suppose Mr Clarkson would have left the country without coming to see him; his cheek was furrowed with tears as he spoke; I did not imagine he had so much sensibility.

There was a very heavy tornado last night, an unusual thing at this time of the year; the roof of my house has become so dry, that the rain had free access through, and I got thoroughly wet.

5th. A remarkable fine ox (sent as a present to the Colony, by King Naimbana) was killed this day; I never saw fatter meat in my life; our acting governor (notwithstanding it was a present) had it sold at 4d. per pound. I suppose he has done this to show us he intends being an œconomist, and thereby reimburse the Company's heavy losses; but that will require more fat oxen than he will be able to procure in this part of Africa for some years. This is not the only instance of his œconomy, or I should say, parsimony, for a few days after Falconbridge died, he came and demanded of me his uniform coat, sword, gun, pistols, and a few other presents that the Directors had made him, which I gave up, they being of no use to me; he also engrosses all the *Yams, Pumpkins, Turtle,* and almost every kind of provisions in the neighbourhood, and has them retailed from the Company's store at an enormous advance; when turtle is killed, he sends his own servant to take an account of the weight, lest the butcher should embezzle a few pounds; but I doubt after all, he will verify the trite proverb, "penny wise and pound foolish," for I have heard it remarked by a Gentleman of information, that the new Fort, if finished on the plan proposed, will cost £20,000.

7th. This day another plantation was begun at Savoy Point, about half a mile from hence, which is intended for the cultivation of cotton; whether it succeeds or not, clearing the wood about the town will certainly be conducive to health.

The manager of Clarkson's plantation complains that most of his gramattos or labourers have left him to attend the cry, or funeral ceremony, of one of their brethren, who lately died by the wound of a shark; it is uncertain how long the cry will last.

9th. Came down from Bance Island, the *Duke of Buccleuch*, bound for Jamaica, with upwards of three hundred slaves. Yesterday arrived two ships, one an American, the other a Frenchman; they have plenty of provisions on board, which the Colony is greatly in want of. Mr Dawes called on most of the gentlemen to request they would not purchase any, saying he intends buying what is wanted by wholesale, and will retail it to them at a *small advance*; such a proposal would have come better from a Jew pedlar, that from the Governor of Sierra Leone, or a Lieutenant of Marines.

11th. The *Duke of Buccleuch* sailed yesterday, and the Frenchman this day.[93] I understand Mr Dawes has purchased some articles of provision from the Frenchman, who would have nothing but slaves in return, and for the sake of accommodation, Mr Dawes gave him an order on Mr. Rennieu, who pays him in slaves. I think if this is not, it borders on, an infringement of the Act of Parliament for incorporating the Company, which says: "the Company shall not, through the medium of their servants, or otherwise, directly, or indirectly, traffic in slaves". It seems as if Providence frowns on this purchase, for an unusual high tide carried away part of the provisions after they were landed.

A small coasting cutter of the Company's called the *Providence* arrived this day from the Turtle islands, about fifteen leagues to leeward; she brought eight goats, four sheep, and twenty-one turtle; sixteen of the

[93] The *Duke of Buccleuch* had 317 slaves on board, 2 of whom died on the passage to Jamaica (HLRO, L5/J/11/2).

latter died since twelve o'clock which has disconcerted the Governor very much; but I am told he has made a *calculation,* and thinks, if he can sell the other five, at *four- pence per pound,* it will be yet a *saving voyage.*

Between eleven and twelve o'clock last night, the Colony was alarmed by the report of guns, beating of drums, and shrill shoutings of our neighbours at King Jemmy's town. Mr Dawes assembled all the men, and had arms and ammunition given them, from a supposition that the natives meant to attack us – but it turned out to be a groundless alarm, and is suspected to have been a contrivance of some ill-disposed persons to get the Settlers armed.

King Jemmy and Signior Domingo being informed of this, came today to enquire why their *good faith* was mistrusted; they dined with Mr Dawes, and after dinner King Jemmy paid me a visit; he seemed much offended, and said it was very foolish to suppose he would make war without a cause – if he had a Palaver with the Colony, he would first come and talk it over, and if it could not be settled in that way, and he was forced to make war, he would give us timely notice, that we might defend ourselves, but it was the custom of his country to compromise disputes amicably, and never to engage in war till there was no other alternative, or words to the same effect. The former assertion, I believe, is not untrue, and his behaviour to the first Settlers is an example; in that dispute, he gave them three days notice of his intention to drive them off, and burn their town; with regard to the latter, I have frequently heard wars were common among the natives for the purpose of obtaining slaves; such may have been the practice, but I have enquired of several Chiefs, who positively deny it; and I am certain, since my first acquaintance in this part of the world, none of those predatory wars have happened hereabouts, notwithstanding upwards of two thousand slaves have been shipped and sent to the West Indies, from this river, within the last twelve months.

15th. Arrived a Cutter belonging to Bance Island, from the Isles de Loss. A Mr M'Auley, Member of Council, and the Reverend Mr Gilbert, came passengers in her. These gentlemen came from England to the River Gambia, in the *Sierra Leone Packet,* where they left her to take in cattle for the Colony. The Settlers are highly pleased at Mr Gilbert's return; indeed every one must rejoice at the society of so amiable a man.

I have not heard any thing of Mr M'Auley, except his lately being an Overseer upon an estate in Jamaica: It is not to be questioned that the prejudices of such an education must impress him with sentiments favourable to the Slave Trade, and consequently I should not suppose him qualified for a Member of Administration in a Colony mostly formed of *Blacks,* founded on principles of *freedom,* and for the *express purpose* of abolishing the Slave Trade.[94]

16th. I heard this morning there was another alarm last night, but as groundless as the last. Seven or eight canoes full of natives, passing the settlement on their way to King Jemmy's, hooping and hallooing as they went, stirred up unnecessary fears in the minds of the Settlers, who flocked to Mr Dawes, requesting he would furnish them with ammunition, which (not thinking requisite) he refused, and they returned home greatly dissatisfied.

I learn those people are come down to make one of their periodical sacrifices to the *Devil* – I should like to witness the ceremony, but strangers (particularly whites) are not admissible; it will be performed between Free Town and King Jemmy's, on the side of a small brook, under a cluster of large trees.[95]

The weather is particularly fine at present – the fogs or smokes are mostly dispelled, a salubrious sea breeze fans us daily, and agreeably tempers the burning sun.

17th. We are prodigiously distressed to understand King Naimbana is so dangerously ill, that his death is hourly looked for: – Mr Dawes, Mr Gilbert, the Physician, and some others, went up to visit him this morning; his death will certainly inconvenience the Colony very much.

Last night arrived the *Lapwing* cutter from the river Carimanca (twelve or thirteen leagues from hence) with a load of Camwood, ivory,[96] and rice – the Company have a small factory there, under the direction of a free mulatto man, but the trade is yet very trifling, not nearly equal to the charges attending it.

[94] Her comment on Zachary Macaulay (as he spelt it) was wide of the mark. Though he had been employed briefly on a plantation in Jamaica he had left in disgust and found more congenial employment with the directors of the Sierra Leone Company whose principles he fully agreed with. Moreover after his return to England in 1799 he became a leading figure in the abolitionist movement.
[95] Probably one of the regular meetings of the *Poro* society which excludes non-members.
[96] Camwood, a hard, red-coloured timber, then used for making red dye, was a valuable commodity in the export trade. Elephants were still plentiful enough in the coastal region to supply ivory for export. "Carimanca" should be "Camaranca".

That river produces the largest and finest oysters I ever eat – not such as are common hereabouts, generated on the mangrove tree, and rocks, but genuine bed oysters – I have been fortunate enough to get a supply of them several times.

The Settlers, having now a number of small boats, are able to furnish the Colony with abundance of capital fish, and they have such plenty of fowls, that the gentlemen get what they require; but propagation of the feathered species is considerably protracted by the multitude of enemies they have here, viz. snakes, rats, wild cats, armadillas,* ants, &c. The most formidable of all these are the ants – in the dead hour of night, they come in swarms, and attack the helpless chickens, while roosting under their mother's wing, who is scarcely able to defend herself. – I have had four or five killed in a night by them; and so prying and assiduous are they after their prey, that I have known them discover two doves, which were hanging in a cage up one pair of stairs, whom they not only killed, but carried off every morsel, except the feathers, before morning.

* A kind of scaly lizard.

19th. Mr Dawes and two or three other gentlemen went to Bunch river this morning to visit Pa Bunkie, who some people imagine will succeed King Naimbana; they took a present, or, as it is termed, Dash, for this Chieftain, by far richer than any yet made King Naimbana or any other Chief.

Returning in the evening, they stopped at Signior Domingo's, where they expected to have seen a late favourite woman of King Jemmy's drink the red water, for suspicion of witchcraft, but their curiosity was disappointed by the ceremony being performed in an inland town; however they were informed the woman had drank the water, and recovered, and in consequence, Jemmy, by the customs of the country, is obliged either to pay the woman's parents a slave, or the value of one in goods.[97]

At half past twelve o'clock, P.M., a spark from the Kitchen fire, kindled in the roof of my house, and before water could be procured, communicated itself in all directions: In a few moments the roof fell in, and in less than fifteen minutes, the whole building was consumed; but by the extraordinary exertions of some labourers who were working hard by, most of my clothes and furniture were saved, so that my loss is trifling.

[97] Winterbottom gave a full account of trial by red water in his *Account*, vol. I, pp. 129–33.

I suppose (from a cursory view of what has escaped), not above £50. As luck would have it, I moved my lodgings some days ago, and only stayed in the thatched house during the day, intending to leave it entirely, when another room was finished in the house where I now am, which will be the case shortly; indeed, it is already so forward, that I have asked a party of two and twenty to dine with me the day after tomorrow, on an *extraordinary occasion*, therefore I cannot complain of *wanting shelter*.

20th. I have been informed that Pa Bunkie was advised by his Pa-laver-Man, not to accept the great *dash*, which Mr Dawes carried him yesterday; and that this Palaver *Gentleman* made use of the following, or similar, language to dissuade him from taking it:

"Father – these people have been here twelve moons now, have they ever taken the slightest notice of you, by inviting you to their camp,* or making you the smallest present heretofore? – No, Father! – And what makes them thus suddenly over generous to you? – Because they think your services will soon be requisite for them. Do not you know white men well enough to be convinced, they never give away their money without expecting it returned many fold? – Cannot you see the drift of this profuse, unlooked for, and unasked for present ? Let me warn you against taking it – for be assured, however disinterested and friendly they appear at this moment, they are aiming at some selfish purposes, and although they may not discover what their wishes are immediately – before twelve moons more you will know them." Bunkie replied, "I know they want something, nevertheless I'll take the *dash* – it rests with me, whether to comply with any request they make or not. I shall not consider the present by any means binding on me."

* The name given *Free Town* by the natives.

Mr Gilbert and Mr Horne went up this afternoon to Signior Dom-ingo's, where Mr Horne preached a sermon to a congregation of natives. How preposterous! Is it possible a sensible man, like Mr Horne, can suppose it in his power to imprint notions of Christianity, or any sort of instruction, upon the minds of people, through the bare medium of a language they do not understand? He might as well expect holding a candle to the eyes of a blind man, or exposing him to the sun, would reclaim his sight! The desire of spreading Christian knowledge through this ignorant land is questionless most praise worthy, but it will require patience and time to effect it.

21st. Last night arrived the *Nassau* (Morley) from Bristol, but last from the Isles de Loss: Captain Morley this day added to the number at our convivial gala: I was highly complimented for the elegance, variety, and richness of my dinner, which, without doubt, was superb, considering where we are; we had three removes, from six and twenty to thirty dishes each; besides an admirable dessert, consisting of a variety of European and tropical fruit, the whole of which was garnished with comfort and pleasantry.[98]

24th. On Sunday last, notice was given that Mr Horne, or Mr Gilbert, would perform divine service, in future, every morning and evening; and every one is desired to attend. I am of opinion the morning service is superfluous. – Why? For many reasons, and I will here enumerate three or four.

Among the Black Settlers are seven religious sects, and each sect has one or more preachers attached to it, who alternately preach throughout the whole night; indeed I never met with, heard or read of, any set of people, observing the same appearance of godliness; for I do not remember, since they first landed here, my ever awaking (and I have awoke at every hour of the night), without hearing preachings from some quarter or other.[99]

Now, those people being so religiously bent, I think it unnecessary, or, as I first said, superfluous, that they should be convened every morning; because the primest part of the day for exercising their worldly vocations is occupied thereby; the vicious and lazy (and some such will creep into every society) are furnished with the plea of being at church; an excuse, I am told, many already make, after skulking an hour or two beyond the customary and proper time, when they have not been within a church door; and it detains the mass of labourers an hour every day, which lost time costs the Company at the rate of £1300 per annum.

Vice and laziness surely ought not to be protected by Religion anywhere; but they should be more especially discountenanced in a new Colony, where success greatly depends on industry.

---

[98] The reason for her convivial gala she will reveal at the end of the next letter. Captain Morley, as we shall eventually see, was her brother-in-law.

[99] As James Walker put it, "And as the chapel was the most important institution in settler life, so their preachers were the true leaders of the colonial population" (*The Black Loyalists*, p. 198).

This day I dined on board the *Nassau,* in company with Mr Rennieu, and some gentlemen of the Colony.

Rennieu says an old man named *Congo Bolokelly* is on his way from the interior country to succeed King Naimbana;[100] and such great pains have been taken to impress him with an unfavourable opinion of our Colony, that he is determined the Company shall re-purchase their land, or he will do every thing in his power to perplex and annoy us.

Mr Dawes met with a circumstance very galling to him this afternoon. He had in contemplation to palisade a piece of ground, for an immediate asylum, in case the natives should take it into their heads to attack us.

The spot fixed upon, unfortunately, took in part of a lot occupied by one of the Settlers, which Mr Dawes, conscious of his unpopularity, did not wish to encroach upon, without obtaining permission, although the Settlers only hold their present Town lots as a temporary accommodation, until their permanent ones are surveyed.

He called on the tenant and took him out to explain what he wanted; many people in the neighbourhood having previously heard of Mr Dawes's intentions, assembled about him, who declared they would not suffer an inch more ground to be enclosed, upon any pretence whatever, before their town and country lots were given them, and most solemnly protested they would destroy every fence which might be erected till such time.

Mr Dawes endeavoured to persuade them by argument, what he wanted to do, was for their protection; but they were deaf to every thing he said, and gave him language in return which he could not stomach: He told them if he had imagined they would have treated him with so much indignity, he should not have come among them: and if they continued to behave in the same way, he would certainly leave them as early as he could. To this, with one voice, they exclaimed, "Go! go! go! we do not want you here, we cannot get a worse after you". He was so disgusted at this, that he turned his back and walked off. It was directly before my door, therefore I witnessed the whole, and could not help feeling for the *Governor,* who seemed dreadfully mortified and out of temper.

[100] Pa Kokelly, as the name was more usually rendered, did not succeed Naimbana, but did eventually succeed King Jemmy when he died in 1796, taking the title King Tom. By then a successor to Naimbana, with the royal title Bai Farama, had already been appointed (Fyfe, *A History,* p. 74).

Feb. 3. Nothing worth recording for these ten days past; yesterday the manager of Clarkson's plantation came over from Bullom; he has had a serious quarrel with the natives, but *reason* was determined on his side. His advances in cultivation, I understand, are very slow; for he is not able to keep any number of labourers together, more than a month at a time; it is customary to pay them every moon, and when they get their wages, like our English tars, they quit work while they have money.

The *Sierra Leone Packet* arrived from Gambia this day, with thirty head of cattle; I have not learned what her European cargo consists of, but it is said to be very trifling.

7th. Since the departure of Mr Clarkson a number of subtle, ungentlemanlike attempts have been made to singe his reputation in the opinion of the people, and to warp away their affections from him, which as yet have proved unsuccessful; but I never heard of so unmanly, unprincipled, and diabolical an assault on any one's character, as was last night made on his. The Settlers were summoned to meet Mr Dawes and the Surveyor in the evening, and being collected, they were informed their permanent *Town Lots* were surveyed and ready for them, and they must relinquish those they at present occupy, immediately; to this they replied, "When placed on the lots we at present occupy, we were informed, they were merely for our temporary accommodation, and we promised, when the plan of the town was fixed upon and surveyed, we would remove, but we were assured no public or other buildings would be erected between our lots and the sea; now, in place of this, the sea shore is lined with buildings, therefore, your promise being broken, we consider ours cancelled, and will not remove unless the new lots are run from the water's edge, and we indiscriminately partake of them. Mr Clarkson promised in Nova Scotia that no distinction should be made here between us and white men; we now claim this promise, we are free British subjects, and expect to be treated as such; we will not tamely submit to be trampled on any longer. Why are not our country allotments of land surveyed! Why are not all the Company's promises to us fulfilled? We have a high regard and respect for Mr Clarkson, and firmly believe he would not have left us, without seeing every promise he made performed, if gentlemen here had not given him the strongest assurances they should be complied with immediately." In answer, they were told, "That it was not uncommon for Mr Clarkson to make prodigal and extraordinary promises without thinking of them afterwards, that the great advantages he held out to them in Nova Scotia he was in no shape authorised by the Sierra Leone Company to make; they all came from himself merely to seduce them here; and he never had an idea of fulfilling of them, nay, he had it not in his power, and more than probable *was drunk* when he made them." Here they groaned and murmured, but said "They believed Mr Clarkson to be a man of honour, and that he never made any promise to them but such as he was authorised by the Company to make". The altercation now ended; I have had it nearly in the same language from more than a dozen people who were at the meeting.[101]

The blacks seem vastly alarmed and uneasy, nothing else is spoken of all this day, and I understand they have determined to send two deputies to the Court of Directors to know from them what footing they are on, and what were the promises Mr Clarkson was authorized to make them; indeed, it is not to be wondered at, for no other conclusion can be formed from such base insinuations, but that a wish exists *somewhere* to do them justice.

12th. We had reason to think, for some days past, King Naimbana was dead, but had no certainty of it until this morning; nor do we exactly know when he died, but it is supposed several days ago. The country custom is to keep a great man's death secret some time; his coffin (the first in all probability any of his family ever had) is making here, and will be sent up to Robana this evening.

14th. Yesterday being the anniversary of the *Harpy's* arrival, a few celebrated it by dining at a house of a late member of Council who came out in her; I think it would have been more *a-propos* to have fasted and mourned on the occasion. The day was cloudy, accompanied with a rumbling thunder and spitting rain,* as if the heavens *were groaning and weeping at the recollection*. It was intended to have fired minute guns in compliment to the remains of Naimbana, which would have been very timely, but that ceremony was postponed until this day, when it was performed.

* A circumstance rarely known at this season.

[101] She fails to make it clear that the "answer" quoted was given by Richard Pepys, the surveyor, not by Dawes (see below Dubois's journal of the same date).

LETTER XI

My dear Madam,

The *Good Intent,* Captain Buckle, affords me the opportunity of sending you the foregoing Journal, which I fear you will think very insipid, but every day produces such a sameness that really there is not subject for high seasoning even a common epistle, and you will allow journalizing still more difficult; however, to avoid tautological writing, as much as possible, I skipped over several days at a time, which of course you will have observed, but after all, it is so dry, that I am almost ashamed to send it to you, and am determined in future to have recourse to my old epistolary mode.

My dinner on the 21st of January will somewhat puzzle you at first, and lest you may not at once hit upon what occasioned it, I must acquaint you I have changed the name of Falconbridge for one a little *shorter* under which I beg to subscribe myself,

Yours sincerely, &c. &c.

Editor's Comment

She now subscribed herself Anna Maria DuBois, having married Isaac DuBois (see *footnote* 67). The marriage licence, signed by John Clarkson on 27 December 1792, just before he left for England, survives in the Clarkson papers (BL, Add. MS 41262A, fol. 224). DuBois seems to have pronounced his name in an anglicised way: a letter from two Nova Scotian settlers refers to him as "Mr Duboz" (*ibid.*, Anderson and Perkins, 26 October 1793).

When Clarkson left he asked DuBois to send him a regular journal of daily events (printed here on pp. 170–189) to keep him informed of what was going on in the Colony. It supplies us with more details of the marriage. On the 3rd of January he made a wedding ring, and on the 6th, after a brief lovers' tiff, she agreed to marry him the following day. On the 7th he wrote,

> At 9 o clock this morning the Reverend Mr Horne performed the Marriage Ceremony and now I am once more, I trust, happily joined in the bands of wedlock, we intended our marriage should be kept a secret till the 21st of this month and Mr Horne had promised to do so, but the *poor* parson was not born to keep secrets, he carried it piping hot to the ears of every one he met, but desired every one he told it to, not to mention it to any one – however in less than two hours it was known over the whole Colony – it made very little difference to me whether it was known today or a fortnight hence – I am happy and the Parson is pleased at telling the news.

The celebration was probably delayed to await the arrival of Captain Morley, captain of the slave ship *Nassau* from Bristol, on its way up the river to Bance Island.

"He seems to be a good honest fellow", wrote DuBois of Morley, "and I am rather gratified by his being highly pleased at his sister [*sic*] marriage". He uses the word "sister" in the then current sense of sister-in-law. The parish registers of All Saints, Bristol, in the Bristol Record Office, show that she had two older sisters, Anne and Christian Jane, one of whom could have been the captain's wife. Though she makes no reference to the relationship, it would have been known to her correspondent in Bristol.

She may have made some use of her husband's journal in writing her own, since many of the events described are the same. But the style and comments are hers, in particular the comments about Dawes's meanness, something

DuBois does not mention in his journal. Nor did she bring into hers the constant complaints he makes in his journal about the way Dawes interfered with his work, nor yet his own long-standing feud with Richard Pepys, the Surveyor.

LETTER XII

My dear Madam,

I finished my last by hinting that I had once more enlisted under the banners of Hymen, but made no apology for my hastiness; or, in other words, for deviating from the usual custom of twelve months *widowhood.* To be plain, I did not make any, because I thought it unnecessary. Narrow minds may censure me, and perhaps the powerful influence of habit might operate against me in your opinion, before you reflected upon my situation, or well digested the many circumstances which plead in my favour; but, having done this, I am mistaken indeed if your heart is not too expanded to sully me with reproach afterwards. My own conscience acquits me from having acted wrong; next to that, I wish for the approbation of my friends, and after them, the charitable construction of the world. I know you wish me happy, and no woman can be more so than I am at present, with every expectation of a continuance.

I must now proceed to give you a summary view of occurrences since the fifteenth of February.

The first thing I shall mention is the universal discontent which has prevailed among the Settlers ever since the altercation they had with Mr Dawes and the Surveyor on the 7th of February, and it must be confessed by every candid person, their murmurs are not excited without cause.

To give you an idea of what their complaints are, I shall state the outlines of a petition which they intend sending to the Court of Directors by two Deputies elected about the middle of March, who, for want of an opportunity, have not sailed, but are just on the eve of embarking in the *Amy,* for England. I have not only seen the petition, but have a copy of it verbatim.[102]

---

[102] The two deputies who brought the petition to London were Cato Perkins, one of the leading preachers, and Isaac Anderson. It is printed in full in Fyfe, *Our Children,* pp. 35–40. Zachary Macaulay alleged (Journal, 25 June 1793) that DuBois had helped the settlers to draw it up and included in it some items they wanted omitted.

It first of all states, "That the Petitioners are sensible of, and thankful for, the good intended by sending them from Nova Scotia to this country, and in return assure the Directors, they are well inclined to assist the Company's views, all in their power.

"That they are grieved beyond expression to be forced to complain of hardships and oppressions loaded on them by the managers of the Colony, which they are persuaded the Directors are ignorant of.

"That the promises made by the Company's Agents, in Nova Scotia, were preferable to any ever held out to them before, and trusting the performance of them, with the Almighty's assistance, and their own industry, would better their condition, induced them to emigrate here. That none of those promises have been fulfilled, and it has been insinuated to them that Mr Clarkson had not authority for making any, they therefore beg to be informed, whether such is the case or not, and that the Directors will point out on what footing they are considered.

"That health and life is valuable and uncertain; that notwithstanding they labour under the misfortune of wanting education, their feelings are equally *acute* with those of *white men*, and they have as great an anxiety to lay a foundation for their children's freedom and happiness, as any human being can possess. That they believe the Directors wish to make them happy, and that they think their sufferings are principally due to the conduct of the Company's Agents here, which they suppose has been partially represented to the Directors.

"That Mr Clarkson had promised in Nova Scotia, among other things, they should be supplied with every necessary of life from the Company's stores, at a moderate advance, of ten per cent on the prime cost and charges. That while Mr Clarkson remained in the Colony they paid no more; but since then they have been charged upwards of 100 per cent. That they would not grumble even at that, if the worst of goods were not sold, and paltry advantages taken of them, particularly in the article of rum. That they had known by Mr Dawes's order several puncheons filled up with thirty gallons of water each, and even, though thus reduced, sold to them at a more extravagant price than they had ever paid before.*

* This is perfectly true, but upon investigation, it appeared to proceed from *religious* motives; Mr Dawes said he ordered a *little* water to be put into each puncheon, from a fear the consumers would neglect to dilute the spirit sufficiently. Had such a trick been played at a *Slave Factory,* how would it be construed?

"That the only means they have of acquiring those goods, is by labouring in the Company's service, and even this they are deprived of, at the whim of Mr Dawes, or any other Gentleman in office, which they consider a prodigious hardship, as it is the only resource whereby they can provide bread for their families; that out of mere pique several have been discharged from service, and not permitted, even with their little savings, to purchase provisions from the Company's store-house, the only one here.

"That Mr Clarkson informed them before he sailed for England, the Company had been mistaken in the quantity of land they supposed themselves possessed of, and in consequence only one fifth part of what was originally promised them (the petitioners) could be at present performed; which quantity the Surveyor would deliver them in a fortnight at furthest, but they should have the remainder at a future time.

"That they should have been satisfied had they got one fifth part of their proportion (*in good land*) time enough to have prepared a crop for the ensuing year, but the rains are now commenced, and the Surveyor has not finished laying out the small allotments, which he might have done, had he not relinquished the work as soon as Mr Clarkson sailed; and the greater part of those he has surveyed, are so mountainous, barren and rocky, that it will be impossible ever to obtain a living from them."

After mentioning many more trifling complaints, and dwelling greatly on the happiness and prosperity of their children, they conclude with words to this effect.

"We wait patiently till we hear from you, because we are persuaded you will do us justice; and if your Honors will enquire into our sufferings, compassionate us, and grant us the privileges we feel entitled to from Mr Clarkson's promises, we will continually offer up our prayers for you, and endeavour to impress upon the minds of our children, the most lasting sense of gratitude, &c &c ..." [103]

This petition is signed by thirty one of the most respectable Settlers in behalf of the whole;[104] and they have raised a small subscription for

---

[103] These extracts from the petition illustrate well how differently the settlers and the directors saw the Colony. The settlers saw it primarily as a new home for themselves and their children. The directors however saw it primarily as a means to enable them to transform West Africa.

[104] The only surviving copy, in the Clarkson papers in the British Library, lacks the signatures.

supporting their representatives while in England: 'tis to be hoped the Directors will pay attention to them, and not suffer themselves to be biased by the mis-representations of one or two plausible individuals, who must of course say all they are able in vindication of their conduct, and who, we have reason to believe, from their hypocritical pretensions to religion, have acquired a great ascendancy over a few of the leading Directors; – but surely they will not be so forgetful of their own characters and interests, as to allow that ascendancy to operate against honesty, truth and justice, and ruin the quiet and happiness of a thousand souls – no ! they must be strangely altered indeed, laying aside their partiality for Ethiopians, if they do not possess too much probity to hesitate a moment when it comes before them.

Besides displeasing the blacks, and rendering them uneasy, Mr Dawes is at constant variance with some one or other of the officers, and since I wrote you last, few days have pass'd over without some fresh feud; one in particular is of so extraordinary a nature I must relate it, that you may have a peep into the disposition of our Governor.

Mr S—[105] a surgeon, who came out in the *Sierra Leone Packet,* was two months here without a room to lodge in on shore, which was attended with great inconvenience to him, and interfered considerably with his duty; he, after some time, interceded with Mr Dawes to let him have a small room fitted up in our house, which he soon got finished, and removed into; the apartment being very comfortable and snug, Mr Dawes took a fancy to it, and the day after Mr S— had taken possession, without any apology or preface, sent his servant to demand the key; Mr S— was surprised at so uncouth and arbitrary a proceeding, and did not feel inclined to treat it with passive obedience, but gave a positive refusal; as such rudeness merited; in consequence, he was immediately dismissed from the service, and here follows an accurate copy of his dismission.

[105] DuBois in his Journal (see below, 6 February 1793) gives his name as Sealy. He also complained to Clarkson (see below, letter of 1 May 1793)) that the government had dismissed "Mr Horwood Mrs DuBois's brother without assigning any reason whatever for so doing". This is the man mentioned in Clarkson's diary as Falconbridge's brother-in-law (see *footnote* 71) whose existence is never even hinted at in the letters.

Council, FREE TOWN, 26th *April,* 1793

SIR,

I am desired to transmit the enclosed resolution of Council to you,

and am, Sir
Your obedient humble Servant
(signed) J. STRAND, Secretary.[106]

Resolved, that Mr S——, who came out to this Colony as Surgeon in the Hon. the Sierra Leone Company's service, has pointedly refused obedience to the commands of the Superintendent, he be dismissed from the service, and that from this day he is no longer considered as a servant of the said Company.

entered

(signed) JAMES STRAND, Secretary.

Did you ever hear of any thing more ridiculously despotic? – but mark the sequel; the day following, Mr Dawes attended by the Secretary and his (Mr Dawes's) servant, came to the Hummums, for by this name I must tell you our house is known.[107] I was sitting in the piazza reading; they took no notice of me, but Mr S—— being present, the Governor addressed him, and demanded the key of his room, which of course was not complied with; he then desired his servant to break open the door, who immediately got to work, and would have done it, but was slyly checked by Mr Dawes, who, with as little ceremony or preface as he had offended, went up to Mr. S—— and said, "I am much concerned, Sir, for what has passed, if you feel offended, I beg your pardon, I have been unwell, or would not have acted so rudely; I wanted your room, because it was retired, that I might be a little quiet; pray, Sir, return my

---

[106] Strand was another of the Swedenborgian Swedes in the Company's service (see *footnote* 79). Neither the incident nor the letter is recorded in the minute book of the Governor and Council (PRO, CO 270/2).

[107] "Hummums", from *hammam,* a Turkish bath (OED). Though she calls it "our" (and earlier, in her journal entry for 15 January, "my") house, it seems to have been intended for the Company's offices (see Dawes' letter in the journal of DuBois, entry for 13 February 1793). The site, the point of land at the east end of the town, became known as "Falconbridge Point", and when Freetown was fortified, the gun battery constructed there was called "Falconbridge Battery". The name "Falconbridge Point" still appears on twentieth century maps.

papers, and forget what has passed, you will greatly oblige and make me happy by doing so".

Mr. S— heard this penitential confession with amazement, and replied, – "Had you asked me in a gentlemanlike manner for my room at first, it would have been much at your service as it is now, I bear no malice – here are your papers".

I could fill up twenty pages was I to acquaint you with all the private quarrels of this sort; but as they can neither afford amusement or instruction, it is best to pass them over in silence.

On the 25th of April we heard of the French King being massacred, and that England had declared war against the blood thirsty banditti who have usurped the reins of government in France. This account came by the *Swift* Privateer Cutter of Bristol, to the Isles de Loss, where she destroyed a French Factory, and made some valuable reprisals.

His Majesty's frigate *Orpheus*, Captain Newcomb, *Sea-flower* Cutter, Lieutenant Webber, and the *African Queen*, a ship chartered by the Company, arrived here the beginning of last month. Captain Newcomb, in his way out, touched at Senegal and Goree, and captured six French ships, four of which arrived safe at this port, and have since been condemned and sold at Bance island; the other two were lost on the shoals of Grandee.

The *Orpheus* came out to protect the British trade on this part of the coast of Africa, as did the *Sea-flower*, in some measure; but she is only to run down the Coast, and proceed to the West Indies. After remaining here a few days, they both went to leeward, unfortunately three or four days too late, or they would have intercepted a French Corsair that has scoured the coast from Cape Mount (about fifty leagues from hence) downwards, considerably annoyed our trade, and taken eight valuable ships clear away, it is supposed to Cayenne; she had captured many more, which have been retaken by the *Sea-flower* and *Robust* (a Privateer from Liverpool); these two vessels, we hear, have consorted and gone to Old Calabar, where they expect to fall in with, and take, a large French Guineaman, that has twelve hundred slaves on board, and is just ready to sail. One of the ships they re-captured was sent in here. I have seen the master of her, who says he never saw such a savage looking set in his life, as were on board the Frenchman. They all had on horseman's caps (having a tin plate in front, with the emblem of *Death's head and marrow bones,* and underneath inscribed, "Liberty or Death"), a leather belt round their waist, with a brace of pistols, and a sabre; and they looked so dreadfully ferocious, that one would suppose them capable of eating every Englishman they met with *without salt or gravy*. Unluckily the *Orpheus* sprung her foremast, which obliged her to give up pursuing those Republican ragamuffins, and returned here.

During her absence, one of the most atrocious infringements on the liberty of British subjects, and the most daring extension of arrogated power that has yet occurred among us, was practised by our Colonial Tribunal, on the persons of three sailors belonging to the *African Queen*.

These thoughtless sons of Neptune came on shore to regale themselves with a walk while their master was away (I believe at Bance Island) and as they strolled through the town, wantonly killed a duck belonging to one of the Settlers; they were immediately apprehended, and taken before the Chief Magistrate, who committed them to prison, and the subsequent day they were tried, not by their Peers, but by *Judge* McAuley, and a *Jury of twelve blacks*, who, without any evidence or defence from the prisoners, found them guilty of stealing and killing the *duck*. The *self-created Judge* then sentenced one of them to receive thirty-nine lashes by the common whipper, fined the other two in a sum of money each, and ordered them to be confined in irons, on board the *York*, till their fines were paid.

These sentences were accordingly put in execution; poor Jack was dreadfully mortified at being whipped by a black man; but his punishment being soon over, I considered it the lightest, for his fellow sufferers were kept ironed in the close hold of a ship, already infested with disease, upwards of three weeks, till the *Orpheus* returned; when the master of the *African Queen* presented a petition from them to Captain Newcomb, who did not hesitate to interpose his authority. He came on shore, waited on the Governors, and without waiting for compliments or paying any himself, he demanded of them, by what authority they tried White Men, the subjects of Great Britain, by a *Jury of Blacks*; it was so novel a circumstance, that it struck him with astonishment. "By Act of Parliament", answered Mr M'Auley. "Show me that Act of Parliament", replied Captain Newcomb; the Act for incorporating the Company being produced, Captain Newcomb read it over carefully, and finding there was no sanction given for holding any Courts of the kind, exclaimed, "Your Act of Parliament mentions nothing of the sort – your Court is a mere usurpation, and a mockery on all law and justice, I desire the prisoners may be released instantly". This, you imagine, was very unpalatable language to our *mighty men*, but they were forced to stomach it, and comply with the orders of their superior.

It is much to be wished, a ship of war was always stationed here; the very sight of her would restrain the exercise of similar abuses, or any extravagant stretches of undelegated power.

The first Sunday in every month is the day appointed for holding this *sham* Court, which, withal, serves very well for regulating any internal quarrels or misunderstandings among the Settlers, by whom it is credited; but extending its functions beyond them, is most iniquitous presumption.

Letters arrived by the *African Queen* from Mr Clarkson, saying he was coming out immediately. The joy this news produced was of short continuance, and suddenly damped by dispatches from the Directors, mentioning Mr Clarkson being *dismissed*, and succeeded by Mr Dawes. This cannot in any way be rationally accounted for, but it is universally supposed the Directors have been betrayed into an act so prejudicial to their interests, and the welfare of the Colony, by listening to some malicious, and cowardly, representations, sent home by certain persons here, who are fully capable of assassinating the most immaculate character, if thereby they can acquire latitude for their boundless ambition, or, for a moment, quench their unconscionable thirst for power.

Editor's Comment

Thornton wrote to John Clarkson on 23 November 1792, "I think you have saved our Colony". Then, when he arrived in London, he was received (so he wrote to DuBois on 1 July 1793) "with every mark of affection and respect and in short the Directors in private made great Professions to me but took care never to mention in public the services I had rendered them". Once again, as with Falconbridge, the Directors were concealing their real feelings. Clarkson's outgoing generosity had endeared him to the Nova Scotian settlers, but it alarmed Henry Thornton, a cautious banker. The Directors were uneasy about the promises he had made, and not without justification. He had, for instance, not knowing that the Company intended to levy quit-rents on the settlers' land, solemnly promised them in Nova Scotia that they would never have to pay quit-rents – a promise that was to embitter relations between the directors and the settlers for the next seven years, and eventually drove some of them into armed rebellion in 1800.

Clarkson, for his part, was impatient with "their want of Method and their want of Exertion, with their strict adherence to nonsensical forms", and told them so. As he wrote to DuBois, "Their general way of doing things is so disgusting that I really could not keep my Temper and very often flew out in abuse of their general plans". When despatches arrived from Dawes and Macaulay contrasting the success of their own style of government by firmness with Clarkson's style of government by persuasion and promises, the Directors decided to be rid of him. They tried to get him to resign, but he refused "to be the *first* to relinquish an Employ wherein my Heart is and has been so deeply interested in its success". So he was dismissed. Then, rather than do anything to bring public discredit on the Colony ("for it has many enemies in this country who would be rejoiced at having an opportunity of prejudicing the minds of the subscribers against it"), he at once left London and took up a new career in business in the country (BL, Add. MS 41263, Clarkson to Thornton, 5 May 1793; Clarkson to DuBois, 1 July 1793).

No language can perfectly describe how much the generality of people are chagrined on this occasion; they have added to their petition the most earnest solicitation for Mr Clarkson to be sent out again.

Numbers, hopeless of such an event, are about to quit the Colony, and ever since the news transpired, they have harassed Mr Dawes with insults, in hopes he may take it in his head to be disgusted and march off. They even went so far as to write a letter, reminding him of the recent melancholy fate of Louis XVI, and threatening something similar to him, if he did not instantly acquiesce with some demand they made relating to provisions, and which, I learn, he complied with without hesitation. I should not be surprised, after obtaining one demand so easily, if they repeated their threats, until all the promises made them were fulfilled: but they say it was the want of provisions, that incited them to *frighten* the Governor, and they will now wait peaceably till their Deputies return from England, or till they know what the Directors mean to do for them.

It will be a monstrous pity if this Colony does not succeed after the immense sum of money expended on it: the original theory of its establishment (so generally known) was praise-worthy and magnanimous, nor do I suppose such a scheme by any means impracticable; but injudicious management, want of method, anarchy, perpetual cabals, and cavils, will thwart the wisest and noblest intentions, which I predict will be the case here, unless some speedy salutary alterations are adopted; if the present system is continued, not only the Settlers, but the Natives will be provoked; all kinds of confidence will cease, the Company's funds will be fruitlessly exhausted, and more than probable, before ten years, we may hear that the Colony is dwindled into a *common* slave factory. Some situations make it necessary for superiors to be feared, and all situations require they should be beloved; but if the present managers continued here their lifetimes, they will never experience the pleasure of the latter, or the honour of the former; and retire when they like, I very much question whether they will leave one friendly thought towards them behind – for this (though an idea well meaning men would blush to foster) must ensue, where the seeds of dissension and rancorous jealousy are sowed and encouraged by those whose province should be to suppress their growth.

The *Amy* it is said will sail in a week, she carries a small cargo of about £1500 value, a laughable return for upwards of £100,000. Being the first remittance, I dare say it will be well puffed off in your newspapers; to see one of those puffs would put me in mind of a person's face distorted with a forced laugh, when the heart felt nought but emotions of agony: for here is a capital stock of more than £200,000 half expended, and this first harvest, I suppose, will barely defray the disbursements of shipping, and carrying itself; what is more lamentable, such as it is cannot be often repeated, for the property is mostly sunk in such a way, that no probable or real advantages can ever revert from it, without the aid of an immense sum most judiciously applied.

The periodical rains are just commencing, and seem to set in very severe, but I am in hopes of escaping its inclemency, being about to turn my back on them, and bid adieu to this distracted land, so you may probably hear of our arrival in England very shortly after the receipt of this letter, although we are to take a round about voyage by way of Jamaica. Mr— had taken our passage in the *Amy,* but the Discontents about to leave the Colony are so numerous, that she will be greatly crowded, and as the *Nassau* has excellent accommodation, sails well and immediately, he thinks we will be more comfortable in her,[108] and less likely to fall in with French Pirates, than we should in the former, which is a dull, sluggish vessel, though it is a prevailing opinion here, should she (the *Amy*) meet with a French man of war, she will be in no danger, as the National Convention have offered protection to all the Company's ships; how true this may be, I cannot say, but is is probable enough, as two of the Directors were some time since nominated Members of the Convention.[109]

---

[108] The *Nassau* was the ship commanded by her brother-in-law Captain Morley, who was taking "a round about voyage by way of Jamaica" to enable him to deliver there the cargo of slaves he had taken on board at Bance Island.

[109] To Wilberforce's horror, the revolutionary French Convention conferred honorary French citizenship on him and Thomas Clarkson for their efforts to abolish the slave trade. But the "prevailing opinion" that the Colony was safe from the French was to prove an illusion. In September 1794, a few months after the first edition of this book was published, Freetown was attacked and ferociously looted by a squadron of the French revolutionary navy. Moreover in succeeding years over a dozen of the Company's ships were captured by the French.

We are to sail in a day or two, and I am very much hurried in packing up, and preparing for our voyage, therefore must bid you farewell, &c. &c. [110]

[110] An hour or so before they sailed DuBois wrote hastily to John Clarkson explaining why they were leaving, sending his letter on a ship that was going direct to England (see his letter of 1 May 1793, below). He wrote :

> Should this reach you before I arrive, it will just serve to inform you I am on my way — You will not be pleased to hear of my leaving the Colony, but I hope it is for the best, believe me unless the Directors will listen to truth their Colony is lost – such Conduct, such every thing you little dream off [sic] — two of the Black Settlers, deputed by the whole, go home in the *Amy* to represent their grievances, they have been shamefully trampled on since you went away ... All the ill-treatment I have received since you left this I am convinced has been due to my not taking a diabolical part which I shudder at — in poisoning the minds of the people against you — but all their efforts have been in vain —the people cry loudly for your return — Adieu.

LETTER XIII

Swan with Two Necks, Lad-lane,
LONDON, 11th *October,* 1793.

My Dear Madam,

I hasten to acquaint you, that after a passage of nine weeks and four days, in the *Alexander* (Shaw) from Jamaica, we landed safe at Dover, the 9th instant. My heart jumped with joy when I found myself once more treading the sod of Old England, which at one time during our voyage, I did not expect would ever be the case, for an ill-natured contagious fever (when we had been but a few days at sea) discovered itself in the ship, and before it could be checked, scourged almost every person on board; however, by the skill and vigilance of the ship's surgeon, only one death happened. We had been out about three weeks, when it attacked me, and was it not for the good nursing and attention I had from every one, particularly the Captain, Surgeon, and my own good man, in all human likelihood I should have fallen a victim to its barbarity; indeed, Captain Shaw's impartial kindness to his sick, was beyond every thing I ever witnessed before, and in my opinion, stamps him a man of genuine humanity.

Our ship was armed with two and twenty guns, and had between fifty and sixty men on board. We sailed from Kingston the 3rd of August, and the following day fell in with thirteen sail of Spanish ships, under convoy of a frigate, who was so very negligent of her charge, as to permit us to intercept seven of them, which, had they been French, we must have taken, in spite of all she could have done, being at that time so far to leeward, as to be scarcely discernable. A Liverpool ship, bound home, had joined them the preceding day, and now begged to be taken under our protection; this was granted, and she kept company with us until we got into the chops of the Channel.

The fever that infested us, broke out among her crew, and hurried a fourth of their number into the other world. Here Captain Shaw displayed his humanity again, in a high degree, by waiting several hours every day, and thus prolonging our voyage, to the prejudice of his own interest, merely for the purpose of rendering them what assistance he could; had he not, their situation would certainly have been extremely comfortless, as the calamity I have just mentioned was aggravated by the ship being so leaky, that the master and crew had it frequently in contemplation to abandon her.[111]

We had little bad or boisterous weather during our voyage, and the time pleasantly vanished after health was restored in the ship; scarcely two days passed away without meeting one or two more vessels; we always brought them to, and though none of them were of the sort wished for, they amused and furnished us with news of some kind. Clearing ship, when a strange sail was seen, as if we really expected a rencounter, and exercising our guns once or twice a week, with all the manœuvres practised in an engagement, were sources of amusement altogether new to me. At first, when a broad side was fired it operated like an electrical shock, but habit soon made it familiar, and at last I was less sensible of vibrations from it, than the awful tremendous thunder we oftentimes had off the coast of America, which was more severe, by far, than any I ever heard on the coast of Africa. This being the substance of every thing worth notice on our way home, I shall therefore turn back to my quitting Sierra Leone, and say something of what occurred from that time till my departure from Jamaica.

We embarked and sailed on the ninth of June; nothing could have reconciled me to the idea of taking my passage in a slave ship, but Mr— being with me, for I always entertained most horrid notions of being exposed to indelicacies too offensive for the eyes of an English woman, on board these ships; however, I never was more agreeably disappointed in my life. In the centre of the ship a barricado was run across, to prevent any communication between the men and the women; the men and the boys occupied the forward part, and the women and girls the after, so I was only liable to see the latter, who were full as well habited as they would have been in Africa, and I had very comfortable apartments, where I could retire, when I chose to be alone.

Having heard such a vast deal of the ill treatment of slaves during the

[111] One of the charges against the slave trade that Thomas Clarkson had made, and that Falconbridge had substantiated from numerous instances, was the brutal way that captains of slave ships ill-treated the members of their crews (see the section on Treatment of the Sailors" in Falconbridge's *Account,* below). It may be that the praise given here to Captain Shaw, who was no doubt returning home from delivering slaves in Jamaica, was a conscious attempt to present a slave-ship captain in a favourable light.

middle passage, I did not omit to make the nicest observations in my power, and was I to give upon oath what those observations were, I would declare I had not the slightest reason to suspect any inhumanity or mal-practice was shown towards them, through the whole voyage; on the contrary, I believe they experienced the utmost kindness and care, and after a few days, when they had recovered from sea sickness, I never saw more signs of content and satisfaction among any set of people, in their or any other country. We had not our complement of slaves by one-third, consequently there was an abundance of room for them. Regularly every day their rooms were washed out, sprinkled with vinegar, and well dried with chafing dishes of coal; during this operation the slaves were kept on deck, where they were allowed to stay the whole day (when the weather would permit) if they liked it; in the morning, before they came up, and in the evening, after they had retired to rest, our deck was always scrubbed and scoured so clean that you might eat off it.

Their provisions were excellent, consisting of boiled rice and English beans, sometimes separate, sometimes mixed, cleanly dressed, and relished with a piece of beef, salt fish, or palm oil, the latter seemed generally to have the preference; a superabundance of this was their constant breakfast and supper; between the two meals each slave had a large brown biscuit, and commonly a dram of rum. Great attention was paid to the sick, of whom, however, there were few; a mess of mutton, fowl, or some fresh meat, was daily prepared for them, and we arrived in Jamaica on the 13th of July, with the loss only of one boy who was ill before we left the coast, and the remainder of the cargo in much higher health than when they had embarked.[112]

Whether slaves are equally well treated in common, I cannot pretend to say, but when one recollects how much the masters are interested in their well doing, it is natural to suppose such is the case, for self-interest so unalterably governs the human heart, that it alone must temper the

---

[112] They had on board 190 slaves (105 men, 52 women, 23 boys (one of whom, as she says, died) and 9 girls (HLRO, L5/J/11/2). The ship seems to have been substantially underloaded. A study of slave loads in the 1790s finds "on average these slavers carried 1.6 slaves per Registered Ship's Ton" (H. S. Klein *et al.* "The allotment of space for African slaves ..." in Serge Daget (ed.), *De la Traite à l'Esclavage*, Paris, 1988, vol II, p. 151). The *Nassau* was registered as 197 tons, which gives an "average" load of 315 slaves. So, perhaps to spare her feeling, and, moreover, enable her to write such a favourable account of the voyage, Captain Morley seems to have given up the profit on a hundred or so slaves.

barbarity of any man, and prevent him from committing violence on, or misusing, his own property, and every cargo of slaves is more or less that of the ship's master's.

A few days before our arrival at Kingston, Mr. W – lb – ce and Tom Paine were burnt in effigy.[113] It would have hurt me had I seen the former coupled with such an incendiary, and thus exposed to public ignominy; for, in my conscience I believe he was impelled by too keen notions of humanity, and too zealous a desire of doing good, to take so active a part as he has done for the abolition.

For a length of time I viewed the Slave Trade with abhorrence – considering it a blemish on every civilized nation that countenanced or supported it, and that this, our happy enlightened country, was more especially stigmatized for carrying it on than any other; but I am not ashamed to confess, those sentiments were the effect of ignorance, and the prejudice of opinion, imbibed by associating with a circle of acquaintances, *bigoted for the abolition,* before I had acquired information enough to form any independent thoughts upon the subject, and so widely opposite are my ideas of the trade from what they were, that I now think it in no shape objectionable either to morality or religion, but on the contrary consistent with both, while neither are to be found in unhappy Africa; and while three-fourths of that populous country come into the world, like hogs or sheep, subject, at any moment, to be rob'd of their lives by the other fourth, I say, while this is the case, I cannot think the Slave Trade inconsistent with any moral or religious law – in place of invading the happiness of Africa, it tends to promote it, by pacifying the murdering, despotic Chieftains of that country, who only spare the lives of their vassals from a desire of acquiring the manufactures of this and other nations, and by saving millions from perdition, whose future existence is rendered comfortable by the cherishing hands of Christian masters, who are not only restrained from exercising any improper or unjust cruelties over their slaves, by the fear of reciprocal injury, but by the laws of the land, and their religious tenets.

All the slaves I had an opportunity of seeing in Jamaica, seemed vastly well satisfied, their conditions appeared to be far preferable to what I had expected, and they discovered more cheerfulness than I ever observed the Blacks show in Africa, unless roused by liquor.

---

[113] There was indeed some irony in bracketing the deeply religious and politically reactionary William Wilberforce with the radical atheist Tom Paine.

The Kingston markets are as abundantly supplied with vegetables, both in variety, and quantity, as any I ever saw; and, I was informed, wholly from the industry of slaves at their by-hours, for their own emolument; and I further heard, that notwithstanding many of them have in this way, amassed money enough to purchase several slaves, yet few instances occur where they show even a desire of ransoming themselves. This is not a matter of much astonishment, when we reflect how little slaves in our Islands are embarrassed with worldly cares: that they are fed when hungry, clothed when naked, and kindly nursed, with every medical care, when sick, solely at their masters' expense, who only exact honesty, and a reasonable task of labour in return, after which, if attended to, they have nothing to fear, but, on the contrary, are certain of being rewarded and encouraged by extraordinary indulgences; and when the thread of life is spun out, they leave this world with the pleasing thoughts that an interested, if not naturally humane and indulgent, master or mistress will supply their place, and prevent their children from experiencing any want of a father or mother's fostering hand.

How very few of our labouring poor can boast, when their mortal bodies become tenants of the grave, that their children have such certain provision secured them, and probably thousands and thousands of themselves may go supperless to bed this very night, and rise tomorrow not knowing where to get a breakfast, or without the means of acquiring a morsel of bread to allay the gnawings of hunger – whether then are their situations, or those of slaves, most preferable? The question, in my opinion, requires but little consideration.

Pray do not misinterpret my arguments, and suppose me a friend to slavery, or wholly an enemy to abolishing the Slave Trade; lest you should, I must explain myself – by declaring from my heart I wish freedom to every creature formed by God, who knows its value – which cannot be the case with those who have not tasted its sweets; therefore, most assuredly, I must think favourably of the Slave Trade, while those innate prejudices, ignorance, superstition, and savageness, overspread Africa; and while the Africans feel no conviction by continuing it. But remove those errors of nature, teach them the purposes for which they were created, the ignominy of trafficking in their own flesh, and learn them to hold the lives of their fellow mortals in higher estimation, or even let me see a foundation laid, whereupon hope itself may be built of their becoming proselytes to the doctrine of Abolition; then, no person on earth will rejoice more earnestly to see that trade suppressed in every shape; nor do I apprehend it would be impracticable, or even difficult, to effect it, for I still admit what I said upwards of two years ago to be strictly just – "That Nature has not endowed the Africans with capacities less susceptible of improvement and cultivation, than any other part of the human race," [114] – and I am sure they thirst for literature; therefore, if seminaries were established on different parts of the coast, and due attention paid to the morals and manners of the rising generation, I do not question but their geniuses would ripen into ideas congenial with our own; and that posterity would behold them, emerged from that vortex of disgrace, in which they have been overwhelmed since time immemorial, establishing social, political, and commercial connections throughout the globe, and even see them *blazing* among the *literati* of their age.[115]

I am heartily glad to get rid of this subject, and am surprised how I came to entangle myself in it: but trust no expressions have slipped from me which will reproach my humanity, or sensibility for the wrongs of mankind; if there have, impute them to mistaken notions of happiness and misery, for I am not conscious of meaning ill.

You will observe, I was in Jamaica from the 13th of July to the 3rd of August, and perhaps may expect some opinion of the country, people's manners, &c. from me, but any remarks of mine cannot be otherwise than trifling and confined, as my stay was too short, and Kingston, with a little of its environs, were the only parts I had a chance of seeing.

Kingston stands on the brink of a bay which forms the harbour; its situation is varied, being partly low and partly high. I suppose it to be about a mile in length, and rather more than half in depth, a regular, well built town, with streets intercepting each other at right angles; but I think many of them quite too narrow for that climate. I am told it is the largest, best built, most opulent, and populous town we have in the West-Indies. The merchants mostly have small country villas, within a couple of miles round, which are called Pens, whither they retire between

---

[114] She quotes a phrase she used on p. 46.

[115] Compare Mungo Park who, on his return from his two and a half year sojourn in West Africa seeking the course of the Niger, wrote in his *Travels,* "If my sentiments should be required concerning the effect which a discontinuance of that commerce [the Atlantic slave trade] would produce on the manners of the natives, I should have no hesitation in observing that, in the present unenlightened state of their minds, my opinion is, the effect would neither be so extensive or beneficial, as many wise and worthy persons fondly expect" (Mungo Park, *Travels,* London, 1799, p. 298).

three and four o'clock in the afternoon, when all business for the day is completed.

I found the heat much more oppressive than I ever felt it in Africa, where I was, including both voyages, upwards of two years without perceiving my skin in any way discoloured by the weather, but before I had been in Kingston a week, I was tan'd almost as brown as a mulatto. This I charge in a great measure to living on the sea side, open to the violent breeze, which sometimes blew a very storm, and which, I am persuaded, is intensely acid, for I never could leave a key, knife, or any piece of steel exposed to it for half an hour, without getting rusted. The people dress mostly after the custom of this country, and their manners are much the same, except in hospitality, which surpasses all I ever met with.

I used commonly to ride out from five to seven o'clock in the morning, and then return to breakfast; in those rides I often observed the country tore up into deep furrows, which I conjectured were passages of rivulets dried up, but was informed they were occasioned by heavy inundations, during the rains; notwithstanding this, I found the roads remarkably good, particularly the road to Spanish Town, which is, without exception, the best I ever travelled upon; but understand, it was made at prodigious expense, being a great part of the way through a morass, which, laying to windward of Spanish Town, must contribute to make that place very unwholesome. This is the capital of Jamaica, about thirteen miles from Kingston, but in comparison with the latter, very insignificant; several public offices, the assembly of the island, and courts of justice are held there; it is also the residence of the Governor, whose house is most spacious and elegant;* a marble statue of our late gallant Rodney is erected there, in memory of that ever famous action on the 12th of April 1782;[116] its ornamental effect is greatly lost by being placed in an obscure corner. I am surprised it was not raised at Kingston, where certainly it would have appeared to more advantage and notoriety; but the House of Assembly determined that it should grace the former, being the metropolis.

* It is said to have cost £30,000 Jamaica currency, £21,428 11s. 6d. sterling.

I have already told you what excellent vegetable markets there are in

[116] The Battle of the Saintes, fought against the French.

Kingston; its flesh markets likewise are very good, plenty of fat beef, but rather dark coloured and coarse grained, excellent mutton, pork, and poultry of all kinds; turtle in high perfection, and a variety of fine fish may be had every day.

Kingston swarmed with emigrants from St Domingo,[117] whose miseries and misfortunes did not fail to draw compassion and charity from its humane inhabitants, who subscribed most liberally to meliorate their sufferings, and I was credibly informed, that even the French prisoners have so handsome an allowance as three and sixpence currency each per day, from the island of Jamaica, for their maintenance. Are not these proofs of generosity ? Can a doubt exist that those people who not only assist the oppressed and injured, but provide so bountifully for their very enemies, are not alive to the nicest definition of humanity ? Only in minds warped by ignorance and prejudice, I presume, and the opinions of such are very immaterial.

A very galling and extraordinary misfortune befell me while at Kingston, which I cannot refrain from mentioning to you. After we had been there about eight or ten days, a genteel dressed man took lodgings in the same house with us, and the following day we went to dine and stay the night at a gentleman's in the country, when this fellow availed himself of our absence, broke into my bed chamber, and rifled a small casket, containing nearly all the trinkets and valuables I had, to some considerable amount; be assured I felt prodigiously mortified at my loss, which was not a little aggravated by finding the knave had eloped, leaving behind him a trunk *half full of stones,* in lieu of his spoils.

Tricks of this sort occur so rarely there, that it made not a little noise, and the Town Vestry offering a handsome reward for apprehending the thief, I had the satisfaction of hearing, just before we sailed, that he was taken; but this was all, for he had disposed of what he stole from me, at least none of the articles were found in his possession; however, it was supposed he would be convicted of other burglaries charged to him, and I cannot say, I should be hurt to hear the world was rid of such a nuisance.[118]

I believe I have now noticed every circumstance meriting attention, from the time of our leaving Sierra Leone, until our arrival here, and having spun this letter out to a greater length than was either expected

[117] The slave war of liberation in St Domingo had broken out in 1791.
[118] Burglary was still punishable by hanging in 1793.

or intended, I must therefore hurry it to a conclusion, and shall only observe that the *Amy* is arrived, with the two black Deputies from Sierra Leone, but I am not informed what kind of reception they have met with from the Directors, none of whom I have yet had the pleasure of seeing.

Mr— has some business with them, which he is in hopes of accomplishing shortly, we then intend paying a visit to you and the rest of my friends in Bristol.

Adieu,
    Believe me always
        Yours sincerely.

LETTER XIV

"Even the declarations made by themselves, seem wholly new and strange to them; they forget not only what they have seen, but what they have said."

Wilberforce on the Slave Trade, 18th April, 1791.[119]

LONDON, 23d. *Dec.* 1793

My dear Madam,

I concluded my last by telling you Mr— had some business to settle with the Directors, part of which was on account of what they were, and yet are, indebted to me as the widow of Mr Falconbridge, for money left in their hands, and for salary due to him when he died.

About a week after we came to town, I called at Mr Henry Thornton's, but not finding him at home, left my address, with a message, that I wished to see him on business. Several days elapsed without a syllable from Mr Thornton, and conjecturing the servant might have omitted delivering my card or message, I called again, when his house-keeper assured me he had received both, but was then at his country seat at Clapham; I now left a note mentioning the circumstance of my having waited on him twice, and begging to be acquainted when I could have the pleasure of seeing him; four or five days more passed away without any answer, which puzzled me very much to account for. Unwilling, however, to nurse any suspicion that either insult or injury could possibly be intended me, by a man who had spontaneously made such declarations of friendship as Mr Thornton did to me before I went last to Africa, and whose character is currently reported to possess as little alloy as frail man can be charged with, I therefore determined to venture another letter before I formed any opinion; the consequence of this was an answer that staggered me a vast deal more than his silence; he informed me I would find him at his banking house, in Bartholomew Lane, from

[119] Here she boldly turns the tables on Wilberforce, a director of the Sierra Leone Company, by quoting back at him from his historic speech in the House of Commons in which he introduced the first motion for the abolition of the slave trade, his own ironic strictures on those who defended it.

ten to twelve the following day, if I *chose to call there.* I was vexed at receiving so affronting a note from Mr Thornton, because it gave me room to question his veracity, and the Directors' good intentions towards me; nevertheless, a consciousness of having done nothing to merit such rudeness, and my interest requiring me to see him, I curbed my nettled pride, collected as much composure as it was possible, and met the gentleman on his own ground. I believe he neither expected or wished for this meeting; when I entered his counting room, he blushed confusion, and with some difficulty he stammered out, "Pray madam, what is your business with me?" "I have been induced to take much pains to see you, Sir, to request you will get the Directors to settle Mr Falconbridge's accounts, and pay what is owing to me", answered I. "Why", said he, "Mr Falconbridge kept no books, and he appears to be considerably in debt to the Company". "Kept no books, Sir, how can that be, when I have a copy of them this moment in my hands, a duplicate of which I know your Accountant at Sierra Leone (in whose possession the original books are) has sent the Directors." "I have never seen them; pray what is the amount of your demand?", replied Mr Thornton. I then produced an abstract account stating the sum. "Why", says he, "it's a large amount; I did not know Mr Falconbridge left any money in our hands, I thought he had received it; and his accounts for the *Lapwing's* first voyage were never settled". This language startled me a good deal, but I refreshed his memory regarding the money left with the Directors; and told him he also laboured under a mistake respecting the *Lapwing's* accounts, for he must recollect they were settled, and that he, fortunately, paid the balance of £74.19s. 6d. to myself. Naked truths thus staring him in the face, made him at a loss what to say; however, after a little reflection, he told me, "Whatever is due to you, madam, must be paid; if you will walk into another room, and wait a few moments, I will send for Mr Williams, the Secretary, who will see every thing set right".

I was then shown into a large cold room, covered with painted floor cloth, where, after waiting some time half frozen, Mr. Williams came. His behaviour was gentlemanlike: when I had recapitulated nearly what I said to Mr Thornton, he enquired if Mr Falconbridge left a will in my favour, which having answered in the affirmative, he wished me joy, as it would prevent others from sharing of the little property he left – desired me to get the will proved, and when that was done, there would be no impediment whatever in my way, and I should be paid immediately.

In a few days after, Mr— saw Mr Williams, who told him he had better omit proving the will till the Court exactly ascertained what amount I had to receive, as it would save expense.[120]

Perhaps Mr Williams intended a kindness by this admonition, for he must have known then, what I am now sure of, that the Directors mean, if they possibly can, to withhold every sixpence from me; at least there is great reason to suppose so from their quibbling conduct.

After detaining us here all this time, and shuffling Mr— off from one Court to another, without assigning any honest, business like reason for doing so; they now wind up their prevarications by saying they must wait for further information from Sierra Leone, which I look upon tantamount to a positive refusal; indeed, it would have been much handsomer had they candidly declared at once, that it was not their intention to pay me – for their evasive answers have increased the injury, by prolonging our stay here to the overthrow of some plans Mr— had in contemplation.

What do you think of their charging me with the presents they particularly directed I should purchase for, and make, Queen Naimbana; with the stores granted by the Court for me to take to Sierra Leone, my journey to Bristol and Falmouth, and every little donation they made either to Mr Falconbridge, or myself.

But besides these paltry, pitiful charges, they bring forward three others of much greater consequence, though founded on equally shameful and frivolous grounds, viz. the *Lapwing's* cargo, with all the expenses of her first voyage, and for eight months before she left the river Thames; the goods sent in the *Duke of Buccleuch*, together with the freight and passage money paid Messrs Andersons, and the *Amy's* cargo when we last went to Africa,

They might, with as much propriety, have included the whole of the Company's funds that have been thrown away, yes, shamefully so – no set of raw boys just let loose from school could have disposed of them more injudiciously. – What had Mr Falconbridge to do with the disbursement of the *Lapwing?* Her master was the ostensible person. The

---

[120] Clarkson had already written to DuBois to say that Richard Phillips, the lawyer who had helped Falconbridge write his book, had custody of the will, which mentioned money of his held by the Company. But "the Company are now so very frugal that I should not wonder if they hesitated paying the Money as they all exclaim against Falconbridge, and say he has deceived them so much, and run them to such immense expenses" (BL, Add. MS 41263, Clarkson to DuBois, 1 July 1793).

trifling goods sent out in her and the *Duke of Buccleuch* were all appropriated conformable to the instructions Mr Falconbridge received; they
were not intended for trading with, but merely as gifts of charity, and
bribes, to pacify the covetous natives; therefore if Mr Falconbridge had
not accounted for them, it would be very easy to find out whether they
had been disposed of that way: but I know every thing was settled
previous to our second voyage, and it is only a poor, mean finesse in
the Directors to say otherwise.

As to the *Amy's* cargo, true – it was consigned to Mr. Falconbridge;
but that consignment was done away, when he received his fresh instructions, after we arrived at Sierra Leone; and before that vessel left
Africa, the Master of her got a receipt for his whole cargo, from the
Governor and Council, which receipt the Directors have at this moment.[121]

I will not interrupt your time with this subject longer than to give
you the sentiments of the late Governor of Sierra Leone, who says, in
a letter of the 15th instant to Mr. —, "I am sorry the Directors should
give you so much trouble, and particularly about the cargo of the *Lapwing*
for her first voyage. They certainly are unacquainted with the circumstances and the situation of Falconbridge on his first voyage, or they
would never be so minute, particularly with his widow, who experienced
such unheard of hardships.

"I hope I speak truth, when I pronounce their late Commercial Agent
an honest man, but a very unfortunate one, not in the least calculated
for the station he filled, which men of discernment might have discovered
at first view. I assure you, had I been on board the *Lapwing* on her first
voyage, by myself, in Sierra Leone river, without a person in the neighbourhood likely to befriend me (which was the case with Falconbridge),
knowing the country as I do, I should have thought myself extremely
happy to have returned safe to my native country without any cargo at
all."

I shall now leave you to make what comments you please on the
vexatious treatment I have received from those Gentlemen, and to turn
in your mind what my prospects would have been had I come home
implicitly confiding in the profusion of friendly promises they bestowed
on me (unsought for) when last in England.

---

[121] The records of the London office of the Sierra Leone Company, which would have
elucidated her claims, have not survived.

I certainly had a right to build some expectations on them; but in place of any, you find those *paragons of virtue and human excellence* unwilling to do me common justice, refusing to pay me what is religiously my right – a little pittance, which, God knows, I gave the highest price for!

However, if there is any comfort in having company in one's misfortunes, or ill usage, I have that satisfaction. – Their treatment to Mr Clarkson (the late Governor), and others, has been highly discreditable, but their behaviour to the two Deputies from Sierra Leone, and consequently to all their constituents, is the most inconsistent part of their conduct, because any injury done them must annoy and jar the Company's interest.

These unfortunate oppressed people (the Deputies) have related to me most minutely every circumstance that has befallen them since their arrival in this country; and, as you seem interested in their behalf, and desire to know what success they have met with, I will repeat their narrative nearly in their own words.

"We landed *pennyless* at Portsmouth", I think they said, "the 16th of August, but we had a small bill on the Directors for the amount of what our fellow sufferers subscribed before we left Free Town. The Company's Agent at Portsmouth gave us two guineas to pay our way here, which were deducted from our bill when it was paid. As soon as we came to Town, we went to Mr Thornton's house, and delivered our Petition to him, he read it over, and seemed at first to be very kind, and to compassionate us very much, but in two or three days time, he told us the Directors had received letters from Africa, stating that our complaints were frivolous and ill grounded. After this we saw several of the Directors who told us the same. We asked who the letters came from, but this they would not tell, however we are sure Dawes and McAuley are the authors, because they must write all the – – they can think of to excuse themselves.

"When we had been here about three weeks, finding our money almost exhausted, we applied to two of the Directors, namely Mr Thornton and Mr Parker,[122] and requested them to supply us with a little. The latter said, 'Yes, I will let you have money, if you will mortgage, or sell, the lands due you by the Company', but the former had *more humanity,* he recommended us to go and labour for our support. To this we replied,

[122] Samuel Parker, a City merchant, was also a neighbour of Thornton's at Clapham.

we were willing to work, if we knew where to get employment. – Mr Thornton then said, 'You shall be at no loss for that, I will give you a line to a person who will employ you'. – This we gladly accepted of, and accordingly got into service, where we wrought for near a month, without hearing the most distant hint of an answer to our Petition. We then began to grow very uneasy, and quite at a loss what to do, having no friend to advise us.

"The Directors never would give us Mr Clarkson's address, though we asked for it frequently; however, in the midst of our distress, accidentally hearing he lived at Wisbeach, we wrote him without hesitation, enclosed a copy of our Petition, requested he would interpose his influence with the Directors, and in vindication of his character, endeavour to get justice done us.[123] We told him all we required was the fulfilment of his promises, which the Gentlemen at Sierra Leone had assured us he made without authority. When Mr Clarkson received this letter, he wrote to Mr Thornton, begging the Directors would appoint some early day to meet him and us together, that he might explain his promises, and thereby acquit himself of having acted dishonourable, in any shape, to the people he carried from America to Sierra Leone.[124]

"We suppose the Directors did not like to see Mr Clarkson and us face to face, for Mr Thornton never answered that letter, which obliged Mr Clarkson to write another; this he sent unsealed, under cover to us, that we might be convinced of his good intentions and integrity towards us."[125]

---

[123] How they "accidentally" heard he lived at Wisbeach is explained in their letter to Clarkson of 26 October 1793 — "we did not know where to write to you till Mr. Duboz let us [sic] and as he is going down we send it by him" (BL, Add. MS 41263).

[124] There is a copy of this letter, dated 24 September 1793, in Clarkson's papers (ibid.).

[125] To Anderson and Perkins he wrote the following covering letter (ibid., copy of letter of 11 November 1793).

> Gentlemen. As the Directors of the Sierra Leone Company, seem unwilling, that I should see you before them, to explain promises made both by the Nova Scotians as well as myself, I have enclosed you a Letter to their Chairman unsealed for your perusal to convince you that the Promises I made you were from authority given me by the Sierra Leone Company, and that you have a just right to their performance — This will I hope convince you, as well as those you represent, that I have done all in *my power* to perform them, and that it must now rest entirely with the Directors, as I have nothing further to do with them. In hopes that you may receive your just due, and that God may Help you and those you represent is the fervent hope of, Gentlemen, Yours as well as their truly affectionate friend, John Clarkson.

They showed me a copy of the letter, which having read, I also transcribed, as I now do again word for word.

"WISBEACH, *Nov.* 11,1793.

"*My dear Sir,*

"As you have given me no answer to my letter, wherein I requested a day to be appointed for the Directors, myself, with Messrs Anderson and Perkins, the Deputies appointed by the inhabitants of Free Town to meet, to explain the promises you authorised me to make them, I am induced to take this method to convince the people at large of your Colony, that I have done all in my power, since I have been in England, to forward the performance of the promises I made them, with as much zeal as I used when I was on the spot; and as I cannot bear to be suspected by them, or the inhabitants of Nova Scotia, who were witnesses of my exertions in their behalf, I am induced to take this method of assuring them of the sincerity of my professions, as well that the promises I made them were from the Directors of the Sierra Leone Company, and that they have as great a right to the performances of them as they have to dispose of their own property.

"I send this letter to you (unsealed) under cover to Messrs Anderson and Perkins, for their perusal, that they may assure those they represent, I have done all in my power to perform my engagements with them, consistent with honour and honesty.

I am, Dear Sir,
        Yours sincerely,
                (signed) JOHN CLARKSON.

To Henry Thornton, Esq.
Chairman of the Court of Directors
of the Sierra Leone Company, London."

"We attended", continued the spokesman, "the first Court after receiving this letter, and delivered it. The Directors did not seem well pleased, but they made no observations on it to us. Before we left the Court, we were informed one of the Company's ships was to sail for Sierra Leone immediately – that we were to return in her, and when *embarked,* we should have an answer to our petition.

"We thought it very strange, they should put off giving us an answer till we had embarked, and therefore objected, saying, we wished not only to have, but to consider, the answer before we left this country, and were proceeding to say much more, when the Court prevented us, by saying, 'Whatever objections you have to make, or whatever you wish to tell us, you must do it in writing'. – In consequence whereof, on the next Court day, we presented an Address as follows:

'To the Honourable the Chairman and
Court of Directors of the Sierra Leone
Company.

'*Honourable Sirs,*

'You have desired us to commit to writing what we wish to tell you.

'We did not think, Gentlemen, any thing more was necessary than the petition we brought, and delivered to you, from the people we represent; but as you do not seem to treat that petition with the attention we expected, you oblige us to say something more on the subject, for we would be very remiss were we to leave this country, without doing all in our power to get some satisfaction, not for the trouble we have been at, but such as will be pleasing and comfortable to our countrymen, and at the same time serviceable to your interest.

'The Settlers at Free Town (those brought from America we mean), whose thoughts we now speak, always believed the promises made them by Mr. Clarkson, in Nova Scotia, were your promises. We are now convinced of the truth of this, by the letter from Mr Clarkson, which we delivered you on Friday last.

'We certainly hope your Honors intend making good those promises, and we beg to know whether you do or not? – We beg to have Grants for the land we at present occupy, and a promise in writing for the remainder, or the value, to be given at a future time named in that instrument of writing.

'When we are able, we shall consider ourselves bound to contribute what we can towards defraying the expenses of the Colony; but this never can be the case until your promises are fulfilled to us; at present you are obliged to give us daily wages to do work, from which no advantage can ever be derived, either to the Company or the Settlers; and we have no choice, but to do this work or starve; whereas if we had our lands, and that support from the Company which was promised, there would be no necessity for employing us except at such work as was really wanting; and we might do as we please, either work on our own lands, or the Company's, whereby there would be mutual advantage, and in a few years, with industry and good management on our parts, the produce of those lands would yield a profitable trade to the Company, and we should have the pleasure of knowing we were providing comfort for our children after us.

'We always supposed we were sent from Nova Scotia to Sierra Leone, by his Majesty (God bless him) the King of this Country; who, no doubt, expected our situation would be made better, from the assurances he had received of what your Honors were to do for us. We wish the Governor of our Colony should be appointed by his Majesty, whose subjects we consider ourselves, and to whom we shall be happy at all times of showing our loyalty and attachment.

'If we are not of importance enough to this Country, to deserve a Governor authorised by the King, we, with due respect to your Honors, think we have a right to a voice, in naming the man who shall govern us, but by this we do not mean to say, that we have a right to inter-fere with the person whom you may choose to direct or manage your property,

'We *will not* be governed by your present Agents in Africa, nor can we think of submitting our grievances to them, which we understand is the intention of your Honors, for it is inconsistent to suppose justice will be shown us, by the men who have injured us, and we cannot help expressing our surprise that you should even hint at such a thing.

'Our Countrymen have told you, in the petition we delivered to his Honor the Chairman – they will wait patiently till we returned, that their religion made them bear the impositions of your Council, and prevented them from doing any thing that might be considered improper, till they heard from your Honors, being convinced they would then have justice shown them; but we are sorry to say, we do not think you seem disposed to listen to our complaints, and if we are obliged to return to Sierra Leone, impressed with those sentiments, and without obtaining any satisfactory answer to the complaints and representations we have made, it is impossible for us to say what the consequences may be, but we will make bold and tell your Honors, on the answer we get, *depends the success of your Colony.*

'We wish to return to our families by the *Amy,* and therefore beg to have your answer time enough for us to consider on it, before we leave this Country.

'We hope your Honors will not think we have said any thing here but what is respectful and proper; we thought it our duty to tell you the truth; we want nothing but justice, which cannot surely be refused us. We have been so often deceived by white people, that we are jealous when they make any promises, and uneasily wait till we see what they will come to.

'We shall conclude, gentlemen, by observing, since we arrived here, we have avoided giving you trouble as much as possible; we did not come upon a childish errand, but to represent the grievances and sufferings of a thousand souls.

'We expected to have had some more attention paid to our complaints, but the manner you have treated us, has been just the same as if we were *Slaves*, come to tell our masters of the cruelties and severe behaviour of an Overseer

'You will pardon us, gentlemen, for speaking so plain; however, we do not think your conduct has proceeded from any inclination to wrong us, but from the influence and misrepresentations of evil minded men, whose baseness will some day or other be discovered to you, for the Great Disposer of events will not suffer them to be hidden long.

> We are gentlemen,
>   With all possible respect
>   Your faithful Servants,

(Signed)
        ISAAC ANDERSON
        CATO PERKINS

            Representatives for the Inhabitants of Free Town'

"When they had read this over, they seemed very much out of humour, and we were desired to leave the Court room, but in a few minutes Mr Thornton sent us this letter.

'Messrs. Anderson and Perkins.

'In consequence of an address sent by you to the Court of Directors this day, I desire to be informed in writing, what are those promises of

Mr Clarkson, which you say were made to you in Nova Scotia, and are still unfilled.

I am,

Your obedient humble servant,

(Signed) H. THORNTON.

SIERRA LEONE HOUSE,
19th *Nov.* 1793.'

"Here is our answer to Mr Thornton.

'To HENRY THORNTON, Esq. Chairman, of the Court of Directors of the Sierra Leone Company.

'Sir,

'As you desire to be informed in writing, what were the promises made by Mr Clarkson to us (the inhabitants of Free Town) in Nova Scotia, we have to acquaint you, they were to the following purpose:

'That his Majesty having heard of the abuses we met with in America, and having considered our loyalty and services, in the late war, wished to make some amends, and proposed, if we were inclined to go to Africa, we should be carried thither free of expense.

'That the part of Africa we were to be carried to, was called Sierra Leone, where a Company of the most respectable gentlemen in England, intended to form a settlement for the purpose of abolishing the Slave Trade.

'That he (Mr Clarkson) was authorised by the Directors of the said Company, to say, each head of a family should have a grant of not less than twenty acres of land, for him or herself; ten acres for a wife and five acres for each child.

'That those grants should be given directly on our arrival in Africa, free of any expense or charge whatever.[126]

'That we should be provided with all tools wanted for cultivation, and likewise the comforts and necessaries of life, from the Company's stores, at a reasonable rate, such as about ten per cent. advance, upon the prime

---

[126] It was this unauthorised promise by John Clarkson that was to embroil the settlers irrevocably with the government, and was ultimately to drive some of them into rebellion (see p. 126).

cost and charges, and should not be distressed for the payment for such goods, until enabled by the produce of our lands; but when we became comfortably settled, we should be subject to such charges and obligations as would tend to the general good of the Colony.

'That we should be protected by the laws of Great Britain, and justice should be indiscriminately shown Whites and Blacks.

'As far as we can recollect those are the heads of Mr Clarkson's promises to us; almost the whole of which remain unfulfilled. There has been one fifth part of the lands distributed to most of the settlers, but they are in general, so mountainous, barren, and rocky, as to be of little or no use to them; nor was the surveying of that fifth part completed when we had left Sierra Leone, at which time the rains had set in, therefore it was impossible to clear or make much progress this year, and you must be sensible, Sir, of the injury we sustain by losing two years in the improvement of those lands.

'We are charged extravagantly for all the goods we purchase from the stores, which we consider, not only a breach of promise, but an unjust and cruel way of imposing a tax on us.

'We certainly are not protected by the laws of Great Britain, having neither Courts of Justice, or officers appointed by the authority of this government. But even the Police which we have formed among ourselves, has not distributed justice impartially to Blacks and Whites, due, as we suppose, to the influence of your Agents; and we think it an unsufferable cruelty, that at the caprice or whim of any Gentlemen in office, at Free Town, we, or any of us, should be subject, not only to be turned away from the service, but prevented from purchasing the common necessaries from the Company's stores, for the support of our families, while it is not in our power to procure them by any other mode.

> We are Sir,
> Respectfully,
> Your obedient, humble servants,

(Signed) ISAAC ANDERSON
        CATO PERKINS

> Representatives for the People of Free Town

LONDON, 20th *Nov.* 1793'."

"What was the consequence of this letter?", said I. – "Why the Directors were no better pleased with it than the first, they seemed quite in a quandary; were very anxious to know whether any person had assisted us in collecting and reducing our thoughts to writing, interrogated us separately on the subject, and appeared greatly disappointed with our answers." [127]

"Have you had any answer from them?" "No, Madam, and imagine they do not intend giving any; indeed we have heard that they mean to keep us from going to Sierra Leone again; if so, it no doubt is a stratagem, to dupe and lull our Countrymen, who have said they will wait peaceable, until we return; but such a poor little artifice is so very unbecoming the characters of gentlemen, that we can hardly believe it; however, if it is the case it cannot avail much, and will in the end do them more injury than us; we have already wrote to our brethren, warning them of our suspicions, and guarding them against signing any paper or instrument of writing, as we have reason to think some thing of the sort will be asked of them, to contradict what we have done; it will be a great hardship on us to be kept here from our families, yet, if it ultimately tends to obtain justice for our constituents, or to secure freedom and happiness to them and their children, we shall think it no sacrifice."

This is fully the substance of the information I have from time to time had from the two Deputies.*

* These two men returned to Sierra Leone, in February or March last, but two others have arrived on the same errand, and are just now (August, 1794) in London; I am told they have many new complaints, among which is one of a serious nature, viz. That an enormous annual tax of two bushels of neat rice, equal to 130lb. has been demanded per acre for their lands, notwithstanding those lands were promised them, *free of every expense, or charge whatever.* Now, rice is sold from the Company's store-house, at Sierra Leone, at the rate of sixteen and eight-pence per hundred pounds, consequently this tax would amount to 21s. 8d., per acre. [128]

[127] Anderson and Perkins could read and write, but the style of their surviving letters in John Clarkson's papers suggests that they must have received some assistance in writing these letters to the Directors — presumably from DuBois.

[128] These settlers who arrived in London in August 1794 had, in fact, not come with grievances, but had been sent there by the government as witnesses in a case of riot — an offence that the Company did not have jurisdiction to try in the colony, and had to have tried in England. A rent of one (not two) bushels of rice an acre on newly occupied land had been proposed, but was subsequently abandoned (Fyfe, *A History*, p. 57).

Is it not almost incomprehensible that Thirteen Men, whose reputations in private life (one or two excepted) [129] have hitherto been esteemed so spotless, that the tarnishing blasts of fame, or the venom'd shafts of malevolence, have seldom ventured to attack them, should, as a corporation, act incompatible with common sense and common – – – ?

The Directors' conduct must really be a subject of consternation wherever it is known; and should they not, of their own accord, fulfil Mr Clarkson's promises to their settlers, which they certainly seem inclinable to, I really think, in my humble opinion, this government ought to feel it a National concern, and enforce a performance.

His Majesty, no doubt, expected he was doing those poor people an actual service, by removing them to a country, which gave birth, not only to their fore-fathers, but many of themselves, and more especially so as they were to be taken under the wing and protection of such patrons of humanity, as the gentlemen conducting the affairs of the Sierra Leone Company *professed* themselves to be, otherwise he never would have hazarded their happiness, by taking them from America, where they were mostly comfortably settled – where they might have been useful and valuable subjects, and where they had been, long before their removal, really an acquisition, besides subjecting this Country to the expense of upwards of £20,000 for their transportation. *

* Those are a part of the very people whom America (it is said) is asking compensation for. [130]

Do you not think that immaculate Member of the House of Commons, who is obstinately persisting to abolish the Slave Trade, [131] would be better employed, and would discover more real humanity, if he exerted himself in getting justice done these poor blacks, whose happiness and comfort he has, in some measure, though innocently, been the means of destroying?

Until all the promises made them are performed, or, at least, a sincere inclination shown to perform them, no kind of confidence can exist between the Company and the Colonists; and unless that is quickly secured, the Colony must fall to nought. It may not be amiss here to

[129] I am unable to identify who her exceptions are.
[130] An issue that was being raised in 1794 during the negotiation of Jay's Treaty between Britain and the United States.
[131] Wilberforce.

give you the sentiments of a Gentleman, zealous for its success, and intimately acquainted with the Directors, and with the progress of the Colony, from its birth.

He says, in a letter sent to a friend of his in Sierra Leone,[132] "I am fearful your present Governors will forget the situation the Nova Scotians were in formerly, the number of times they have been deceived, and will not make allowances for the great change they have made; and I am more fearful of their not having patience or moderation enough to put up with their ignorance. It is an easy thing for the Governor and Council to leave them to themselves, if they are wickedly inclined; but I should consider such behaviour as the greatest species of wickedness on their parts, (the Governor and Council) and should think their education ill bestowed upon them, and their religion but skin deep. What ! are they not sent out to instruct them, and to set a good example to the unenlightened Africans? Ought they not to make the same allowances for them as our schoolmasters did for us in our infancy ? And ought they not to know that ignorant people, situated as they are, with the bad example set before their eyes by those who were sent out to instruct them at the commencement of the Colony, are liable to be riotous and unruly, particularly when so many have resided together, and but little employment to keep their minds amused, with the promises made them by the Company entirely neglected, and not the least appearance of a speedy completion, or even a *desire* to perform them. I say, had the Nova Scotians acted different from what they have done, under all these circumstances, it would have astonished me, and I should have requested those who consider themselves more enlightened, and stood forward as their friends and protectors, to have taken a lesson from so singular an example.

"Should you quarrel with the Nova Scotians, who do you think I shall blame? Your Government and the Company – your *Government,* for want of patience, and for not showing an inclination to perform promises, which will always set ignorant people at variance with their leaders, and particularly those who have been so often deceived before; and the *Company,* for not enforcing their orders relative to promises, and for their dilatory manner of sending out the means to perform them with dispatch.

"If you should have a war with the Natives, it will certainly be the fault of your Government, because you have it in your power, by a particular conduct, to make your Colony unanimous – and then you

---

[132] Clarkson to DuBois, writing after his dismissal, 1 July 1793 (BL, Add. MS 41263). The letter arrived after DuBois had left and was sent back to Clarkson

have nothing to fear. – You can always keep the Natives quiet if you have peace at home, which you may do, and at the same time gain their esteem and confidence; and if your Government should not, in every instance, do their utmost to preserve peace and harmony, and make every degree of allowance for the ignorance and bad example hitherto set to the poor Natives, and, I may add, the Nova Scotians, they will, in my opinion, have a greater crime to answer for than they may be aware of – for should your Colony, from bad management, not succeed, after *all the advantages it has had,* the friends to the civilization of Africa will have reason to repent of their having made an attempt to instruct that unenlightened part of society; it will depress the spirits of those whose hearts were warmly engaged in the cause, and deter them from making future attempts.

"These considerations have been so forcibly impressed on my mind, that I do not remember, since my arrival in England, of having written to, or conversed with, the Directors, either as a body or in private, but I have taken care to enforce, in as strong language as I could, the necessity of performing, as soon as possible, their promises to the Nova Scotians.

"I have been almost ready to expose people who are deserving of blame, but the situation of the Colony is such, that I am obliged to be silent, for it has many enemies in this Country, who would be rejoiced at having an opportunity to prejudice the minds of the Subscribers against the measures adopted by the Directors."

I have given you those extracts, corroborant to many assertions I have made, that you may not impute any of them to a wrong cause; and I must give you another from the same letter, very interesting to the Company's servants and officers employed in the Colony.

"I find there is a religious influence in the Colony, that will carry every thing their own way with a majority of the present Directors, and whatever they say, will be a law with them; and I really believe that religion, which ought to have been the support and sheet anchor of the Colony, will be its ruin, from its being practised with too great enthusiasm and inconsistency; and I am fearful that those possessed of honest hearts and independent spirits, who will speak their sentiments as truth dictates, will always be neglected by the Government there, and the Directors at home; and will never be done that justice which their readiness and exertions on every occasion to promote the prosperity of the Colony, entitles them to."

Can the Company ever expect to prosper, or have officers of probity or worth, while such is the case ? No – Sycophantic Hypocrites are the only servants who will continue in their service, and those will always drain the purses of their employers, by any means, however scandalous or dishonourable, to fill their own.

ADIEU.

Editor's Comment

By now Isaac DuBois had also been dismissed from the Company's service. Thornton wrote to Clarkson explaining that Dawes had passed on to the directors a disrespectful letter DuBois had written to him which they could not overlook. Nor could they overlook his having left the Colony for Jamaica as a passenger on board a slave ship. (Add. MS 41263, Thornton 16 September 1793). A further unmentioned offence in their eyes must have been his supporting the settlers' complaints. Clarkson replied in dismay, "With respect to DuBois I am to [*sic*] much hurt to say anything about him – His behaviour was so exemplary, his Manners so engaging, and his zeal and industry to promote the Happiness and Comfort of the Colony so conspicuous that I assure you I attribute the first foundation of the Colony in great part to him" (*ibid.* Clarkson, 24 September 1793).

To DuBois, who wrote asking him for a character reference, Clarkson replied, "Truth obliges me to say, that I attribute the commencement of regularity, order and the comfort of the Colony, principally to your exertions, and your readiness to comply with every request of mine for the good of the Company with respect and cheerfulness – I must also thank you for your kind and humane treatment of those committed to your care, and the great allowances you made for their Situation, as well as for your firmness in enforcing a just and proper behaviour of the People towards the Company – all this I informed the Directors upon my arrival in England" (*ibid.* Clarkson 3 November 1793).

And in a letter to a friend in Nova Scotia he wrote, " .... the Government there has induced a man to resign whom I can justly say has done more good in the Colony than all the rest put together, but he happened to have rather a more enlarged Mind than his Superiors and would not brook their behaviour to him .... I fear altho' I mentioned him so handsomely upon my arrival and specified the numerous works he had undertaken and completed yet they will not listen to any thing he may have to say to vindicate his behaviour in quitting the Colony. The Nova Scotians were doatingly fond of him, he kept them at a proper distance, behaved kind to them and made them do their duty – besides he was known to many of them when they were slaves in America" (Clarkson to Hartshorne, September 1793).

Thornton made no reply. As we shall see, he was preparing to line up DuBois with Falconbridge as scapegoats for the Colony's early misfortunes.

To HENRY THORNTON, *Esq.* M.P. *and Chairman of the Court of Directors of the* Sierra Leone Company, &c. &c.

BRISTOL, *April* 4, 1794.

SIR,

Being earnestly solicited, by several friends, to publish the History of my *Two Voyages to Africa,* and having, with some reluctance, consented, I feel it incumbent on me to address this letter to you (which is hereafter intended for publication), by way of acquitting a tribute truth and candour demands, in support of what I have, necessarily, mentioned regarding the Directors' behaviour to me.

It is needless, Sir, to take a more distant retrospect of the subject matter, than to the time of our arrival from Sierra Leone, in 1791.

If you will turn over to that period, and search into your personal behaviour, as well as the Court of Directors, to Mr Falconbridge, I am persuaded you will find it marked with repeated testimonies of approbation and applause for the services you were pleased to say he had rendered the common interest and original views of the Company.

For what purpose did the Directors vote us a compensation for our losses? Or for what purpose did they remove Mr Falconbridge out of his particular province as a medical man, and make him their Commercial Agent?

Were these not tokens of satisfaction, and rewards for his extraordinary exertions to serve the Company; or were they mere tricks of chicane and deception, to inveigle him to return to Africa, and answer the desirable end of securing a footing for the Emigrants then expected from America? Let your own heart, Sir, decide upon these questions.

I understand the Directors persist to say, Mr Falconbridge had not settled the accounts of his first voyage before he left England the second time; and that they impeach his memory, by saying he has not accounted for the cargo of the *Amy,* consigned to him as Commercial Agent. Is it so, Sir ? Are these paltry subterfuges made use of for withholding the poor pittance I am entitled to ? – If they are, I shall charitably suppose, for a moment, they proceed from error, and endeavour once more to set you to right – though, believe me, not with the smallest expectation of profiting thereby.

To the first I shall observe – You must labour under the misfortune of a very careless memory, if you cannot recollect that all Mr Falconbridge's accounts, anteceding the 25th of December, 1791, were adjusted to that time, and that I received from *yourself* a balance of £74.19s. 6d. which appeared on the face of the account in his favour.

Can you deny the truth of this assertion, and say there was no such settlement ? If you can, I will not attribute it to any harsher cause than bad memory, for I yet think it impossible Mr Thornton would be so pitiful, *willingly,* to utter an untruth.

But if this pointed circumstance had not happened, and I was wholly ignorant of the affair, I should suppose men of business (as some of the Directors must be) would never have suffered him, or any person else, to commence the transactions of a new concern till those of the old were clearly concluded, but more especially so, in this instance, as the charities Mr Falconbridge had the distribution of on his first voyage, were the property of the St George's Bay Company, whose original funds and effects were taken in account by the Sierra Leone Company, upon their incorporation, and therefore it was certainly necessary that the Directors should be made acquainted with the true state of their affairs.

To the second, I have to remind you that Mr Falconbridge never received the Cargo of the *Amy,* and consequently cannot account for what he was not in possession of; upon his arrival in Africa, he got instructions from the Directors, placing him entirely under the control of the Superintendent and Council, and the property of the Company solely under their direction, consequently the first consignment and unlimited instructions given him became nugatory; furthermore, the master of the *Amy* got a receipt for his whole Cargo from the Governor and Council, previous to his leaving Sierra Leone, which is just now in possession of the Directors.

Mr Falconbridge had no independent authority or management over the Company's goods after he received those instructions, nor did he give any orders of himself, as other hair-brained members of the Council did, but got written instructions from the Superintendent and Council for every sixpence worth he had, either from ship-board or else where, all of which is accounted for in his books, delivered Mr. Grey by the particular desire of Mr Dawes.[133]

I am inclined to believe the Directors are already acquainted with these circumstances, indeed it is almost impossible they can be ignorant of them.

But admitting they are, what excuse can they have for swelling up an account against me with fictitious niggardly charges, such as charging me with disbursements for the *Lapwing's* first voyage, not only during her voyage, but for six or seven months before she left the river Thames. The freight and passage money of the *Duke of Buccleuch* paid Messrs Anderson. The presents I was desired to purchase and make Queen Naimbana, for which I have your letter as authority. The stores I was allowed to take with me for our use at Sierra Leone. Our Journey to Bristol, Falmouth, &c. &c.

How can your *Honourable* Court, formed, as it is, of Members of Parliament, Bankers, and some of the first Merchants in the City of London, all professing the quintessence of philanthropy, thus depreciate its worth by being guilty of such gross meanness ? I verily believe it would be impossible to cull from the Migratory Chapmen of *Rag Fair*, any number of men who would not blush to be detected in a similar transaction.

That the Directors had cause to be displeased with Mr Falconbridge, for not extending their commercial views, may be in some measure true; but tied up as he was, to obey the dictates of the Superintendent and Council, who would not listen to any arrangements of the kind until comfort and regularity were established in the Colony – what was he to do ? However if he was altogether at fault, was he not punished by annulling his appointment as Commercial Agent ? Could the Directors do more ? If they had blindly (as they certainly did in many instances) made improper appointments what more could they do than annul them when they discovered their mistake?

But I should suppose it did not require any great discernment, to

---

[133] Macaulay however reported to Thornton that 'there is no document whatever of Falconbridge's transactions' (Journal, 29 August 1793). John Gray [sic] the government accountant, had arrived in Freetown in 1792. He remained there until 1802 when, 'after having devoted the best ten years of my life' to the Sierra Leone Company, he resigned and moved to the rivers north of the colony to trade in slaves (PRO, CO 270/8, Council minutes, 27 January 1802, 8 December 1802).

know that a Surgeon, unacquainted with mercantile affairs, would make but as poor a figure in that line, as a Merchant, who had not studied physic or anatomy, would make in the practice of surgery.

Mr Falconbridge's dismission did not charge or accuse him with any *crime,* but wanting knowledge of his business; and what information the Directors could get on that score must have been from a quarter as ignorant, if not more so, than himself; – but surely, it was their province to have convinced themselves, when they made their appointment, whether he was equal to it or not.

Did not Mr Falconbridge's dismission stipulate that his salary was to continue till the Governor and Council procured him a passage to England ? Could there have been the smallest idea, at that time, of detaining either the money left in the hands of the Directors, or his wages? Surely not. – Then why do the Directors now (for he is no more) withhold payment from me ?

For shame, Mr. THORNTON, for shame!!! – How can you wink at my being so shabbily treated, after the unexampled sufferings I have undergone, and after the prodigality of fair promises I had from you, to induce me to return a second time to Africa. Did you not tell me, if any accident befell Falconbridge, I should be handsomely provided for by the Company ? Surely you cannot forget making such a promise – which you not only forgo fulfilling, but shamefully keep back (all I require of you) the trifling sum so justly due to me.

If the Directors were not fearful of subjecting their conduct (towards me) to the investigation of impartial men, they would never have refused submitting the affair to arbitration, as was offered; nor would they have threatened, or boasted, that they would ruin me with an expensive law-suit in Chancery, when I signified my intention of trying the cause at Common Law, if they meant to do the fair thing.

I cannot help forming those conjectures, for how are we to calculate the principles of men but by their actions ? Though, believe me, Mr Thornton, notwithstanding all I have said of the Court of Directors, I yet firmly believe, if the decision was left wholly to yourself, I should have ample justice, and I cannot avoid thinking, from the opinion I have heretofore formed of your benevolence of heart, that you are secretly ashamed of the Directors' nefarious treatment to me.

I will not trespass on your time any longer, but shall quit the subject, with referring my cause to the loftiest of Tribunals, where reigns a Judge of mercy, vengeance and justice, who, I am persuaded, will not let such turpitude go unpunished, and who has, probably, already begun to show his displeasure.

Pray, Sir, receive this letter with temper, and consider it comes from a Woman, aggravated by insults and injury.

I am, &c &c,

ANNA MARIA —

Henry Thornton, Esq. M.P.
King's Arms Yard,
Coleman Street, London.

Appendix[134]

In the Preface, the Public is referred to the Directors of the Sierra Leone Company, for the authenticity of the Author's assertions, who now thinks proper, as a further vindication, to annex the following letter, which speaks for itself.

Moreover, she avails herself of this supplement to express her vexation at the number of typographical errors throughout the forgoing pages; besides those enumerated [in the *Errata*, not reproduced here] she has discovered several others, such as – Preface, *allmost* for almost; page 35, *spinnage*, for spinage; page 80 *maddern* for madder; page 176, *least* for last – and one or two more, which she hopes the reader has mercifully looked over, and not charged to her pen.

BRISTOL, August 11, 1794.

SIR,

Your not answering my last letter, and the disdain you have shown me on other occasions, since I came last to England, has not deterred me from doing what I considered honourable and upright.

Conscience, never wandering Monitor, advised me I should fall short of that sincerity I now boast to possess, and proudly nourish, if I omitted sending you a copy of my Voyages to Africa, before they were presented to the World.

This admonition (which no doubt grew from a desire "to hide the fault I see," [135] and a persuasion of having adhered most scrupulously to truth) prompted me to present a Copy to that valuable and ever to be esteemed Divine Mr GILBERT, who will give the same to you, for your perusal, immediately on his arrival in London, for which place he sets off this morning.

---

[134] The Appendix was omitted from the 1802 edition.
[135] 'Teach me to feel another's woe / To hide the fault I see': Alexander Pope, *The Universal Prayer*.

Would to God! you may read with calmness! but I fear a prepossession of the author's obscurity and insignificance will betray you; nay, I already anticipate your reproachful smiles at my mean diction and trite remarks, but remember, Sir, Truth, though unadorned, never fails to attract notice – it carries its own value – always shelters the innocent, and brands conviction on the malefactor's threshold.

Search the secret recesses of your bosom, and enquire if the Directors' conduct to me, has not been a violation of those fundamental principles, which *should* govern the actions of every man, or body of men? – Yes, Sir, ask there, if I am not an injured Woman ?

Remember, for a moment, my little patrimony has been expended in your service – remember my matchless sufferings – and remember likewise your own honour and credit, I say, remember these things, and they may point out what you ought to do.

The second document of Christianity is to make contrition for our offences. *All,* from the Palace to the Cottage, are liable to err, and none of us should blush to confess our penitence; however let the impulse of your own heart guide you – What I have done exonerates mine.

I am, Sir,
Your obedient Servant,
ANNA MARIA —

To Henry Thornton, Esq.
M.P. and Chairman of
the Court of Directors of
the Sierra Leone Company.

Editor's Comment

The title page of the book proclaimed that it was not merely a narrative of the author's travels. It began *Two Voyages to Sierra Leone during the years 1791–2–3, In a Series of letters, by Anna Maria Falconbridge*, and went on *To which is added, A letter from the Author to Henry Thornton, Esq. M.P. And Chairman of the Court of Directors of the Sierra Leone Company*. Then followed the quotation "If I can hold a Torch to others, / 'Tis all I want – – ". It was published in London, and "Printed for the author, and sold by different booksellers throughout the kingdom", price five shillings.

Mrs Falconbridge had an ally in Carl Bernhard Wadstrom, another Swedenborgian Swede (see *footnotes* 73, 79) who, also in 1794, published *An Essay on Colonization,* a vast tome replete with numerous appendices on various colonization projects, including a detailed account of Sierra Leone. He too had a grievance against the Company, for not giving any financial support to the widow and children of his countryman Nordenskiöld, who had died in its service, or any remuneration to the botanist Afzelius. To Clarkson and DuBois he gave high praise, adding -

> The resolution of Mrs Falconbridge (now Mrs Dubois) in accompanying her former husband twice to S. Leona, and the hardships she suffered at the unpromising commencement of the colony, destitute as it *then* was of every thing necessary to the comfort of a well educated English lady, prove that even the tender sex, under the influence of conjugal attachment, may be so much interested in a great undertaking, as to forget the delicacy of their frame, and to face danger and distress in every terrifying shape. That this lady possesses not only patience and fortitude to endure difficulties, but ability to describe them, will not be doubted by those who have read her interesting account of Sierra Leona, which she published after her second return from that colony. If any excess of warmth should be observed in some parts of this spirited little work, it will be remembered that the writer is a woman who generously sacrificed her ease and comfort, to a principle of duty to her husband, and enlightened zeal in a great cause; that she certainly suffered many trials; and that, she might think, some of them might have been prevented by human prudence and foresight. (*Essay,* § 782).

Thornton however had already given his own version to the public. On 17 March 1794 he presented his director's report to the Court of Directors, a discursive 175-page history and description of the colony, subsequently published for the general public to read. In it, as in his letter telling Clarkson that Falconbridge had been dismissed (see pp. 92–3), Falconbridge was again, by implication, made responsible for all the disasters of the early period of settlement, and the directors absolved from responsibility:

> Whether the directors erred in dividing the authority among so many as eight persons, or whether the blame belonged more properly to the Governor and Council, it is not perhaps material now to canvas. The Directors acquit the body of acting counsellors of all wilful misconduct, with the exception indeed of one person detained in their employ, but not originally appointed by them, whose knowledge of the natives and of the country made him appear a person of importance at the outset of the undertaking, but whose habits of intoxication, idleness and irregularity, as well as want of accuracy in his information, are necessary to be mentioned as one chief cause of the first difficulties of the colony, and of the first commercial disappointments of the Company. It is partly to be ascribed to the extraordinary neglect of this person (whom it was the duty of the Governor and Council to direct and control) that the colony was not supplied with any fresh provisions before the sickly season arrived. The Company's ships were not employed for this purpose as was directed to be done, and the original body of instructions to the Governor and Council, drawn up by the Court of Directors and read to the Proprietors, received little or no consideration till long after this period. Confusion in the accounts, in the stores, in the government, in the information sent home, and in the operations of every kind prevailed; and this confusion not only tended to aggravate in many ways the distress of the sickly season, but it ought, perhaps, to be stated as one principal occasion of the extraordinary mortality. (*Substance of the Report delivered to the Court of Directors of the Sierra Leone Company*, London, 1794, pp. 10–11).

DuBois's turn came next. Having mentioned the Nova Scotians' grievances, Thornton went on,

> The secret cause however, to which the Directors have been informed that much of the dissatisfaction prevailing at this period may be traced, was the unbecoming conduct of one of the Company's servants who, on Mr Clarkson's leaving the colony, took occasion to prejudice a considerable party of labourers working under him against the succeeding government: this body of men made an attempt to raise the price of labour in the colony, which was already very high, by combining to leave their work; but not finding the government inclined to yield in any measure to their wishes, they returned after a week's interval to their employments, and the Company's servant who was supposed to have sowed the seeds of this dissension, and had also manifested the greatest disrespect towards the

government, having come to England, was dismissed from the service. (*ib.* p. 18).

A second edition of the book appeared later in 1794, identical with the first, except that it was differently paginated. A third appeared in 1795, also identical except that the title page showed it "Printed for the author: and sold by J. Parsons, No. 21 Paternoster Row".[136]

But no attempt was made to answer the author, or to make her "with all due deference, kiss the rod of correction" (see p. 10). Only two of the substantial reviews noticed it, *The Monthly Review*, although it had a year earlier given a sympathetic notice of Falconbridge's *Account*, nevertheless welcomed her "amusing volume" with its "plain and artless language", but made no comment on her denunciation of the Company (*Monthly Review*, xvi, 1795, 102–3). *The British Critic*, included in its brief, acerbic notice the misinformation (and this must surely have been a piece of deliberate and cruel malice), "Before we go far in the book we find the lady's name changed from Falconbridge to Dawes" (*The British Critic*, iv, 1794, 555). I gratefully owe this reference to Deirdre Coleman). *The Gentleman's Magazine* which was hostile to the abolitionist cause, and had praised Matthews's book (calling the slave-trader author "humane') gave it no notice, wary perhaps of antagonising the wealthy and highly respectable Thornton. Nor do the reports of the parliamentary debates of 1799 and 1802 in which Sierra Leone was brought up suggest that any of the Company's opponents in Parliament were aware of the book and the damaging evidence it contained – certainly none of them quoted from it.

In Freetown the returned delegate Isaac Anderson had a copy, and used it when in dispute with the government. Macaulay reported him quoting from "his favourite book DuBois" (Journal 22 August 1797, 26 August 1797). But there is no indication, from their surviving letters, that any of the other settlers read it.

In 1802 another edition, misleadingly called "The Second Edition" appeared. The text was the same (with the typeface tending to wear thin, and the Errata listed in the previous editions still uncorrected). But the final letter to Thornton was suppressed, and his name no longer appeared on the new title page which firmly located the book in the anti-abolitionist camp. It now read *Narrative of Two Voyages to the River Sierra Leone, during the years 1791–2–3, performed by A.M.Falconbridge. With a Succinct account of the Distresses and proceedings of that Settlement; a description of the Manners, Diversions, Arts, Commerce, Cultivation, Custom, Punishments, &c. And Every interesting Particular relating to the Sierra Leone Company. Also The present State of the Slave Trade in the West Indies, and the improbability of its total*

---

[136] I am grateful for this bibliographical information to James Green, Curator of the Library Company of Philadelphia, which holds a copy of the second edition, and to Peter Berg of the Michigan State University Library which holds a copy of the third.

Abolition. It too was published in London, printed for L. I. Higham, No. 6 Chiswell Street.

This time the *British Critic* ignored it, as did *The Monthly Review* and *The Gentleman's Magazine*. So did *The Critical Review*, even though it had by 1802 become sceptical about abolition, and *The Anti-Jacobin Review*. So did the newly founded *Edinburgh Review* – unsurprisingly, since its first number contained a respectful, thirty-page review of a book by Thornton on monetary policy. And again, when Sierra Leone was debated in the House of Commons, in 1804 and 1807, none of the hostile speeches contained references to it. No one stood up in Parliament to confront Wilberforce and Thornton with the wrongs of Mrs Falconbridge.

When the Sierra Leone Company was wound up in 1807, and Sierra Leone transferred to the Crown as a British colony, the Company's aim of spreading "the Blessings of Industry and Civilization" to Africa was carried on by a newly founded African Institution, with which Thornton, Wilberforce and Macaulay were closely associated. It was persistently attacked, in seven vituperative pamphlets, by Robert Thorpe, first (and summarily dismissed) Chief Justice of the Colony, who raked up the Company's treatment of John Clarkson, with various other charges. But there is only one reference to *Two Voyages* in them – quoting the hostile first impression given by Macaulay (see p. 108). Moreover Thorpe supposed the book authored by a man ('. . . his account of Sierra Leone'), misled perhaps by the title page of the 1802 edition which bore only the author's initials. Nor was it referred to in a series of pamphlets by Joseph Marryat M.P., attacking the African Institution and upholding Thorpe's strictures.

During the 1820s the scurrilous high-Tory newspaper *John Bull* mounted a long-running campaign against "the Saints", particularly Zachary Macaulay, and "that pest-house of the world", Sierra Leone. But it made no use of the ready-made evidence *Two Voyages* could have provided. And a long series of pamphlets, and articles in *Blackwood's Magazine*, hostile to Sierra Leone, by the Glasgow geographer James M'Queen contained only one reference from the book – the story of the "Gothic infringement on human Liberty" (see p. 39–40), quoted with heavily emphasized type-faces added, " . . . upwards of ONE HUNDRED unfortunate women were *seduced* from England to practise their iniquities MORE BRUTISHLY IN THIS HORRID COUNTRY!!" (*Blackwood's Magazine*. XXI, 1827, p. 315).

Not until 1836 was it given some recognition, in a book with the eye-catching title *The White Man's Grave: A Visit to Sierra Leone in 1834*, by F. Harrison Rankin, who quoted on the title page (from her p. 82), "it is quite customary to ask in the morning, how many died last night". One of Rankin's informants, an elderly Nova Scotian, recalled the Company's mistreatment of John Clarkson: his story is substantiated with a footnote reference to *Two Voyages*. Rankin also gave a brief account of the disasters of the early days (including the story of the garden watering pots), referring his

readers to her narrative "for a minute account of the settlers' sufferings and
their causes" (vol. I, p. 88; vol. II, pp. 164–7).

From then on, writers on Sierra Leone have made occasional use of it,
usually picking up the early mortality and the "Gothic infringement". But the
author herself has remained veiled. The late Averil Mackenzie-Grieve included
a chapter on her in *The Great Accomplishment: The Contribution of five English
Women to 18th century Colonisation* (London, 1953), and she is mentioned
in Moira Ferguson, *Subject to Others* (London, 1992), and in Mary Louise
Pratt, *Imperial Eyes* (London, 1992). There is also a brief account in Jane
Robinson's *Wayward Women* (Oxford, 1990). Frank Cass and Co published
a facsimile reprint of the 1802 edition of the *Narrative* in 1967, but without
any introduction or notes. And in 1999 Deirdre Coleman published *Maiden
Voyages and Infant Colonies: Two Women's Travel Narratives of the 1790s*
(London, 1999) reprinting together the first edition of the *Narrative*, with
annotations, and *A Voyage Round the World* (1795) by Mary Ann Parker, who
accompanied her husband on a voyage to Botany Bay (the two ladies were
coincidentally in sight of one another in Portsmouth harbour in January 1791
(see p. 15).

And now in the same year this belated tribute to Anna Maria Falconbridge
also appears. It is a tribute less complete than her editor feels she deserves,
for her subsequent life he has been unable to unveil. Some details of DuBois's
later activities can be found. He still wanted to return to Africa, and applied
in 1794 for service with the ill-fated Bulama Company. But his application
was turned down as the result of a private letter discrediting him — written
by the Reverend Melville Horne, who had performed their marriage ceremony, and now was Thornton's ally against him and Clarkson (Horne to
Thomas Haweis, 27 January 1794, letter in private collection). The couple
then moved to Bristol: he is listed in the *Bristol Directory* for 1795, living in
Alfred Place. But his name is absent from subsequent volumes. In 1801 he
was briefly in Dublin (BL, Add. MS 35731, fol. 62).

He still went on renewing his claim against the government for compensation for the losses he had suffered through loyally embracing the British
cause in America (see *footnote* 74). His father, who had died when he was
a boy, had been one of the wealthiest men in Wilmington, and the family
property, including houses, warehouses, a bakery and a mill, as well as "a
great number of valuable Boat Negroes and Tradesmen', was valued at nearly
£30,000, yielding an income of about £4,000 a year. He petitioned the
Treasury in 1801, but only received £5,320. Feeling this inadequate, he
petitioned Parliament for a further grant, claiming not only for himself but
on behalf of fifteen dependent relatives. It was 1807 before his petition came
before a committee of the House of Commons, supported by two retired
generals who testified to the valuable part he had played in the campaign in
North Carolina. The committee was sympathetic and recommended that he
be granted £10,000, in addition to the £5,320 granted already.

But the government, now engaged in the long war against Napoleon, was retrenching all expenditure. It was pointed out that DuBois had in 1804 been appointed Barrack Master at Tenterden in Kent (with a meagre salary of £150 a year) and subsequently Comptroller of Customs in Curaçoa, recently captured from the Dutch (though there is no sign in the Curaçoa records that he ever went there). So he was granted only £5,000 (*House of Commons Journals*, vol. lxii (1807), pp. 277–8, 845, 954- 56).

And there my knowledge of Anna Maria Falconbridge-DuBois and her husband ends. The name of her brother-in-law, Captain Morley, turns up from time to time in the Sierra Leone records, when he was calling in at Freetown on his way up the river to load a cargo of slaves at Bance Island. By comic coincidence, the Reverend Cato Perkins, the Nova Scotian delegate whom she and DuBois had befriended, came one day to complain to Zachary Macaulay that his wife had eloped with Morley (Macaulay, Notebook, 26 September 1796) But what happened to Anna Maria and Isaac DuBois in later years, where they lived, and what they did, and when they died, I do not know. Perhaps this reprint of her work may inspire some reader to find out.

7 Freetown, 10 November 1792, watercolour by John Beckett.
(Below, left, Robana Island, right, the French factory on Gambia Island).

8 Portrait of Thomas Clarkson, by A. E. Chalon.

9 Portrait of Granville Sharp,
by G. Dance,
engraved by Henry Meyer.

10 Portrait of John Clarkson.

11 Portrait of Zachary
    Macaulay,
    by F. Slater.

12 Portrait of Henry
Thornton, by John Hoppner,
engraved by T. Blood.

The Journal of Isaac DuBois

Before leaving the Colony Clarkson had asked Isaac DuBois to keep and send him a daily journal, to let him know what was going on in the Colony. It survives among the Clarkson Papers (British Library, Add. MS 41263, fols 1–17) and is reproduced here to complement the *Narrative*. Though addressed to Clarkson, it refers to him in the third person. DuBois's idiosyncratic punctuation and spelling have been retained: corrections,` in square brackets, have been inserted only when the sense demands it. The passages he underlined, to bring them to Clarkson's special attention, have been italicised. Three subsequent letters he wrote to Clarkson have been added at the end (Add. MS 41263, fols 30–1, 38–40, 45–6).

Free Town Sierra Leone 31st December 1792

My dear Sir

We arrived safe and well in the hours after parting with you last night but to be sure I found my spirits much *more oppressed* then usual. This morning I resolved to begin the Journal you desired me to keep in your Absence, tho I greatly fear it will neither be so satisfactory as I could wish, or as it might be, was not my time continually occupied with business, however you may be assured of a fair and ingenuous statement of every thing as it happens, or as I come acquainted with it — it is not my intention to keep a diary of the weather, that I shall leave for my friend Afzellius, who has less to do than I have, or in other words who makes that a part of his vocations — but I shall confine myself merely to the affairs and occurances in the Colony.

Jany 1st 1793

Our Neighbour Paa: Queit brought me six Gramattas[1] this morning — Mr Dawes *called on me* this morning — and *last night* also — This being New Years Day little or no work is done in the Colony — except by a

---

[1] Free labourers (from Portuguese *grumete* 'cabin-boy, deck hand').

few — Mr Dawes called on me again this evening and asked me to accompany him to King Naimbannas tomorrow which I have promised to do — every thing quiet!!

January 2d. Having a small fever last night am prevented from accompanying Mr Dawes to King Naimbannas today — he breakfasted with me and went up alone — Charming weather — I find myself much better in the evening. Sat at my *Neighbours* till Nine OClock, came home, made these remarks & so I'll go to bed, & comfort myself, for I am vastly sleepy.

Jany 3d

Mr Dawes returned from King Naimbannas at 3 OClock this morning with the Ox the King gave to Mr Clarkson — *Made my wedding ring this day* — had a visit from King Jammy he seemed to regret very much not seeing Mr Clarkson before he went away — nay I saw several tears fall from his eyes. I comforted the King with a Glass of wine & he went away in good humour, *every thing quiet — but the people are rather dissatisfied that neither their Town or Country Lotts are now run out, the Engineer very busy with his New Fort.* The Providence Sloop arrived from the Carrimancas, has on board 3½ tons of Camwood three goats some rice etc. I am informed that Captain Paterson has turned his second mate, Mr Torry, before the mast, but that Mr Dawes has desired he go down to the Carrimancas as first mate of the Lapwing — which I am much pleased at — the Amy sent the last of her Cargoe on shore this afternoon — get three Gramattas today, I have in all 19 — I feel in better health & spirits this night then I have done for some time — Amused myself till ½ past 10 OClock at my *Neighbours* & am just going to bed — but I recollect one or two more occurrences of the day — the bales of Goods from the Amy which are lodged in the new Cellar are all more or less damaged some of them considerably so — I called on Mr Dawes & requested he would order a Survey on them — *Yesterday I began to cut down the side of the Hill & to level the foundation for the Grand Store House but have had a hint, that the Masons are to be taken from me to build the Fort, surely this cannot be true — Querie — will not one room in that store house be of more consequence than twenty Forts? have we any thing to dread or have we soldiers to occupy a Fort?* ½ past 11 OClock thunder & lightning the first we have had for two months past the weather looks wild & squally.

Jany 4th A heavy tornado last night the roof leaked so intolerably that I was forced to take shelter in Mr Afzelliuss house — the Ox which came from King Naimbannas was killed — it was remarkable fat — Two ships in the offing we suppose one to be the Nassau, Capt Morley & the other the Sierra Leone Packet — I mean tomorrow to go to Bance Island — called on Mr Dawes to ask if he had any objection — None —

Bance Island Jany 5th Mr Grey accompanied me here today was very politely received & entertained by all the Gentlemen — went to Tasso am much pleased with the soil, but the Cotton appears of a very inferior Quality — Appologize for the newspapers supposed to be taken away by Mr Clarkson — drank tea on board the Duke of Bucklieu she has 300 slaves on board & will sail Tuesday next.

Free Town Jany 6th Returned from Bance Island at three OClock this afternoon, called at King Naimbannas in my way down, found the King much indisposed but he received my visit very kindly & I was entertained with palaver sauce and different kinds of fruits. *His Majesty* took a fancy to my snuff box which I made him a present of & by his request engraved his name on the lid — hear such shamefull accounts of my workmens Idleness during my absence yesterday that it puts me out of humour — which my *Neighbour* takes for indifference towards her, and gets quite in a *pet* however a Reconsiliation is quickly brought about, and we agree to be married to morrow — *all well,* Good Night —

Jany 7th At 9 OClock this morning the Reverend Mr Horne performed the Marriage Ceremony and now I am once more, I trust, happyly joined in the bands of wedlock,[2] we intended our marriage should be kept a secret till the 21st of this month & Mr Horne had promised to do so, but the *poor* parson was not born to keep secrets, he carried it piping hot to the ears of every one he met, but desired every one he told it to, not to mention it to any one — however in less than two hours it was known over the whole Colony — it made very little difference to me whether it was known today or a fortnight hence — I am happy & the Parson is pleased at telling the news — Mr Dawes & Mr Pepys went to Signior Domingos upon some business respecting the lands — I began at four OClock this afternoon to clear a field at Savoy point [3] for Cotton, I have in all 21 Gramattas, 2 Chief men and two Settlers.

---

[2] I have not found any other reference to his previous marriage.
[3] East of Freetown – today Mabella Point – where the *Duke of Savoy,* a ship chartered by the Company, had been anchored.

Jany 8th — Mr Dawes returned last night from Sigr Domingos and I understand the business he went upon was settled to the satisfaction of all parties — *Mr Dawes hinted to me this morning that he did not wish I should go on with the Grand Store House under the Hill, this no doubt was the advice of Pepys yesterday — I pointed out to Mr Dawes that there was already sufficient stone cut to compleat the building which was the worst of the labour over* also that it was Mr Clarksons particular wish for me to go one with that work — to this he made no reply — and I mean to go on with it, till I have his positive written orders to *stop* — *I am rather of Oppinion there is no other objection than the Masons being wanted for the Fort* — *Which of the two buildings does the Colony stand most in need of?* Mr Dawes took a walk with me this afternoon to see where my Gramattas are clearing the field and took a look at where I am digging the foundation of my Store, in the course of all the afternoon he neither *approved* nor disapproved of any thing I showed him which was rather unpleasant.

Jany 9th — I cannot help thinking Mr Dawes has behaved in a very strange & illiberal manner with respect to Mr Afzellius. It was Mr Clarksons desire that Mr Afzellius should mess with me, Mr Afzellius also wishes — Mr Dawes says he must mess with him, Mr Afzellius says he has promised Mr Clarkson to mess with me & that he prefers it to any other mess — Mr Dawes insists that he messes with him, & poor Afzellius is left in an auquard situation — he tells me — & begs to know what he can do — I immediately said — tho it would be a pleasure for me to have his Compy — yet sooner then it should cause any shyness from Mr Dawes I would wish him to dine there, he could otherwise be with me as often as was agreable to himself — this he agrees to — I turned several men away from work on account of their sulky behaviour — the Duke of Bucklieu came down from Bance Island. Mr Tylly came on shore & dined with me — I went on board with him in the afternoon & wrote several letters to my friends in the West Indies & in Europe — stayed till 10 OClock at night — drank bad wine, got a violent head ache & came home sick.

Jany 10th — the two vessels which were off the Cape a few days ago proved to be a french man & an American both of them come in the 7th — they have a variety of Articles such as provisions & other Comforts wanted in the Colony, but very few have been purchased notwithstanding — there is neither beef — Pork — flower — or any kind of provision sufficient to last the Colony a week — a few *hams & Onions* are purchased for the officers — The French man sailed this day the American goes tomorrow. I am yet indisposed, tho not from the quantity, but from the badness of the wine I drank last night, for two Glasses was all I took when on board. Sent Mr King a dozen of wine, he returned me a Message by the boy that unless I sent another dozen he would send it back, or might send for that, again [sic] as he never would drink it — indeed there is an extraordinary change in the behaviour of Mr King — in place of the civil obliging manner he carried with him a few weeks ago, nothing but haughtiness and unbecoming airs are to be seen, nay I fear much from the way he conducts himself, he will shortly find his time unpleasant here —

11th Jany — Had occasion to send this morning for some paint of different kinds to the store, but Mr King refused to let me have such as I wanted without having any reasonable excuse whatever, & immediately after he went to Mr Dawes & told him, he had offered me such as I wanted — but that I was displeased & would not take it, by telling the *wilful mistake* he did not mend the matter much — Mr Dawes is very polite but very reserved the people seem to like him better —

Jany 12th 1793 — The American sailed last night — we got one cask of Molasses, two of beef, & two of Pork from her, but one of the Casks of beef was washed away by the tide after it was landed — I called on Mr Dawes respecting some of the works this morning — he again repeated his intention or wish to stop the New Store House in Susans Bay — but gave no positive order so I shall go on — *however he has desired me to call on him during the course of the ensuing week, as he wishes to speak to me relative to the several works I am conducting — and means to stop some of them, the reason he assigns is the poverty of the Company — if that is the case why in Gods name build such an expensive fort as Mr Pepys is now about — or why purchace useless vessels when we cannot employ them to avantage* — The Providence returned from the Turtle Islands with 8 Goats — 4 sheep & had in her when she left 21 Turtle but 16 of them died about noon this day in the course of an hour —

13th — I was alarmed about 11 OClock last night by one of the Settlers — thundering at my door & calling me frequently by name — begging for Gods sake, I would get up as the Town was attacked by the Natives — I did not at first rightly understand him, but on enquiring — he said I must make haste & turn out, that King Jemmys people were in the Town — and that Mr Dawes was sending for every body and arming them — by this time I began to awaken & consequently [was] less alarmed — nor was there any other reason for apprehension then the

Drum and a few Guns being heard from King Jammys Town — in a little while I went to bed & slept comfortably till morning. King Jemmy and Signior Doming came to town this forenoon — & said they were much offended that such doubts were enertained of their friendship as to suppose that they would make war without a cause — they dined with Mr Dawes & after dinner came to see me [4]— Jemmy observed, it was not this country fashion to make war with their friends — but it was very foolish in us to harbour thoughts of the kind unless he gave us reason to think so — that if he had a Palaver in the Colony he would come & talk it over — & if it could not be settled without war, he would tell us so — at the same time he hoped allways to be friends — I find Mr Elliotte has been the cause of this alarm and it strikes me he has some scheme at bottom — I wish it may not be to get arms & ammunition into the hands of the people, in hopes of making some improper use of them — indeed I am sorry to say Mr Elliotte has a prodigious sway over them just now —

Jany 14th — Mr Dawes, his Secretary, & Mr Horne went in the Yorks boat to visit several of the neighbouring Chiefs — before they set out Mr Dawes sent Mr Strand to acquaint me that he had authorised *Mr Pepys to supply his place in his absencee and in case I wanted any thing — I was to apply to him — this to be sure did not go down well with me — and is it not scandalous to see so villainous a Character as an Atheist[5] Govern a Christian Colony — is there a doubt but Pepys is an Atheist — nor is there the smallest doubt but he rules every thing here just now — but leave him to himself — Ill warant in time he works his own ruin — all idea of laying out the lotts of land seem to be vanished — nothing but fortification is thought off.* Mr Pepys has asked several of his friends to dine with him the 28th of February in the *New Fort* & in commemoration of the great day — *when the Flag was first hoisted in the same spot where the Fort is now buiding — but if he has any thing like a fort for twelve months after that time I shall think it a miracle — the people grumble exceedingly — & not without cause, about their lands — I am surprised at Mr Dawes but really he & the Engineer are Fort Mad.*

[4] But see p. 107 above — 'and after dinner King Jemmy paid me a visit'. It does indeed seem more likely that he came to visit his old acquaintance, the former Mrs Falconbridge, whom he knew was well informed about "country fashion", than her new husband who had only been a few months in the Colony.

[5] A letter among Clarkson's papers from John Gray, the accountant, repeats the charge (unexpected against an employee of the Sierra Leone Company) that Pepys was an atheist, but that it did not stop him attending the daily church services (BL, Add. MS 41263, fol. 18).

Memorandum

Mr Dawes has never called on me since I was *married* — Would Mr Clarkson have done so? — Non Opposite!!

Jany 15th — Mr Tylly returned from the Isles Deloss, I saw several strangers on board his Cutter — but supposed them to be Captain Morley & others as Mr Tylly sayed he would bring him up — As the Cutter came opposite the Fort she saluted with eleven Guns which I thought was extraordinary — but it instantly occurred that some of our Gentlemen from England was on board which proved to be the case — The Battery returned the Salute — Mr Tylly & the strangers came on shore — they proved to be Mr Gilbert & Mr McAuley who had left the Packet at Gambia & getting to the Isles Deloss — took passage with Mr Tylly here — I cannot help saying I am fond of the first appearance of Mr Gilbert — I have had the pleasure of seeing Mr McAuley before — cannot say there is any thing unpleasant in his Countenance but rather the reverse — however he is *young* & I shall not be hasty in forming my Oppinion[6] — Gladness seems to shine in the countenance of every one today — for my part I am disappointed as I have not received the scrape of a pen from a single friend in England or elsewhere — for which reason I determine from this moment never to write one of them again — at least those I have wrote to before.

Jany 16th — There was another alarm last night (as I was informed this morning) but with as little foundation as the last — King Jemmy had been up to Bunch River to see some of his friends & a number of them came down with him in their cannoes — which Mr Elliotte again took the Opportunity of hinting to the Settlers, had the appearance of Hostility and desired they would be on their Guard — consequently the Nova Scotians came all in crowds to Mr Dawes begging for arms and ammunition which being refused them, they all returned home much dissatisfyed — however Mr Dawes the same night sent on board the York & ordered three hundred stand of arms on shore — but I will not at the same time venture to assert, he thought there was real danger — however nothing *frightfull* happened during the night — I wish to God Mr Dawes would see into the *Character of Elliotte* for he is surely an errand rogue — This day having sent to the store for some nails wanted for the Hummums — Mr King refused to let me have them, & gave

[6] They may have met at the Company's office before DuBois left London. His, on the whole, favourable assessment contrasts with his wife's (p. 108) which looks like a later addition inserted to discredit Macaulay.

for reason that Mr Dawes had desired him to deliver no more goods *to me* unless I had an order from him specifying such articles as I wanted — which being sure was a *falsehood* I wrote the following letter to Mr Dawes —

Sir

I just now sent to the store for some nails, but Mr King refused them to me & sayed he had your instructions to deliver nothing more to me unless I had a particular order for the purpose from you — Now knowing that you have given general instructions for the Store to furnish me with whatever I stood in need of for Public Service — I am *persuaded* you would not do any thing so *inconsistent* as to contradict these orders, without first giving me notice such were your wishes or intentions — therefore I beg leave to acquaint you with this Circumstance & have to request you will have the Goodness to see the Business rectifyed —

I am Sir etc /IDB

As soon as Mr Dawes recd. this letter he went in person to Mr King & desired I might have whatever I wanted as usual — the nails consequently were sent immediately — in the evening Mr Afzellius & self took a walk to see where my Gramattas were working — we met Mr Dawes, Mr Gilbert, Mr McAuley & Mr Strand — after the usual Compliments Mr Dawes called me *aside* & apologized for the behaviour of the Storekeeper as well as he could, & requested I would take no further notice of it, sayed he had put every thing to rights — Afzellius & self proceeded on our walk & after we had gathered several plants & viewed what work my Gramattas had done, returned home to Tea — Afzellius is a worthy Character.

Jany 17 — Mr Dawes, Mr MacAuley, Mr Gilbert, Doctor Winterbottom & Mr Pepys went in the *Yorks boat* to see King Naimbanna who we understand is dangerously ill — This day I sent cards of invitation to all the Gentlemen in the Colony for dinner on Monday Next — The Lapwing Cutter arrived from the Carimancas last night, loaded with Camwood, Ivory & rice — The Amy lays ashore in Thompsons bay refitting — the Gentlemen who went to King Naimbannas in the morning returned in the evening at 7 OClock.

Jany 18th — Recd a note from Mr King refusing my invitation to dinner, with a very frivolous appology — had polite cards from Mr Dawes & Mr McAuley accepting the same — Mr Watt came over from Clarksons Plantation —

19th — Mr Dawes, Mr McAuley, Mr Watt, Mr Strand, Doctor Winterbottom and Mr Elliotte went up to Pa Bunkies and returned in the evening — they intended to have stop'd at Signior Domingos to see one of King Jemmys women drink the *Red Water*, a sentence denounced against her on suspicion of witchcraft — but the ceremony was performed at an inland town — however they heard that the woman had drunk the water and recovered — consequently King Jemmy is brought into a serious palaver and by the Customs of his Country has to pay the parents of his *woman* the value of a slave in Goods — about ½ past 12 OClock a spark of fire was discovered in the thatch of our house at the Point, & before any water could be procured, it communicated it self to the whole roof — which in a few minutes fell in — the building was shortly consumed — I was much alarmed for the Hummums, but most fortunately in the morning I had cleared away all the shavins & trash between the two buildings as tho I had forseen what was going to happen — the wind was about S.W. and carried the flames clear of the Hummums — I saved a great many things, but notwithstanding must have lossd £40 or £50 at least — the only thing I seriously regret is Mr Clarksons *china* which tho saved from the fire did not escape destruction, most of them were broken — I hope when he reads this part of my journal he will recollect what confusiuon fire makes, & not suppose that his china suffered from carelessness.

Jany 20th — Being sunday went to hear Divine service which was performed by Mesrs Gilbert & Horne, in the afternoon they went up to Signior Domingos where Mr Horne [preached] for the first time to the natives, but I fear it did not make much impression on them — and *is it not truly ridiculous, to preach to any set of people in a language they do not understand* — The Nassau Captn Morley arrived from the Isles Deloss — he seems to be a good honest fellow & I am rather gratifyed by his being highly pleased at his sister [*sic*] Marriage[7] -

21st Gave my wedding dinner this day to such gentlemen in the Colony as chose to attend — Mr Horne was absent — sent word that he was unwell — such a dinner in all probability was never seen in the Grain Coast of Africa[8] — Mr Dawes invited us to dine with him on Wednesday.

22d Mr Dawes & several Gentlemen went up to Signior Domingos

---

[7] See comment on p. III.

[8] A by then old-fashioned name (normally for the coast of modern Liberia and not including Sierra Leone) which DuBois is using rhetorically rather than geographically.

with a vast deal of abusive language not only against me but every officer in the Colony he continued to use for a length of time without my taking the smallest notice of him, as soon as Mr Dawes came home, I called & mentioned the business to him — he said any reasonable satisfaction I wished should be complyed with — I desired no other punishment then that he should not in future be employed by the Company — which Mr Dawes readily agreed to — & the same was made known to Patrick[9] — Mr Watt returned this day to the Bullom Shore —

Jany 23d — dined with Mr Dawes according to appointment — last sunday Divine service was ordered to be performed twice a day throughout the week — the inconvenience of this is already felt & the Company in the end will pay dear for it, for the workmen are an hour later in coming to their work then they used to be & *the Church is the excuse*, I suppose the morning service costs the Sierra Leone Company just now at the rate of £1500 pr annum — tho not more than twenty people ever attend — is it not a pity that religion should be a cloak to vice & idleness ? —

24th — By accounts from Robanna this morning King Naimbanna is not expected to live — Mrs DuBois, Grey & Self dined on board the Nassau — Messieur Rennieu & three or four french men were there — Rennieu told me that there is another King now on his way down the Country to succeed King Naimbanna, & I also understand the slave factories have been giving him large dashes, & prejudicing him against the settlement — that in consequence he is determined we shall make a new purchace of the Country as soon as he comes to the *Throne* his name is *Congo, Bolikie* — I learn that Mr Dawes has been very liberal in his dashes to Paa Bunkie & other chiefs — however I do not disapprove

[9] Francis Patrick was to be one of the two settlers hanged after the rebellion of 1800 (Fyfe, '*Our Children ...*', pp. 18, 78).

of that — for surely the Sierra Leone Compy should be at least as liberal as the slave factorys in the Neighbourhood.

25th Jany — *Cabba* the Mandingo Priest came from Rochelle but did not bring any thing to discharge his debt — I sent his daughter home with him — Mossieur Rennieu paid me a visit — invited him to dinner but business prevents him — *An unpleasant circumstance happened yesterday — Mr Dawes wished me to take in about twenty feet from Wm Grants lot into the fence I am making round the Hummums — Grant refused the Ground — & while Mr Dawes was speaking the whole Neighbourhood assembled, & unanimouslsy said if we offered to fence in another inch of Ground then what we had, they would pull the fence down — at the same time cried out loudly for their Town & Country lotts — till they got them they would not resign an inch of what they had in possession — Mr Dawes said if they would not shew him more respect then they did he would leave the Country — with one voice — that you may do as soon as you please, God almighty will take case of us. —*

Jany 26th — Captain Buckle in the ship Good Intent arrived from the Isles Deloss.

27th — being Sunday as usual attended Divine Service. Captn. Buckle & Morley dined with me, also Mr Afzellius — Mr Gilbert went to the old settlement [10] & preached a sermon — he was attended by several persons from the Colony.

28th — The *Alpha* parted her Cable and drove in shore — we got her off without much damage, sent on board the York for a Grapnel & Cable — got the Grapnel but no Cable I am sure the old one will not hold her 24 hours — I was told by Mr Dawes today that Mr McAuley will in future pay all the workmen — this will save me a vast deal of trouble & vexation —

29th *As I expected the flat [sic] broke from her Anchor last night & was this morning laying on the rocks with part of her bottom stove in & otherwise much wrecked — at high water we floated her & sent her to Thompsons bay to be repaired — its a pity Captn Hebden did not send a new rope for her —*

Capn Morley went to Bance Island yesterday —

[10] Falconbridge's Granville Town.

Jany 30th Mr Bellingall from Bance Island s
Sherborough river, he remained about two hour

31st Got one Gramatta from the Bullom Sh

Feby 1st Am a good deal plagued with the Gramattas

2d Mr Watt came this day from the Bullom Shore, I learn he has had
a serious Palaver with his People but got the better of them.

3d The Sierra Leone Packet arrived from Gambia has 30 head of Cattle
on board she was very near getting ashore on the middle ground—

Mr Watt & Mr Afzellius dined with me —

4th Mr McAuley commenced paying the workmen, I imagine he will
find it more troublesome then he apprehends.

5th Mr Watt & Mr McAuley went to the Bullom Shore. Doctor
Winterbottom & Mr Horne to King Naimbannas — Mr McAuley
returned in the evening from Clarksons Plantation.

6th *I have understood, tho I could not credit it, that the lotts of land are
not to be laid off till next year — however this day I am persuaded it is
the case as Mr Dawes told me that Mr Pepys having little or nothing to do
just now, wished to resume his place as Surveyor of Works, and that he was
disposed to take a part of what I was about, & that he wished him to take
the direction of the old wharf — I observed it was unpleasant not to finish
what I had begun & that it was Mr Clarksons last promise to me — to
this I had no reply but he told me Mr Pepys would take direction of the
wharf on Monday next* — Mr Dawes at this time asked me what com-
mutation I would take in lieu of the Compy finding my Table etc —
to this I replyed that I did not wish to say any thing on that subject,
as I had spoken to Mr Clarkson before he sailed — that it was a desirable
thing to have a Table of ones own — & that I was sure Mr Clarkson
would do every thing necessary concerning sallery — this subject being
ended we parted — & after recollecting myself a few minutes, wrote the
following letter to Mr Dawes —

Sir

You no doubt are acquainted that I have written orders from Mr
Clarkson for all the works I am carrying on in the Colony — therefore
as you intimated to me this day — that it was your intention to put a
part of them immediately under the directions of Mr Pepys — I shall

feel myself much obliged — if yourself & Mr McAuley will signify your wishes on that subject in writing before any event of the kind takes place.

I am Sir with much respect
Your Obt Servt/IDB

To Wm Dawes Esqr

I shortly after received the following note

Messieurs Dawes and Mac Auley are total strangers to any orders which Mr Clarkson may have thought proper to give Mr DuBois before his departure for England — but Mr DuBois may depend on having written directions from them for every measure they may deem it expedient for the Good of the Colony — he should take.

Wednesday afternoon

Memorandum — If I am not to have the credit of finishing the works I have begun I shall quit the Colony — Mr Pepys talks of going home in a month or two — is it not evident that taking the works from me is merely to fill up his reports & to inhance his value, & depreciate mine with the Directors — I grant that Mr Pepys came out as Surveyor of Works but who can tell me of any work he has done in that department except his own Kitchen and that noble Monument to his memory The Grass House Store, which would long ago have tumbled down & which would at this moment fall to the ground was it not for the repairs I gave it very recently after it was erected — Why does he not finish laying out the lotts of land that has already cost the Company upwards of £2000 & which must cost as much more, besides the injustice done to the Nova Scotians in keeping them out of their lotts — should the compleating of them be posponed to next year — Yesterday received a few lines from Mr Kingston [11] — the first I have had from any of the Directors since my arrival here — it was deld. me by Mr Sealy a Surgeon who came in the Packet — he dined with me today —

Feby 7th — *I understand there was a great palaver with the Settlers last night — The Town Lotts was the subject —* The people were called together to be informed that their town lotts were ready & that those they at present occupied they were to quit directly — they asked how far the front lotts were from the water — to which they were answered 500 feet — they then said they would not move back so far, *but had*

---

[11] John Kingston, a City merchant, was a director of the Company from its foundation to its dissolution in 1808.

the Promises originally made them been attended to — they in that case would have had no objection to moving — they meant those promises made respecting buildings on the sea shore — for Mr Pepys told them when the present lotts were laid out — they were only temporary — that their proper lotts would be given them at a future time or as soon as the rains was over — they would be at some distance from the waterside but that no houses were to be between them & the river — Now as this promise was broke by the number of buildings on the river side they looked upon it any obligation they were under on that score was also cancelled and they were determined not to give up those habitations *they now possess unless the lotts were run from the water — they said none of the promises made them by Mr Clarkson in Nova Scotia were performed — they did not blame him for it, he could not lay out the lotts himself — Mr Clarkson told them they would be treated as free men & as well as white men — they believed Mr Clarkson, they said, to be an honourable man & they were sure he would never have left them without performing his promises to them — had he not been assured by the Gentlemen he left behind they should all be complyed with — Mr Pepys then told them that whatever promises Mr Clarkson had made them in Nova Scotia, were all from himself — that he had no authority whatever for what he said & that he believed Mr Clarkson was drunk at the time he made them — this he repeated several times — and added that Mr Clarkson seldom knew or thought of what he said — so it was not to be wondered he should make extraordinary promises, or words to that effect — besides many disrespectfull things — With respect to the sea side being filled with houses — he said Mr DuBois had assumed an authority he had no right to — of building houses & that it was my fault all the houses were built — that every thing I was doing in the Colony was without any Authority whatever, but that he was to have the works directly & he meant to pull them all down — but to this the people replyed he had better let that alone or he would bring himself into bad head for they would not see what had caused* [cost] *so much money destroyed, unless there was a good reason for it and at present they saw none — I can bring 20 of the best men in the Colony to prove all I have said — I do not mind what he has said against me so much as his ingratitude in endeavouring to poison the people against my friend.*

Memorandum — He *Richard Pepys* is as black a Hearted insinuating a *Villain* as this day exists — if he offers to take any more libertys with my Character I shall perhaps put him in mind of all at once, but for the sake of peace I will be quiet now — however I think Ill tell him of it the first time I meet him & Mr Dawes together.

8th Feby — We hear today that King Naimbanna is speechless.

9th — I dislike the proceedings here more & more — in my life I never lived among such an illiberal set — Mr McAuley is taken suddenly ill today — finished one field of 20 Acres at Savoy Point.

10th being sunday I attended divine Service.

11th began to clear the woods between the Town & King Jemmys bay — (12th) it was rumoured yesterday that King Naimbanna was dead — this morning the news is confirmed, and a Coffin is just now making for *His Majesty* which Mr Dawes takes up with him — my Gramattas have almost all left me to go to the Cry — they do not like cutting down the woods where they are just now working — as they say the *Devil* lives there & they do not wish to offend him [12] —

13th — received the following Note from Mr Dawes —

Mr Dawes will be obliged to Mr DuBois for his Weekly Reports that they may be coppyed & transmitted to the Directors by this Opportunity together with those of the other Officers. Wednesday 13th Feby 93

To this note I sent the following answer —

Sir

From the Multiplicity of business I have had and for want of proper assistance in the Cleark way, my weekly reports are in arrear from the 6th of September last — However Mr McAuley paying the workmen gives me more leisure time and as soon as it is convenient for Mr Grey to furnish me with my store Accounts, I shall dedicate every moment I can spare to make up the reports & accts: I am behind hand — till then it will be impossible for me to make so satisfactory a statement of things as I could wish —

I appologised to Mr Clarkson before he sailed for England, & as he was intimately acquainted, & knew the excuses I made were not feigned, I trust what he will say to the Directors on that score will sufficiently exculpate me — up to the time of his leaving the Country — since which time I hope Mr Dawes is persuaded that notwithstanding I have no reports ready —I have never been Idle.

I am Sir/your obdt Servt/I DuBois

[12] See p. 108, *footnote 95.*

Wm Dawes Esqr etc etc etc

Mr Dawes was perfectly sensible I could have no reports ready but he wrote that note merely to see if he could draw from me a confession that I had too much business which would be sufficient excuse for his giving part of the work to Pepys — however I saw through the business directly, & being disappointed there he sent me the following Letter —

Sir

I have received your Letter of this day & have to observe that the weekly reports and an exact state of your accounts are not at present the chief things required. What Mr McAuley & myself particularly wish to have it in our power to inform the Directors off, are,

First, A rough guess of the expence which has been already incurred by, & is still likely to attend, the execution of each of the works now under your direction, that is to say

1. The old landing place from the time you took charge of it —

2. The new landing place from the time it was begun —

3. The new Wharf & Store House intended to be erected in Susans bay —

4. The House fitting up for the Companys Offices called the Hummums —

Secondly, A rough guess at the time which each of them will require to compleat it —

It is also necessary to send home duplicates of such public papers as you sent home by the Felicity if they can be got ready in time

(signed) William Dawes

To Mr DuBois

This is my answer to the foregoing —

Sir

At the moment I received your letter I was making out such extracts from my letter to Mr Clarkson as I apprehend will be useful to you & such as I had promised to do — I shall also endeavour by tomorrow to furnish me with an estimate of what I think will be the expence of the different works I am at present directing, but I will not answer for the exact accuracy of it — tho I shall endeavour to come as nigh the business as I can —

I am Sir etc/ I DuBois/14th Feby 1793

Wm Dawes Esqr

King Jemmy came and teased me all this morning that I have not been able to do any thing — he says we must not cut down the bush on the point — unless we pay him eighty Barrs — I told him I had nothing to with [*sic*] he must go to Mr Dawes —

15th Feby received a line from Mr Dawes desiring me not to cut any more between the Town & King Jemmys — till further notice — Performed my promise of yesterday to Mr Dawes — & I suppose Mr Clarkson will see my Estimates in London, at least I hope so for I have not time to coppy them just now —

Free Town February 16th 1793

I am affraid my dear Sir you will neither take time to read, or pleasure in receiving this strange kind of Journal — pray look over my faults with your usual goodness — I am sorry to tell you your presense is much wanted & unless you or some one of your disposition comes out, *this Colony is loss'd* — I shall stay quietly till I know whether you do really come or not — but should you not come I cannot possibly remain here a week after I know it — pray let me hear from you — Mrs DuBois begs her best wishes — Adieu My dear Sir, do not forget that you have left one man behind you, who would cheerfully sacrafise his life, to do you & this Colony a *real Service* — & that he is your sincere friend & Huml. Servant

Isaac DuBois

[Add. MS 41263, fols 30–1]

Free Town 7th March 1793

My dear Sir,

I did myself the pleasure of writing you by the Ship Good Intent, Capn. Buckle, she sailed from here on the 15th Ult — and am in hopes may have a short passage.

I very much fear that you will find that journal so insipid that you will scarcely have patience to read it through, but am persuaded any faults or errors contained in it you will endeavour to skim — *even from yourself* — tho in reallity I would prefer you to discover my errors before any man in existence, as I am sure that your Goodness would readily look over them — I did intend by this conveyance to have wrote you very fully but am this morning informed from Mr Dawes that there is an opportunity direct for London in ten days or a fortnight — therefore as I think it probable the letters I write by that vessel which I suppose will be the *New* Cutter, or *rather the Cutter lately bought*, will reach you before this, I shall not say any thing particular just now — except acquainting you that the Colony is in vast confusion & disorder — the people in General are much dissatisfyed, and appear every day more ripe for mischief — *of some kind* — the carpenters have all left off work in the Colony — & the Hummums as well as every other public work are left in a ruinous & distressed situation, the whole cause & reasons you shall have in my next — which as I have before mentioned, will in all probability reach you before this.

Mrs DuBois joins me in best respects & good wishes to you — hoping by this time you are as *happy* as I am.[13] I remain unalterably /yours/ I DuBois

---

[13] He married his *fiancée*, Susan Lee, on 25 April (Wilson, *John Clarkson*, p. 137).

[Add. Ms 41263, fols 38–40]

Free Town Sierra Leone
1st May 1793

My dear Sir

The Endeavour, Wyatt, having touched here and as it is probable she will be among the first vessels that will sail direct for England, I would not let the opportunity slip me without writing you a few lines — As to the state of the Colony, I shall only say, that things are *not ordered* as they should be, that discontent & Chagrin are painted in the countenances of every one, both blacks and whites, that unless you do come out immediately, or some other system be quickly adopted, it will be impossible for any one to live here, all your orders are laughed at, & I even apprehend that *our people* in power wish *nay intend* to disannul the few appointments you have made, many circumstances tend to confirm me in this Oppinion but one more Glaring than the rest fully convinces me — which is the dismissal of Mr Horwood, Mrs DuBois's brother, without assigning any reason whatever for so doing — and after dismissing him, telling him he might *be re-appointed* in the service if he chose — be assured I did not let it drop in silence, and after some altercation on the subject, I told Mr Dawes that as Mr Horwood was appointed by you I certainly should mention the circumstance to you in my first letter — to which I was answered they were not accountable to *Mr Clarkson* for their conduct but to the Directors of the Sierra Leone Company only —

Captain Hebden died the 17th ulto. there are many sick in the Colony but none dangerously ill — an ugly accident happened a few days ago — Mr Pepys gave some shells to Ben Francis (whom you may remember) to dry over the fire & load, in executing these orders one of the shells went off & killed Francis & a native boy — I have not time to go on in giving you all our news but I shall write you by way of the West Indies next week — but I will not finish without telling you that the Colony is in a starving condition — we have had no letters from England since the Sierra Leone Packet arrived — but I feign flatter myself that we shall have the pleasure of seeing you here shortly — which will be the best *provision* we could have.

The Orpheus frigate arrived on the coast a few days ago after a few weeks passage from Plimouth, she sent in two prises here & we expect her & four more prises that she has taken at Goree — every moment.

Mrs DuBois desires her best Compliments — I wish I knew whether I could send mine to *Mrs Clarkson* but I rather suppose it is so by this time. Adieu my dear Sir/ believe me as ever/ yours sincerely/ Isaac DuBois

[Add. MS 41263, fols 45–6]

My dear Sir

Should this reach you before I arrive, it will just serve to inform you I am on my way — You will not be pleased to hear of my leaving the Colony, but I hope it is for the best, believe me unless the Directors will listen to truth their Colony is lost, such conduct — such every thing — you little dream off — two of the Black settlers deputed by the whole, go home in the Amy to represent their Grievances, they have been shamefully trampled on since you went away — I sail in about an hour with Captn Morley — Mr Afzellius goes home in the Amy who will deliver you this with a large bird — the Ocean arrived two days ago — why did you not write me by her ? as I make no doubt you are by this time married let me assure you there is no man in the world who I sincerely wish should enjoy more happiness in that state than your self — & be pleased to make my best respects to Mrs Clarkson.

All the ill treatment I have received since you left this I am convinced has been due to my not taking a diabolical part which I shudder at — in poisoning the minds of the people against you — but all their affairs have been in vain — the people cry loudly for your return — Adieu/ & believe me/ most sincerely/ & affectionately/yours/ Isaac DuBois

Mrs DB begs her best respects to your self & Mrs Clarkson

Free Town 9th June 1793

Alexander Falconbridge
An Account of the Slave Trade
on the Coast of Africa

AN ACCOUNT

of the

SLAVE TRADE

on the

COAST of AFRICA,

by

ALEXANDER FALCONBRIDGE,

Late Surgeon in the African Trade.

LONDON :

Printed and sold by James Phillips, George-Yard,

Lombard Street. 1788

Editor's Introduction

Alexander Falconbridge, like his wife, was a native of Bristol. Wishing to adopt a medical career, he spent a year as a student at the Bristol Infirmary.[1] Then, having no financial means to set up a practice of his own, he signed on as a surgeon on a slave ship, a potentially lucrative position, since surgeons received, as well as their pay, a bounty of a shilling a head for each slave landed, and, if they survived a few voyages, might then be taken on as a captain.

Between 1780 and 1787 he made four voyages. 'In my first and second voyage', he later declared, 'I reflected but little on the justice or injustice of the Trade; in my last voyage I reflected more, and the more I did so the more I was convinced it is an unnatural, iniquitous and villainous trade, and could not reconcile it to my conscience'.[2] He therefore gave it up, and when Clarkson met him, was living at home, in debt to his father, hoping to improve his chances by studying with a well known Bristol doctor.[3]

Clarkson passed on Falconbridge's devastating evidence to the newly constituted Committee for the Abolition of the Slave Trade. It was decided to publish it, and circulate it widely as propaganda. Falconbridge came to London, supporting himself by working in a dissecting establishment, and was helped by Richard Phillips, a Quaker lawyer, to put his evidence into publishable form. Phillips's daughter recalled long after —

> I have often heard my father speak of the great quantity of paper which he filled by writing down the Answers to the Questions which were put to Alexander Falconbridge. He had been a surgeon on board a slave-ship, and was an important witness; but would not have been able to furnish much information, in a connected form, himself. It was therefore necessary to draw it from him, by numerous interrogations; to write it down; and subsequently to arrange it; — a long and tedious process.[4]

Falconbridge also gave evidence to a Committee of the Privy Council set up to investigate the trade in slaves.[5]

---

[1] *House of Commons Papers, vol. 72 (Slave Trade)*, 1790 (reprinted Wilmington, 1975), p. 600.

[2] *ibid.*, p. 601.

[3] *ibid.*, p. 616.

[4] [Mary Phillips], *Memoir of a Life of Richard Phillips*, London, 1841, pp. 24–5.

[5] *Report of the Lords of the Committee of the Privy Council ... concerning ... the Trade in Slaves*, London, 1789.

His *Account* was published in February 1788 by James Phillips, his editor's cousin, a London printer and a member of the Abolition committee, for circulation as propaganda.[6] On the title page appeared the Wedgwood medallion of a kneeling slave, with the superscription 'Am I not a Man and a Brother', which the committee had adopted for its seal. Three thousand copies were printed in a quarto edition, then another three thousand in duodecimo. Falconbridge assigned to the Committee the copyright, and received sixpence per copy for the first edition, seven pence for the second.[7] It was presumably these payments that enabled him to set up in medical practice in Lodway — and to marry Anna Maria Horwood.

* * *

The story of Falconbridge's years in the slave trade can be put together from his own *Account* and from the evidence he gave to the House of Commons Committee in 1790. On three of his four voyages he sailed, first in the *Tartar*, then in the *Emilia*, under Captain James Fraser whom he described as 'one of the very best men in the trade',[8] and on his third voyage, in the *Alexander*, under Captain Mactagart whose brutalities he describes in the *Account*. They took him along the coast of the modern Liberia, to the Gold Coast, to the Niger Delta, and to Ambriz, north of Luanda, then claimed, but not yet occupied, by the Portuguese, which had become an important slave-export centre during the eighteenth century. Most of his descriptions however concentrate on Bonny and New Calabar in the Niger Delta, the main centre of export.

Despite Richard Phillips's efforts, the *Account* remains poorly organised. The section entitled 'A short Description of such Parts of the coast of Guinea, as are before referred to', instead of forming an introduction to the work, appears at the end. So the reader is plunged straight away into into a detailed description of the trade at Bonny and New Calabar — how the ships were organised in the Delta, how slaves were procured, and how they were treated on board ship. Then follows a description of how they were sold in Jamaica, where the ships in which Falconbridge sailed landed their cargoes.

He then considers in detail an associated topic — how the sailors in the slave trade were treated by their employers and ship's officers. One of the chief arguments in favour of the slave trade was that it constituted 'a nursery

[6] Its success as propaganda may be judged from a notice in *The Monthly Review or Literary Journal Enlarged*, 78, 1788, p. 343: 'It is a horrid detail, abounding with anecdotes sufficient to make his readers conclude that the Europeans who carry on this infernal trade are devils, and not human beings'.

[7] British Library, Add. MS 21254, fols. 16, 34, 41; Add. MS 21255, fols 25, 33, 47. Proceedings of the Committee for the Abolition of the Slave Trade.

[8] *House of Commons Papers, vol. 71 (Slave Trade)*, 1790 (reprinted, Wilmington, 1975), p. 538.

of seamen', training up experienced sailors for the merchant navy. Overwhelming evidence is produced to prove the contrary, showing that the callous, brutal treatment the sailors received resulted in a tragic loss of life and health — an argument that might move those uninterested in the sufferings of African slaves, but concerned for those of their own fellow countrymen.

The following reprint appears with James Phillips's spelling and punctuation unchanged.

Preface

The following sheets are intended to lay before the publick the present state of a branch of British commerce, which, ever since its existence, has been held in detestation by all good men, but at this time more particularly engages the attention of the nation, and is becoming the object of general reprobation.

Leaving to abler pens to expatiate more at large on the injustice and inhumanity of the *Slave Trade,* I shall content myself with giving some account of the hardships which the unhappy objects of it undergo, and the cruelties they suffer, from the period of their being reduced to a state of slavery, to their being disposed in the West India islands; where, I fear, their grievances find little alleviation. At the same time, I shall treat of a subject, which appears not to have been attended to in the manner its importance requires; that is, the sufferings and loss of the seamen employed in this trade; which, from the intemperature of the climate, the inconveniences they labour under during the voyage, and the severity of most of the commanders, occasion the destruction of great numbers annually.

And this I shall endeavour to do by the recital of a number of facts which have fallen under my own immediate observation, or the knowledge of which I have obtained from persons on whose veracity I can depend.

And happy I shall esteem myself, if an experience obtained by a series of injuries and observations, made during several voyages to the coast of Africa, shall enable me to render any service to a cause, which is become the cause of every person of humanity.

Before I proceed to the methods of obtaining slaves, and their subsequent treatment, the treatment of the sailors, and a concise account of the places on the coast of Africa, where slaves are obtained (which I purpose to annex), it may not be unnecessary to give a short sketch of the usual proceedings of the ships employed in the slave trade.

An Account
of the
Slave Trade, &c.

Proceedings during the Voyage

On the arrival of the ships at Bonny, and New Calabar, it is customary for them to unbend the sails, strike the yards and topmasts, and begin to build what they denominate *a house*. This is effected in the following manner: The sailors first lash the booms and yards from mast to mast, in order to form a *ridge-pole*. About ten feet above the deck, several spars, equal in length to the ridge-pole, are next lashed to the standing rigging, and form a wall-plate. Across the ridge-pole and wall-plate, several other spars or rafters are afterwards laid and lashed, at the distance of about six inches from each other. On these, other rafters or spars are laid length-wise, equal in extent to the ridge-pole, so as to form a kind of lattice, or net-work, with interstices of six inches square. The roof is then covered with mats, made of rushes of very loose texture, fastened together with rope-yarn, and so placed, as to lap over each other like tiles. The space between the deck and the wall-plate, is likewise enclosed with a kind of lattice, or net-work, formed of sticks, lashed across each other, and leaving vacancies of about four inches square. Near the main-mast, a partition is constructed of inch deal boards, which reaches athwart the ship. This division is called a *barricado*. It is about eight feet in height, and is made to project near two feet over the side of the ship. In this barricado there is a door, at which a centinel is placed during the the time the negroes are permitted to come upon deck. It serves to keep the different sexes apart; and as there are small holes in it, wherein blunder-busses are fixed, and sometimes a cannon, it is found very convenient for quelling the insurrections that now and then happen. Another door is made in the lattice or net-work at the ladder, by which you enter the ship. This door is guarded by a centinel during the day, and is locked at night. At the head of the ship there is a third door, for the use of the sailors, which is secured in the same manner as that at the gang-way. There is also in the roof a large trap-door, through which the goods intended for barter, the water casks, &c. are hoisted out or in.

The design of this house is to secure those on board from the heat of the sun, which in this latitude is intense, and from the wind and rain, which at particular seasons, are likewise extremely violent. It answers these purposes however but very ineffectually. The slight texture of the mats admits both the wind and the rain, whenever it happens to be violent, though at the same time, it increases the heat of the ship to a very pernicious degree, especially between decks. The increased warmth occasioned by this means, together with the smoke produced from the green mangrove, (the usual firewood) which, for want of a current of air to carry it off, collects itself in large quantities, and infests every part of the ship, render a vessel during its stay here very unhealthy. The smoke also, by its acrimonious quality, often produces inflammations in the eyes, which terminates sometimes in the loss of sight.

Another purpose for which these temporary houses are erected, is, in order to prevent the purchased negroes from from leaping overboard. This, the horrors of their situation frequently impel them to attempt; and they now and then effect it, notwithstanding all the precautions that are taken, by forcing their way through the lattice-work.

The slave ships generally lie near a mile below the town, in Bonny river, in seven or eight fathom water. Sometimes fifteen sail, English and French, but chiefly the former, meet here together. Soon after they cast anchor, the captains go on shore, to make known their arrival, and to inquire into the state of the trade. They likewise invite the kings of Bonny to come on board, to whom, previous to breaking bulk, they usually make presents (in that country termed *dashes*)[9] which generally consist of pieces of cloth, cotton, chintz, silk handkerchiefs, and other India goods, and sometimes of brandy, wine, or beer.

When I was at Bonny a few years ago, it was the residence of two kings, whose names were *Norfolk* and *Peppel.* The houses of these princes were not distinguished from the cottages or huts of which the town consists, in any other manner, than by being of somewhat larger dimensions, and surrounded with warehouses, containing European goods, designed for the purchase of slaves. These slaves, which the kings procure in the same manner as the black traders do theirs, are sold by them to

[9] From Portuguese *dar* 'to give', *dás* (pronounced 'dash') 'you give'.

the ships. And for every negroe sold there by the traders, the kings receive a duty, which amounts to a considerable sum in the course of a year. This duty is collected by officers, stationed on board the ships, who are termed *officer-boys*; a denomination which it is thought they received from the English.

The kings of Bonny are absolute, though elective.[10] They are assisted in the government by a small number of persons of a certain rank, who style themselves *Parliament gentlemen*; an office which they generally hold for life. Every ship, on its arrival, is expected to send a present to these gentlemen, of a small quantity of bread and beef, and likewise to treat them as often as they come on board. When they do this, their approach to the ship is announced by blowing through a hollow elephant's tooth, which produces a sound resembling that of a post-horn.

After their kings have been on board, and have received the usual presents, permission is granted by them for trafficking with any of the black traders. When the royal guests return from the ships, they are saluted by the guns.

From the time of the arrival of the ships to their departure, which is usually near three months, scarce a day passes without some negroes being purchased, and carried on board; sometimes in small, and sometimes in large numbers. The whole number taken on board, depends, in a great measure, on circumstances. In a voyage I once made, our stock of merchandise was exhausted in the purchase of about 380 negroes, which was expected to have procured 500. The number of English and French ships then at Bonny, had so far raised the price of negroes, as to occasion this difference.

The reverse (and a *happy reverse* I think I may call it) was known during the late war. When I was last at Bonny, I frequently made inquiries on this head, of one of the black traders whose intelligence I believe I can depend upon. He informed me that only one ship had been there for three years during that period; and that was the *Moseley-Hill*, Captain Ewing, from Liverpool, who made an extraordinary purchase, as he found negroes remarkably cheap from the dulness of trade. Upon further inquiring of my black acquaintance, what was the consequence of this

---

[10] Falconbridge, like most Europeans, misunderstood the political structures of the Delta peoples. For a comprehensive account of Delta trade and politics at this period (which contains references to Falconbridge's work) see David Northrup, *Trade without Rulers: Pre-colonial Economic Development in South-Eastern Nigeria*, Oxford, 1978.

decay of their trade, he shrugged up his shoulders, and answered, *only making us traders poorer, and obliging us to work for our maintenance.* One of these black merchants being informed, that a particular set of people, called the Quakers, were for abolishing the trade, he said, *it was a very bad thing, as they should then be reduced to the same state they were in during the war, when, through poverty, they were obliged to dig ground and plant yams.*

I was once upon the coast of Angola also, when there had not been a slave ship at the river Ambris for five years previous to our arrival, although a place to which many usually resort every year; and the failure of trade for that period, as far as we could learn, had not any other effect, than to restore peace and confidence among the natives; which, upon the arrival of any ships, is immediately destroyed, by the inducement then held forth in the purchase of slaves. And during the suspension of trade at Bonny, as above-mentioned, none of the dreadful proceedings, which are so confidently asserted to be the natural consequence of it, were known. The reduction of the price of negroes, and the poverty of the black traders, appear to have been the only *bad* effects of the discontinuance of the trade; the *good* ones were, *most probably,* the restoration of peace and confidence among the natives, and a suspension of kidnapping.

When the ships have disposed of all their merchandize in the purchase of negroes, and have laid in their stock of wood, water, and yams, they prepare for sailing, by getting up the yards and top-masts, reeving the running rigging, bending the sails, and by taking down the temporary house. They then drop down the river, to wait for a favourable opportunity to pass over the bar, which is formed by a number of sand-banks lying across the mouth of the river, with navigable channels between them. It is not uncommon for ships to get upon the bar, and sometimes they are lost.

The first place the slave ships touch at in their passage to the West-Indies, is either the Island of St. Thomas, or Princes Island,[11] where they usually carry their sick on shore, for the benefit of the air. and likewise replenish their stock of water. The former of these islands is nearly circular, being one hundred and twenty miles round, and lies exactly under the equator, about forty-five leagues from the African continent. It abounds with wood and water, and produces Indian corn, rice, fruits,

[11] Both were Portuguese colonies.

sugar and some cinnamon. The air is rather prejudicial to an European constitution, nevertheless it is well peopled by the Portuguese. Princes Island, which is much smaller, lies in one deg. 30 min. north latitude, and likewise produces Indian corn, and a variety of fruits and roots, besides sugar canes. Black cattle, hogs, and goats are numerous there; but it is infested with a mischievous and dangerous species of monkeys.

During one of these voyages I made, I was landed upon the Island of St Thomas, with near one hundred sick negroes, who were placed in an old house, taken on purpose for their reception. Little benefit however accrued from their going on shore, as several of them died there, and the remainder continued nearly in the same situation as when they were landed, though our continuance was prolonged for about twelve days, and the island is deemed to be on the whole healthy.

Upon the arrival of the slave ships in the West-Indies. a day is soon fixed for the sale of their cargoes. And this is done by different modes, and often by one they term a *scramble*, of which some account will be given, when the sale of the negroes is treated of,

The whole of their cargoes being disposed of, the ships are immediately made ready to proceed to sea. It is very seldom, however, that they are not detained for want of a sufficient number of sailors to navigate the ship, as this trade may justly be denominated the grave of seamen. Though the crews of the ships upon their leaving England, generally amount to between forty and fifty men, scarcely three-fourths, and sometimes not one-third of the complement ever return to the port from whence they sailed, through mortality and desertion; the causes of which I shall speak of under another head.

The time during which the slave ships are absent from England, varies according to the destination of the voyage, and the number of ships they happen to meet on the coast. To Bonny, or Old and New Calabar, the voyage is usually performed in about ten months. Those to the Windward[12] and Gold Coasts, are rather more uncertain, but in general from fifteen to eighteen months.

[12] The Windward Coast was taken to stretch from Cape Mount, the northern limit of modern Liberia, to Assini in modern Côte d'Ivoire (see Philip Curtin, *The Atlantic Slave Trade: A Census*, Madison, 1969).

The Manner in which the Slaves are procured.

After permission has been obtained for *breaking trade,* as it is termed, the captains go ashore, from time to time, to examine the negroes that are exposed to sale, and to make their purchases. The unhappy wretches thus disposed of, are bought by the black traders at fairs, which are held for that purpose, at the distance of upwards of two hundred miles from the sea coast; and these fairs are said to be supplied from an interior part of the country. Many negroes, upon being questioned relative to the places of their nativity, have asserted, that they have travelled during the revolution of several moons (their usual method of calculating time) before they have reached the places where they were purchased by the black traders. At these fairs, which are held at uncertain periods, but generally every six weeks, several thousands are frequently exposed to sale, who had been collected from all parts of the country for a very considerable distance round. While I was upon the coast, during one of the voyages I made, the black traders brought down, in different canoes, from twelve to fifteen hundred negroes, which had been purchased at one fair. They consisted chiefly of men and boys, the women seldom exceeding a third of the whole number. From forty to two hundred negroes are generally purchased at a time by the black traders, according to the opulence of the buyer; and consist of those of all ages, from a month to sixty years and upwards. Scarce any age or situation is deemed an exception, the price being proportionable. Women sometimes form a part of them, who happen to be so far advanced in their pregnancy, as to be delivered during the journey from the fairs to the coast; and I have frequently seen instances of deliveries on board ship. The slaves purchased at these fairs are only for the supply of the markets at Bonny, and Old and New Calabar.

There is great reason to believe, that most of the negroes shipped off from the coast of Africa, are *kidnapped.*[13] But the extreme care taken by

[13] This varied in the different parts of the coast. The Reverend John Newton who worked as a young man in the slave trade in the Sherbro country, then became a slave-ship captain, and eventually an abolitionist, declared in his *Thoughts on the African Slave Trade* (London, 1788, p. 31) that 'with regard to the Natives, to steal a free man or woman, and to sell them on board a ship, would, I think, be a more difficult and dangerous attempt in Sherbro than in London'. A famous Delta kidnapping was that of Olaudah Equiano (see *The Interesting Narrative of the Life of Olaudah Equiano, or Gustavus Vassa the African, Written by Himself,* London, 1789 (reprinted, London, 1969), pp. 47–9).

the black traders to prevent the Europeans from gaining any intelligence of their modes of proceeding; the great distance inland from whence the negroes are brought; and our ignorance of their language (with which, very frequently, the black traders themselves are equally unacquainted) prevent our obtaining such information on this head as we could wish. I have, however, by means of occasional inquiries, made through interpreters, procured some intelligence relative to the point, and such, as I think, puts the matter beyond doubt.

From these I shall select the following striking instances: — While I was in employ on board one of the slave ships, a negroe informed me, that being one evening invited to drink with some of the black traders, upon his going away, they attempted to seize him. As he was very active, he evaded their design, and got out of their hands. He was, however, prevented from effecting his escape by a large dog, which laid hold of him, and compelled him to submit. These creatures are kept by many of the traders for that purpose; and being trained to the inhuman sport, they appear to be much pleased with it.

I was likewise told by a negroe woman, that as she was on her return home, one evening, from some neighbours, to whom she had been making a visit by invitation, she was kidnapped; and, notwithstanding she was big with child, sold for a slave. This transaction happened a considerable way up the country, and she had passed through the hands of several purchasers before she reached the ship. A man and his son, according to their own information, were seized by professed kidnappers, while they were planting yams, and sold for slaves. This likewise happened in the interior parts of the country, and after passing through several hands, they were purchased for the ship to which I belonged.

It frequently happens, that those who kidnap others, are themselves, in their turns, seized and sold. A negroe in the West-Indies informed me, that after having been employed in kidnapping others, he had experienced this reverse. And he assured me, that it was a common incident among his countrymen.

Continual enmity is thus fostered among the negroes of Africa, and all social intercourse between them destroyed; which most assuredly would not be the case, had they not these opportunities of finding a ready sale for each other.

During my stay on the coast of Africa, I was an eye-witness of the following transaction:— A black trader invited a negroe, who resided a little way up the country, to come and see him. After the entertainment was over, the trader proposed to his guest, to treat him with a sight of one of the ships lying in the river. The unsuspicious countryman readily consented, and accompanied the trader in a canoe to the side of the ship, which he viewed with pleasure and astonishment. While he was thus employed, some black traders on board, who appeared to be in the secret, seized the unfortunate man, and dragging him into the ship, immediately sold him.

Previous to my being in this employ, I entertained the belief, as many others have done, that the kings and principal men *breed* negroes for sale, as we do cattle. During the different times I was in the country, I took no little pains to satisfy myself on this particular; but notwithstanding I made many inquiries, I was not able to obtain the least intelligence of this being the case, which is more than probable I should have done, had such a practice prevailed. All the information I could procure, confirms me in the belief, that to *kidnapping,* and to crimes (and in many of these fabricated as a pretext) the slave trade owes its chief support.

The following instance tends to prove, that the last mentioned artifice is often made use of. Several black traders, one of whom was a person of consequence, and exercised an authority somewhat similar to that of our magistrates, being in want of some particular kind of merchandize, and not having a slave to barter for it, they accused a fisherman, at the river Ambris, with extortion in the sale of his fish; and as they were interested in the decision, they immediately judged the poor fellow guilty, and condemned him to be sold. He was accordingly purchased by the ship to which I belonged, and brought on board.

As an additional proof that kidnapping is not only the general, but almost the sole mode, by which slaves are procured, the black traders, in purchasing them, chuse those which are the roughest and most hardy; alledging, that the smooth negroes have been *gentlemen.* By this observation we may conclude they mean, that nothing but fraud or force could have reduced these smooth-skinned gentlemen to a state of slavery.

It may not be here unworthy of remark, in order to prove that the wars among the Africans do not furnish the number of slaves they are supposed to do, that I never saw any negroes with recent wounds; which must have been the consequence, at least with some of them, had they been taken in battle. And it being the particular province of the surgeon to examine the slaves when they are purchased, such a circumstance could not have escaped my observation. As a further corroboration, it might be remarked, that on the Gold and Windward Coasts, where fairs are not held, the number[s] of slaves procured at a time are usually very small.[14]

The preparations made at Bonny by the black traders, upon setting out for the fairs which are held up the country, are very considerable. From twenty to thirty canoes, capable of containing thirty or forty negroes each, are assembled for this purpose; and such goods put on board them as they expect will be wanted for the purchase of the number of slaves they intend to buy. When their loading is compleated, they commence their voyage, with colours flying, and musick playing; and in about ten or eleven days, they generally return to Bonny with full cargoes. As soon as the canoes arrive at the trader's landing-place, the purchased negroes are cleaned, and oiled with palm-oil; and on the following day they are exposed to sale for the captains.

The black traders do not always purchase their slaves at the same rate. The speed with which the information of the arrival of ships upon the coast is conveyed to the fairs, considering it is the interest of the traders to keep them ignorant, is really surprising. In a short time after the ships arrive upon the coast, especially if several make their appearance together, those who dispose of the negroes at the fairs are frequently known to increase the price of them.

These fairs are not the only means, though they are the chief, by which the black traders on the coast are supplied with negroes. Small parties of them, from five to ten, are frequently brought to the houses of the traders, by those who make a practice of kidnapping; and who are constantly employed in procuring a supply, while purchasers are to be found.

When the negroes, whom the black traders have to dispose of, are shown to the European purchasers, they first examine them relative to their age. They then minutely inspect their persons, and inquire into the state of their health; if they are afflicted with any infirmity, or are deformed, or have bad eyes or teeth; if they are lame, or weak in their joints, or distorted in the back, or of a slender make, or are narrow in

[14] Here too there was variation in the different parts of the coast. In Dahomey, for instance, 'Dahomian military organisation was clearly geared to the gathering of slaves' (Robin Law, *The Slave Coast of West Africa, 1550–1750*, Oxford, 1991, p. 348).

the chest; in short, if they have been, or are afflicted in any manner, so as to render them incapable of much labour; if any of the foregoing defects are discovered in them, they are rejected. But if approved of, they are generally taken on board the ship the same evening. The purchaser has liberty to return on the following morning, but not afterwards, such as upon re-examination are found exceptionable.

The traders frequently beat those negroes which are objected to by the captains, and use them with great severity. It matters not whether they are refused on account of age, illness, deformity, or for any other reason. At New Calabar, in particular, the traders have frequently been known to put them to death. Instances have happened at that place, that the traders, when any of their negroes have been objected to, have dropped their canoes under the stern of the vessel, and instantly beheaded them, in the sight of the captain.

Upon the Windward Coast, another mode of procuring slaves is pursued; which is, by what they term *boating*, a mode that is very pernicious and destructive to the crews of the ships. The sailors, who are employed in this trade, go in boats up the rivers, seeking for negroes, among the villages situated on the banks of them.[15] But this method is very slow, and not always effectual. For, after being absent from the ship during a fortnight or three weeks, they sometimes return with only from eight to twelve negroes. Numbers of these are procured in consequence of alleged crimes, which, as before observed, whenever any ships are upon the coast, are more productive than at any other period. Kidnapping, however, prevails here.

I have good reason to believe, that of one hundred and twenty negroes, which were purchased for the ship to which I then belonged, then lying at the river Ambris, by far the greater part, if not the whole, were kidnapped. This, with various other instances, confirms me in the belief that kidnapping is the fund which supplied the thousands of negroes annually sold off these extensive Windward and other Coasts, where boating prevails.

---

[15] There were not, on this part of the coast, any settled European traders to whom the captains could apply for slaves as there were further north, at Bance Island and along the rivers of modern Sierra Leone and Guinée.

Treatment of the Slaves.

As soon as the wretched Africans, purchased at the fairs, fall into the hands of the black-traders, they experience an earnest of those dreadful sufferings which they are doomed in future to undergo. And there is not the least room to doubt, but that even before they can reach the fairs, great numbers perish from cruel usage, want of food, travelling through inhospitable deserts &c. They are brought from the places where they are purchased to Bonny, &c. in canoes; at the bottom of which they lie, having their hands tied with a kind of willow twigs, and a strict watch is kept over them. Their usage in other respects, during the time of the passage, which generally lasts several days, is equally cruel. Their allowance of food is so scanty, that it is barely sufficient to support nature. They are, besides, much exposed to the violent rains which frequently fall here, being covered only with mats that afford but a slight defence; and as there is usually water at the bottom of the canoes, from their leaking, they are scarcely ever dry.

Nor do these unhappy beings, after they have become the property of the Europeans (from whom, as a more civilized people, more humanity might naturally be expected) find their situation in the least amended. Their treatment is no less rigorous. The men negroes, on being brought aboard the ship, are immediately fastened together, two and two, by hand-cuffs on their wrists, and by irons rivetted on their legs. They are then sent down between decks, and placed in an apartment partitioned off for that purpose. The women likewise are placed in a separate apartment between decks, but without being ironed. And an adjoining room, on the same deck, is besides appointed for the boys. Thus are they all placed in different apartments.

But at the same time, they are frequently stowed so close, as to admit of no other posture than lying on their sides. Neither will the height between the decks, unless directly under the grating, permit them the indulgence of an erect posture; especially where there are platforms, which is generally the case. These platforms are a kind of shelf, about eight or nine feet in breadth, extending from the side of the ship towards the centre. They are placed nearly midway between the decks, at the distance of two or three feet from each deck. Upon these the negroes are stowed in the same manner as they are on the deck underneath.

In each of the apartments are placed three or four large buckets, of a conical form, being near two feet in diameter at the bottom, and only one foot at the top, and in depth about twenty-eight inches; to which, when necessary, the negroes have recourse. It often happens, that those who are placed at a distance from the buckets, in endeavouring to get to them, tumble over their companions, in consequence of being shackled. These accidents, although unavoidable, are productive of continual quarrels, in which some of them are always bruised. In this distressed situation, unable to proceed, and prevented from getting to the tubs, they desist from the attempt; and, as the necessities of nature are not to be repelled, ease themselves as they lie. This becomes a fresh source of broils and disturbances, and tends to render the conditions of the poor captive wretches still more uncomfortable. The nuisance arising from these circumstances, is not unfrequently increased by the tubs being much too small for the purpose intended, and their being usually emptied but once every day. The rule for doing this, however, varies in the different ships, according to the attention paid to the health and convenience of the slaves by the captain.

About eight o'clock in the morning the negroes are generally brought upon deck. Their irons being examined, a long chain, which is locked to a ring-bolt-hole, fixed in the deck, is run through the rings of the shackles of the men, and then locked to another ring-bolt, fixed also in the deck. By this means, fifty or sixty, and sometimes more, are fastened to one chain, in order to prevent them from rising, or endeavouring to escape. If the weather proves favourable, they are permitted to remain in that situation till four or five in the afternoon, when they are disengaged from the chain, and sent down.

The diet of the negroes, while on board, consists chiefly of horse-beans, boiled to the consistence of a pulp; of boiled yams and rice, and sometimes, of a small quantity of beef or pork. The latter are frequently taken from the provisions laid in for the sailors. They sometimes make use of a sauce, composed of palm-oil, mixed with flour, water, and pepper, which the sailors call *slabber-sauce*. Yams are a favourite food of the Eboe, or Bight negroes, and rice or corn, of those from the Gold and Windward Coasts; each preferring the produce of their native soil.

In their own country, the negroes in general live on animal food and fish, with roots, yams, and Indian corn. The horse-beans and rice, with which they are fed aboard ship, are chiefly taken from Europe. The latter, indeed, is sometimes purchased on the coast, being far superior to any other.

The Gold Coast negroes scarcely ever refuse any food that is offered to them, and they generally eat larger quantities of whatever is placed before them, than any other species of negroes, whom they likewise excel in strength of body and mind. Most of the slaves have such an aversion to the horse-beans, that unless they are narrowly watched, when fed upon deck, they will throw them overboard, or in each other's faces when they quarrel.

They are commonly fed twice a day, about eight o'clock in the morning, and four in the afternoon. In most ships they are only fed with their *own food* once a day. Their food is served up to them in tubs, about the size of a small water-bucket. They are placed round these tubs in companies of ten to each tub, out of which they feed themselves with wooden spoons. These they soon lose, and when they are not allowed others, they feed themselves with their hands. In favourable weather they are fed upon deck, but in bad weather their food is given them below. Numberless quarrels take place among them during their meals; more especially when they are put upon short allowance, which frequently happens, if the passage from the coast of Guinea to the West-India islands, proves of unusual length. In that case, the weak are obliged to be content with a very scanty portion. Their allowance of water is about half a pint each at every meal. It is handed round in a bucket, and given to each negroe in a pannekin; a small utensil with a strait handle, somewhat similar to a sauce boat. However, when the ships approach the islands with a favourable breeze, they are no longer restricted.

Upon the negroes refusing to take sustenance, I have seen coals of fire, glowing hot, put on a shovel, and placed so near their lips, as to scorch and burn them. And this has been accompanied with threats, of forcing them to swallow the coals, if they any longer persisted in refusing to eat. Those means have generally had the desired effect. I have also been credibly informed, that a certain captain in the slave trade poured melted lead on such of the negroes as obstinately refused their food.[16]

Exercise being deemed necessary for the preservation of their health,, they are sometimes obliged to dance, when the weather will permit their coming on deck. If they go about it reluctantly, or do not move with agility, they are flogged; a person standing by them all the time with a cat-o'-nine-tails in his hand for that purpose. Their musick, upon these

[16] During his evidence to the House of Commons Committee he was asked, 'Are compulsive means used to induce these slaves to take their food?', and replied, 'In every ship I have been it has been the case' (*House of Commons Papers, vol. 72*, p. 588).

occasions, consists of a drum, sometimes with only one head; and when that is worn out, they do not scruple to make use of the bottom of one of the tubs before described. The poor wretches are frequently compelled to sing also; but when they do, their songs are generally, as may be naturally expected, melancholy lamentations of their exile from their native country.

The women are furnished with beads for the purpose of affording them some diversion. But this end is generally defeated by the squabbles which are occasioned, in consequence of their stealing them from each other.

On board some ships, the common sailors are allowed to have intercourse with such of the black women whose consent they can procure. And some of them have been known to take the inconstancy of their paramours so much to heart, as to leap overboard and drown themselves. The officers are permitted to indulge their passions among them at pleasure, and sometimes are guilty of such brutal excesses as disgrace human nature.

The hardships and inconveniences suffered by the negroes during the passage, are scarcely to be enumerated or conceived. They are far more violently affected by the sea-sickness, than the Europeans. It frequently terminates in death, especially among the women. But the exclusion of the fresh air is among the most intolerable. For the purpose of admitting this needful refreshment, most of the ships in the slave-trade are provided, between the decks, with five or six air-ports on each side of the ship, of about six inches in length, and four in breadth; in addition to which, some few ships, but not one in twenty, have what they denominate *wind-sails.* But whenever the sea is rough, and the rain heavy, it becomes necessary to shut these, and every other conveyance by which the air is admitted. The fresh air being thus excluded, the negroes rooms very soon grow intolerably hot. The confined air, rendered noxious by the effluvia exhaled from their bodies, and by being repeatedly breathed, soon produces fevers and fluxes, which generally carries off great numbers of them.

During the voyages I made, I was frequently a witness to the fatal effects of this exclusion of the fresh air. I will give one instance, as it serves to convey some idea, though a very faint one, of the sufferings of those unhappy beings whom we wantonly drag from their native country, and doom to perpetual labour and captivity. Some wet and blowing weather having occasioned the port-holes to be shut, and the grating to be covered, fluxes and fevers among the negroes ensued. While they were in this situation, my profession requiring it, I frequently went down among them, till at length their apartments became so extremely hot, as to be only sufferable for a very short time. But the excessive heat was not the only thing that rendered their situation intolerable. The deck, that is, the floor of their rooms, was so covered with the blood and mucus which had proceeded from them in consequence of the flux, that it resembled a slaughter-house. It is not in the power of the human imagination to picture to itself a situation more dreadful or disgusting. Numbers of the slaves having fainted, they were carried upon deck, where several of them died, and the rest were, with great difficulty, restored. It had nearly proved fatal to me also. The climate was too warm to admit the wearing of any clothing but a shirt, and that I had pulled off before I went down; notwithstanding which, by only continuing among them for about a quarter of an hour, I was so overcome with the heat, stench, and foul air that I had nearly fainted; and it was not without assistance, that I could get upon deck. The consequence was, that I soon after fell sick of the same disorder, from which I did not recover for several months.

A circumstance of this kind, sometimes repeatedly happens in the course of a voyage; and often to a greater degree than what has just been described; particularly when the slaves are much crowded, which was not the case at that time, the ship having more than a hundred short of the number she was to have taken in.

This devastation, great as it was, some few years ago was greatly exceeded on board a Liverpool ship. I shall particularize the circumstances of it, as a more glaring instance of an insatiable thirst for gain, or of less attention to the lives and happiness, even of that despised and oppressed race of mortals, the sable inhabitants of Africa, perhaps was never exceeded; though indeed several similar instances have been known.

This ship, though a much smaller ship than that in which the event I have just mentioned happened, took on board at Bonny, at least six hundred negroes; but according to the information of the black traders, from whom I received the intelligence immediately after the ship sailed, they amounted to near *seven hundred*. By purchasing so great a number, the slaves were so crowded, that they were even obliged to lie on one another. This occasioned such mortality among them, that, without meeting with unusual bad weather, or having a longer voyage than common, nearly one half of them died before the ship arrived in the West-Indies.

That the publick may be able to form some idea of the almost incredible small space into which so large a number of negroes were crammed, the following particulars of this ship are given. According to Leverpool custom she measured 235 tons. Her width across the beam, 25 feet. Length between the decks, 92 feet, which was divided into four rooms, thus :

Store room, in which there were not any negroes placed	15 feet
Negroes rooms — mens room —	about 45 feet
womens ditto	about 10 feet
boys ditto	about 22 feet
Total room for negroes	77 feet

Exclusive of the platform before described, from 8 to 9 feet in breadth, and equal in length to that of the rooms.

It may be worthy of remark, that the ships in this trade, are usually fitted out to receive only one third women negroes, or perhaps a smaller number, which the dimensions of the room allotted to them, above given, plainly shew, but in a greater disproportion.

One would naturally suppose, that an attention to their own interest, would prompt the owners of the Guinea ships not to suffer the captains to take on board a greater number of negroes than the ship would allow room sufficient for them to lie with ease to themselves, or, at least, without rubbing against each other. However that may be, a more striking instance than the above, of avarice, completely and deservedly disappointed, was surely never displayed: for there is little room to doubt, but that in consequence of the expected premium usually allowed to the captains, of £6 per cent. sterling on the produce of the negroes, this vessel was so thronged as to occasion such a heavy loss.

The place allotted for the sick negroes is under the half deck, where they lie on bare planks. By this means, those who are emaciated, frequently have their skin, and even their flesh, entirely rubbed off, by the motion of the ship, from the prominent parts of the shoulders, elbows and hips, so as to render the bones in those parts quite bare. And some of them, by constantly lying in the blood and mucus, that had flowed from those afflicted with the flux, and which, as before observed, is generally so violent as to prevent their being kept clean, have their flesh much sooner rubbed off, than those who have only to contend with the mere friction of the ship. The excruciating pain which the poor sufferers feel from being obliged to continue in such a dreadful situation, frequently for several weeks, in case they happen to live so long, is not to be conceived or described. Few, indeed, are ever able to withstand the fatal effects of it. The utmost skill of the surgeon is here ineffectual. If plaisters be applied, they are very soon displaced by the friction of the ship; and when bandages are used, the negroes very soon take them off, and appropriate them to other purposes.

The surgeon, upon going between decks, in the morning, to examine the situation of the slaves, frequently finds several dead; and among the men, sometimes a dead and living negroe fastened by their irons together. When this is the case, they are brought upon the deck, and being laid on the grating, the living negroe is disengaged, and the dead are [*sic*: is] thrown overboard.

It may not be improper here to remark, that the surgeons employed in the Guinea trade, are generally driven to engage in so disagreable an employ by the confused state of their finances. An exertion of the greatest skill and attention could afford the negroes little relief, so long as the causes of their diseases, namely the breathing of a putrid atmosphere, and wallowing in their own excrements, remain. When once the fever and dysentery get to any height at sea, a cure is scarcely ever effected.

Almost the only means by which the surgeon can render himself useful to the slaves, is, by seeing that their food is properly cooked, and distributed among them. It is true, when they arrive near the markets for which they are destined, care is taken to polish them for sale, by the application of the lunar caustic to such as are afflicted with the yaws. This, however, affords but a temporary relief, as the disease most assuredly breaks out, whenever the patient is put upon a vegetable diet.

It has been asserted in favour of the captains in this trade, that the sick slaves are usually fed from their tables. The great number generally ill at a time, proves the falsity of such an assertion. Were even a captain *disposed* to do this, how could he feed half the slaves in his ship from his own table? for it is well known, that *more than half* are often sick at a time. Two or three may perhaps be fed.

The loss of slaves, through mortality, arising from the causes just mentioned, are frequently very considerable. In the voyage lately referred to (not the Liverpool ship before mentioned) one hundred and five, out of three hundred and eighty, died in the passage. A proportion seemingly very great, but by no means uncommon. One half, sometimes, two-thirds, and even beyond that, have been known to perish. Before we left Bonny River, no less than fifteen died of fevers and dysenteries, occasioned by their confinement. On the Windward Coast, where slaves are procured more slowly, very few die, in proportion to the numbers which die at Bonny, and at Old and New Calabar, where they are obtained much faster; the latter being of a more delicate make and habit.

The havock made among the seamen engaged in this destructive commerce, will be noticed in another part; and will be found to make no inconsiderable addition to the unnecessary waste of life just represented.

As very few of the negroes can so far brook the loss of their liberty, and the hardships they endure, as to bear them with any degree of patience, they are ever upon the watch to take advantage of the least negligence of their oppressors. Insurrections are frequently the consequence; which are seldom suppressed without much bloodshed. Sometimes these are successful, and the whole ship's company is cut off. They are likewise always ready to seize every opportunity for committing some act of desperation to free themselves from their miserable state; and notwithstanding the restraints under which they are laid, they often succeed.

While a ship, to which I belonged, lay in Bonny River, one evening, a short time before our departure, a lot of negroes, consisting of about ten, was brought on board; when one of them, in a favourable moment, forced his way through the network on the larboard side of the vessel, jumped overboard, and was supposed to have been devoured by the sharks.

During the time we were there, fifteen negroes belonging to a vessel from Liverpool, found means to throw themselves into the river; very few were saved; and the residue fell a sacrifice to the sharks. A similar instance took place in a French ship while we lay there.

Circumstances of this kind are very frequent. On the coast of Angola, at the river Ambris, the following incident happened:— During the time of our residing there, we erected a tent to shelter ourselves from the weather. After having been there several weeks, and being unable to purchase the number of slaves we wanted, through the opposition of another English slave vessel, we determined to leave the place. The night before our departure the tent was struck; which was no sooner perceived by some of the negroe women on board, than it was considered a prelude to our sailing; and about eighteen of them, when they were sent between decks, threw themselves into the sea through one of the gun ports; the ship carrying guns between decks. They were all of them, however, excepting one, soon picked up; and that which was missing, not long after, taken about a mile from the shore.

I once knew a negroe woman, too sensible of her woes, who pined for a considerable time, and was taken ill of a fever and dysentery; when declaring it to be her determination to die, she refused all food and medical aid, and in about a fortnight after, expired. On being thrown overboard, her body was instantly torn to pieces by the sharks.

The following circumstance also came within my knowledge. A young female negroe, falling into a desponding way, it was judged necessary, in order to attempt her recovery, to send her on shore, to the hut of one of the black traders. Elevated with the prospect of regaining her liberty by this unexpected step, she soon recovered her usual chearfulness; but hearing, by accident, that it was intended to take her on board the ship again, the poor young creature hung herself.

It frequently happens that the negroes, on being purchased by the Europeans, become raving mad; and many of them die in that state; particularly the women. When I was one day ashore at Bonny, I saw a middle aged stout women, who had been brought down from a fair the preceding day, chained to the post of a black trader's door, in a state of furious insanity. On board a ship in Bonny River, I saw a young negroe woman chained to the deck, who had lost her senses, soon after she was purchased and taken on board. In a former voyage, on board a ship to which I belonged, we were obliged to confine a female negroe, of about twenty-three years of age, on her becoming a lunatic. She was afterwards sold during one of her lucid intervals.

One morning, upon examining the place allotted for the sick negroes, I perceived that one of them, who was so emaciated as scarcely to be able to walk, was missing, and was convinced that he must have gone overboard in the night, probably to put a more expeditious period to his sufferings. And, to conclude on this subject, I could not help being sensibly affected on a former voyage, at observing with what appparent eagerness a black woman seized some dirt from off an African yam, and put it into her mouth; seeming to rejoice at the opportunity of possessing some of her native earth.

From these instances, I think it may be clearly deduced, that the unhapy Africans are not bereft of the finer feelings, but have a strong attachment to their native country, together with a just sense of the value of liberty. And the situation of the miserable beings above described, more forcibly urges the necessity of abolishing a trade which is the source of such evils, than the most eloquent harangue, or persuasive arguments could do.

Sale of the Slaves

When the ships arrive in the West-Indies (the chief mart for this inhuman merchandize), the slaves are disposed of, as I have before observed, by different methods. Sometimes the mode of disposal, is that of selling them by what is termed a *scramble* ; and a day is soon fixed for that purpose. But previous thereto, the sick, or refuse slaves, of which there are frequently many, are usually conveyed on shore, and sold at a tavern by vendue, or public auction. These, in general, are purchased by Jews and surgeons, but chiefly the former, upon speculation, at so low a price as five or six dollars a head. I was informed by a mulatto woman, that she purchased a sick slave at Grenada, upon speculation, for the small sum of one dollar, as the poor wretch was apparently dying of the flux. It seldom happens that any, who are carried ashore in the emaciated state in which they are generally reduced by that disorder, long survive their landing. I once saw sixteen, conveyed on shore, and sold in the foregoing manner, the whole of whom died before I left the island, which was within a short time after. Sometimes the captains march their slaves through the town at which they intend to dispose of them; and then place then in rows, where they are examined and purchased.

The mode of selling them by scramble having fallen under my observation the oftenest, I shall be more particular in describing it. Being some years ago, at one of the islands in the West-Indies, I was witness to a sale by scramble, where about 250 negroes were sold. Upon this occasion all the negroes scrambled for bear an equal price; which is agreed upon between the captains and the purchasers before the sale begins.

On the day appointed, the negroes were landed, and placed altogether in a large yard, belonging to the merchants to whom the ship was consigned. As soon as the hour agreed upon arrived, the doors of the yard were suddenly thrown open, and in rushed a considerable number of purchasers, with all the ferocity of brutes. Some instantly seized such of the negroes as they could lay hold of with their hands. Others, being prepared with several handkerchiefs tied together, encircled with these as many as they were able. While others, by means of a rope, effected the same purpose. It is scarcely possible to describe the confusion of which this mode of selling is productive. It likewise causes much animosity among the purchasers, who, not infrequently on these occasions, fall out and quarrel with each other. The poor astonished negroes were so much terrified by these proceedings, that several of them, through fear, climbed over the walls of the court yard, and ran wild about the town; but were soon hunted down and retaken.

While on a former voyage from Africa to Kingston in Jamaica, I saw a sale there by scramble on board a snow. The negroes were collected together upon the main and quarter deck, and the ship was darkened by sails suspended over them, in order to prevent the purchasers from being able to see, so as to pick or chuse. The signal being given, the buyers rushed in as usual, to seize their prey; when the negroes appeared to be extremely terrified, and near thirty of them jumped into the sea. But they were all soon retaken, chiefly by boats from other ships.

On board a ship, lying at Port Maria, in Jamaica, I saw another scramble; in which, as usual the poor negroes were greatly terrified. The women, in particular, clang to each other in agonies scarcely to be conceived, shrieking through excess of terror, at the savage manner in which their brutal purchasers rushed upon, and seized them. Though humanity, one should imagine, would dictate the captains to apprize the poor negroes of the mode by which they were to be sold, and by that means to guard them, in some degree, against the surprize and terror which must attend it, I never knew that any notice of the scramble was given to them. Nor have I any reason to think that it is done; or that this mode of sale is less frequent at this time, than formerly.

Various are the deceptions made use of in the disposal of the sick slaves; and many of these, such as must excite in every humane mind, the liveliest sensations of horror. I have been well informed, that a Liverpool captain boasted of his having cheated some Jews by the following stratagem: A lot of slaves, afflicted with the flux, being about to be landed for sale, he directed the surgeon to stop the anus of each of them with oakum. Thus prepared, they were landed, and taken to the accustomed place of sale; where, being unable to stand but for a very short time, they are usually permitted to sit. The Jews, when they examined them, oblige them to stand up, in order to see if there be any discharge; and when they do not perceive this appearance, they consider it as a symptom of recovery. In the present instance, such an appearance being prevented, the bargain was struck, and they were accordingly sold. But it was not long before a discovery ensued. The excruciating pain which the prevention of the discharge of such an acrimonious nature occasioned, not being to be borne by the poor wretches, the temporary obstruction was removed, and the deluded purchasers were speedily convinced of the deception.

So grievously are the negroes sometimes afflicted with this troublesome and painful disorder, that I have seen large numbers of them, after being landed, obliged, by the virulence of the complaint, to stop almost every minute, as they passed on.

Treatment of the Sailors

The evils attendant on this inhuman traffick, are not confined to the purchased negroes. The sufferings of the seamen employed in the slave-trade, from the unwholesomeness of the climate, the inconveniencies of the voyage, the brutal severity of the commanders, and other causes, fall very little short, nor prove in proportion to the numbers, less destructive to the sailors than negroes.[17]

The sailors on board the Guinea ships, are not allowed always an equal quantity of beef and pork with those belonging to other merchant ships. In these articles they are frequently much stinted, particularly when the negroes are on board; part of the stock laid in for the sailors, being, as before mentioned, appropriated for their use.

With regard to their drink, they are generally denied grog, and are seldom allowed any thing but water to quench their thirst. This urges them, when opportunity offers, at Bonny and other places on the coast,

[17] John Newton, after reading Falconbridge's *Account*, wrote to Richard Phillips, 'The very ill-treatment the seamen receive from the captains, or those who act under his authority, is often fatal ... A savageness of spirit, not easily conceived, infuses itself (though, as I have observed, there are exceptions) into those who exercise power on board an African slave-ship, from the captain downwards' (Phillips, *Memoir*, p. 30).

to barter their clothes with the natives, for English brandy, which the Africans obtain, among other articles, in exchange for slaves; and they frequently leave themselves nearly naked, in order to indulge an excess in spirituous liquors. In this state, they are often found lying on the deck, and in different parts of the ship, exposed to the heavy dews, which in those climates fall during the night; notwithstanding the deck is usually washed every evening. This frequently causes pains in the head and limbs, accompanied with a fever, which generally, in the course of a few days, occasions their death.

The temporary house constructed on the deck, affords but an indifferent shelter from the weather; yet the sailors are obliged to lodge under it, as all the parts between decks are occupied by, or kept for, the negroes. The cabin is frequently full, and when this is the case, or the captain finds the heat and the stench intolerable, he quits his cot, which is usually hung over the slaves, and sleeps in the round-house, if there is one, as there is in many ships.

The foul air that arises from the negroes when they are much crowded, is very noxious to the crew; and this is not a little increased by the additional heat which the covering over the ship occasions. The mangrove smoke is likewise, as before observed, productive of disorders among them.

Nor are they better accommodated after they leave the coast of Africa. During the whole of the passage to the West-Indies, which in general lasts seven weeks, they are obliged, for want of room between decks, to keep upon deck. The exposure to the weather, is also found very prejudicial to the health of the sailors, and frequently occasions fevers, which generally prove fatal. The only resemblance of a shelter, is a tarpawling thrown over the booms, which even before they leave the coast, is generally so full of holes, as to afford scarce any defence against the wind or the rain, of which a considerable quantity usually falls during this passage.

Many other causes contribute to affect the health of the sailors. The water at Bonny, which they are obliged to drink, is very unwholesome; and, together with their scanty and bad diet, and the cruel usage they receive from the officers, tends to impoverish the blood, and render them susceptible of putrid fevers and dysenteries.

The seamen, whose health happens to be impaired, are discharged, on the arrival of the ships in the West-Indies; and as soon as they get on shore, they have recourse to spirituous liquors, to which they are the more prone, on account of being denied grog, or even any liquor but water, during their being aboard; the consequence of which is, a certain and speedy destruction. Numbers likewise die in the West-India islands, of the scurvy brought on in consequence of poverty of diet, and exposure to all weathers.

I am now come to a part of the sufferings of the sailors who are employed in the slave-trade, of which, for the honour of human nature, I would willingly decline giving an account; that is, the treatment they receive from their officers, which makes no inconsiderable addition to the hardships and ailments just mentioned, and contributes not a little to rob the nation annually, of a considerable number of this valuable body of men. However, as truth demands, and the occasion requires it, I will relate some of the circumstances of this kind, which fell under my own immediate observation, during the several voyages I made in that line.

In one of these, I was witness to the following instance of cruel usage: Most of the sailors were treated with brutal severity; but one in particular, a man advanced in years, experienced it in an uncommon degree. Having made some complaint relative to his allowance of water, and this being construed as an insult, one of the officers seized him, and with the blows he bestowed upon him, beat out several of his teeth. Not content with this, while the poor old man was yet bleeding, one of the iron pump-bolts was fixed in his mouth and kept there by a piece of rope-yarn tied round his head. Being unable to spit out the blood which flowed from his wound, the man was almost choaked, and obliged to swallow it. He was then tied to the rail of the quarter-deck, having declared, upon being gagged, that he would jump overboard and drown himself. About two hours afterwards he was taken from the quarter deck rail, and fastened to the grating companion of the steerage, under the half deck, where he remained all night with a centinel placed over him.

A young man on board one of the ships, was frequently beaten in a very severe manner, for very trifling faults. This was done sometimes with what is termed a *cat* (an instrument of correction, which consists of a handle or stem, made of a rope three inches and a half in circum-ference, and about eighteen inches in length, at one of which are fastened nine branches, or tails, composed of log-line, with three or more knots upon each branch), and sometimes was beat with a bamboo. Being one day cruelly beaten with the latter, the poor lad, unable to endure the severe usage, leaped out of one of the gun ports on the larboard side of the cabin, into the river. He, however, providentially escaped being devoured by the sharks, and was taken up by a canoe belonging to one of the black traders then lying along-side the vessel. As soon as he was brought on board, he was dragged to the quarter-deck, and his head forced into a tub of water, which had been left there for the negroe women to wash their hands in. In this situation he was kept till he was nearly suffocated; the person who held him, exclaiming, with the malignity of a demon, "if you want drowning, I will drown you myself". Upon my inquiring of the young man, if he knew the danger to which he exposed himself by jumping overboard, he replied, "that he expected to be devoured by the sharks, but he preferred even that, to being treated daily with so much cruelty."

Another seaman having been in some degree negligent, had a long chain fixed round his neck, at the end of which was fastened a log of wood. In this situation he performed his duty (from which he was not in the least spared) for several weeks, till at length he was nearly exhausted by fatigue; and after his release from the log, he was frequently beaten for trivial faults. Once, in particular, when an accident happened, through the carelessness of another seaman, he was tied up, although the fault was not in the least imputable to him, along with the other person, and they were both flogged till their backs were raw. Chian pepper was then mixed in a bucket, with salt water, and with this the harrowed parts of the back of the unoffending seaman were washed, as an addition to his torture.

The same seaman having at another time accidentally broken a plate, a fish-gig was thrown at him with great violence. The fish-gig is an instrument used for striking fish, and consists of several strong barbed points fixed on a pole, about six feet long, loaded at the end with lead. The man escaped the threatening danger, by stooping his head, and the missile struck in the barricado. Knives and forks were at other times thrown at him; and a large Newfoundland dog was frequently set at him, which, thus encouraged, would not only tear his clothes but wound him. At length, after several severe floggings, and other ill treatment, the poor fellow appeared to be totally insensible to beating, and careless of the event.

I must here add, that whenever any of the crew were beaten, the Newfoundland dog, just mentioned, from the encouragement he met with, would generally leap upon them, tear their clothes and bite them. He was particularly inveterate against one of the seamen, who, from being often knocked down, and severely beaten, appeared quite stupid and incapable of doing his duty. In this state he was taken on board another ship, and returned to England.

In one of my voyages, a seaman came on board the ship I belonged to, while on the coast, as a passenger to the West Indies. He was just recovered from a fever, and notwithstanding this, he was very unmercifully beaten during the passage, which, together with the feeble state he was in, rendered him nearly incapable of walking, and it was but by stealth, that any medical assistance could be given to him.

A young man was likewise beaten and kicked almost daily, for trifling, and even imaginary faults. The poor youth happening to have a very bad toe, through a hurt, he was placed as a centry over the sick slaves, a situation which required much walking. This, in addition to the pain it occasioned, increased a fever he already had. Soon after he was compelled, although so ill, to sit on the gratings, and being there over-come with illness and fatigue, he chanced to fall asleep; which being observed from the quarter-deck, he was soon awakened, and with many oaths, upbraided for neglect of duty. He was then kicked from the gratings, and so cruelly beaten, that it was with great difficulty he crawled to one of the officers who was more humane, and complaining of the cruel treatment he had just received, petitioned for a little barley-water (which was kept for the sick slaves) to quench the intolerable thirst he experienced.

Another seaman was knocked down several times a day for faults of no deep dye. It being observed at one time, that the hen coops had not been removed by the sailors who were then washing the deck, nor washed under, which it was his duty to see done, one of the officers immediately knocked him down, then seized and dragged him to the stern of the vessel, where he threw him violently against the deck. By this treatment, various parts of his body was [sic: were] much bruised, his face swelled, and he had a bad eye for a fortnight. He was afterwards severely beaten for a very trifling fault, and kicked till he fell down. When he got on shore in the West-Indies, he carried his shirt, stained with the blood which had flowed from his wounds, to one of the magistrates of the island, and applied to him for redress; but the ship being consigned to one of them, all the redress he could procure, was his discharge.

Many other instances of similar severity might be produced; but the foregoing will suffice, to give some idea of the treatment seamen are liable to, and generally experience in this employ; the consequence of which is usually desertion or death.

Of the former I will give one instance. While a ship I belonged to lay at Bonny, early one morning near a dozen of the crew deserted in one of the long boats. They were driven to this desperate measure, as one of them afterwards informed me, by the cruel treatment they had experienced on board. Two of them, in particular, had been severely beaten and flogged the preceding day. One of these having neglected that the arms of the ship were kept fit for use, was tied up to the mizen shrouds, and after being stripped, very severely flogged on the back; his trowsers were then pulled down and the flogging was repeated. The other seaman, who was esteemed a careful, cleanly, sober fellow, had been punished little less severely, though it did not appear that he had been guilty at that time of any fault.

It is customary for most of the captains of the slave ships to go on shore every evening to do business with the black traders. Upon these occasions many of them get intoxicated, and when they return on board, give proofs of their inebriation, by beating and ill using some or other of the crew. This was the present case; the seaman here spoken of, was beaten, without any reason being assigned, with a knotted bamboo, for a considerable time; by which he was very much bruised, and being before in an ill state of health, suffered considerably.

Irritated by the ill usage which all of them, in their turn, had experienced, they resolved to attempt an escape, and effected it early in the morning. The person on the watch discovered, that the net-work on the main deck had been cut, and that one of the long-boats was gone; and, upon further examination it was found, that near a dozen of the seamen were missing. A few hours after, the captain went in the cutter in pursuit of the deserters, but without success.

On my return to England, I received from one of them, the following account of their adventures during this undertaking.

When they left the vessel, they proposed going to Old Calabar, being determined to perish, rather than return to the ship. All the provisions they took with them was, a bag containing about half a hundred weight of bread, half a small cheese, and a cask of water of about 38 gallons. They made a sail of a hammock, and erected one of the boat's oars for a mast. Thus slenderly provided, they dropt down the river of Bonny, and kept along the coast; but mistaking one river for another, they were seized by the natives, who stripped them, and marched them across the country, for a considerable distance, to the place to which they themselves intended going. During the march several were taken ill, and some of them died. Those who survived, were sold to an English ship which lay there. Every one of these deserters, except three, died on the coast, or during the passage to the West-Indies; and one of the remaining three died soon after his arrival there. So that only two out of the whole number lived to arrive in England, and those in a very infirm state of health.

While I am on the subject of the desertions among the sailors, I must add, that the captains in this trade generally take out with them tobacco and slops, which they sell at an exorbitant price to the sailors. And in the case of their desertion or decease, they have it in their power to charge to the seamens accounts, whatever quantity they please, without contradiction. This proves an additional reason for cruel usage. In case of desertion, the sailors forfeit their wages, by which the expenses opf the voyage are lessened, and consequently the merchants reap benefit from it.

The relation just given of the barbarities exercised by the officers in the slave trade, upon the seamen under their command, may appear to those who are unacquainted with the method in which this iniquitous branch of commerce in conducted, to be exaggerated. But I can assure them, that every instance is confined within the strictest bounds of truth. Many others may likewise be brought to prove, that those I have recited are by no means singular. Indeed the reverse of this conduct would be esteemed a singularity. For the common practice of the officers in the Guinea trade, I am sorry to say it, will, with a very few exceptions, justify the assertion, that to harden the feelings, and to inspire a *delight in giving torture* to a fellow creature, is the natural tendency of this unwarrantable traffick. It is but justice however, that I except from this general censure, one captain with whom I sailed. Upon all occasions I found him to be a humane considerate man, and ever ready to alleviate the evils attendant on the trade as far as they were to be lessened.

The annual diminution of British seamen by all the foregoing causes, is what next claims attention, and upon due investigation will be found, I fear, to be much more considerable than it is generally supposed to be. As this is a question of great national importance, and cannot fail to evince the necessity of an abolition of the slave trade; in order to convey to the public some ideas of the destructive tendency of it, I will give an account of the statement of the loss of a ship, to which I belonged, during one of her voyages. And though this statement may not be considered as an average of the loss upon each voyage, which I have before estimated, as I would not wish to exceed the mark, at one fourth, and oftentimes one third. I have known instances where it has been greatly exceeded, as I shall presently show.

The crew of the ship I speak of, upon its departure from England, consisted of forty-six persons, exclusive of the captain, chief mate, and myself. Out of this number, we lost on the coast eleven by desertion (of whom only two, and those in a very infirm state, ever arrived in England) and five by death. Three perished in the middle passage, of whom one was a passenger. In the West-Indies two died, one of which was a passenger from Bonny. Five were discharged at their own request, having been cruelly treated, and five deserted, exclusive of two who shipped themselves at Bonny; of these ten, several were in a diseased state; and probably, like most of the seamen who are discharged or desert from the Guinea ships in the islands, never returned to their native country. One died in our passage from the West-Indies to England; and one, having been rendered incapable of duty, was sent on board another ship while we lay at Bonny.

Thus, out of the forty-six persons before-mentioned, only fifteen returned home in the ship. And several, out of this small number, so enervated in their constitutions, as to be of little service in future; they were, on the contrary, reduced to the mournful necessity of becoming burthensome to themselves and to others. Of the ten that deserted, or were discharged in the West-Indies, little account can be taken; it being improbable that one half, perhaps not a third, ever returned to this country.

From hence it appears, that there was a loss in this voyage of thirty-one sailors and upwards, exclusive of the two sailors who were passengers, and not included in the ship's crew. I say *a loss of thirty-one,* for though the whole of this number did not die, yet if it be considered, that several of those who returned to England in the ship, or who might have returned in other ships, are likely to become a burthen, instead of being useful to the community, it will be readily acknowledged, I doubt not, that the foregoing statement does not exceed reality.

How worthy of serious consideration is the diminution here repre-sented, of a body of people so valuable in a commercial state! But how much more alarming will this be, when it appears, as is really the case, that the loss of seamen in the voyage I am speaking of, is not equal to what is experienced even by some other ships trading to Bonny and Calabar; and much less than by those employed in boating on the Windward Coast; where frequently there happens such a mortality among the crew, as not to leave a sufficient number of hands to navigate the ships to the West-Indies. In the year 1786, I saw a ship belonging to Miles Barber, and Co. at Cape Monsurado, on the Windward Coast, which had lost all the crew except three, from *boating;* a practice that proves extremely destructive to sailors, by exposing them to the parching sun and heavy dews of Africa, for weeks together, while they are seeking for negroes up the river, as before described.

It might naturally be asked, as such are the dangers to which the sailors employed in the slave trade are exposed from the intemperature of the climate, the inconveniencies of the voyage, and the treatment of the officers, how the captains are able to procure a sufficient number to man their ships ? I answer, that it is done by a series of finesse and imposition, aided not only by allurements, but by threats.

There are certain publick-houses, in which, for interested purposes, the sailors are trusted, and encouraged to run in debt. To the landlords of these houses the captains apply; and a certain number being fixed on, the landlord immediately insists upon their entering on board such a ship, threatening, in case of refusal, to arrest and throw them into prison. At the same time the captain holds out the allurements of a month's pay in advance above the ships in any other trade, and the promise of satisfying their inexorable landlords. Thus terrified on the one hand by the apprehensions of a prison, and allured on the other by the promised advance, they enter. And by this means a very great proportion of the sailors in the slave trade are procured; only a very small number of landmen are employed. During the several voyages I have been in the trade, I have not known the number to exceed one for each voyage. The few ships that go out in time of war, generally take with them, as other merchant ships do, a greater proportion of landmen. And with regard to apprentices, we had not any on board the ships I sailed in, neither to my knowledge have I ever seen any. So far is this trade from proving a nursery for our seamen.

By their articles, on entering on board some Guinea ships, the sailors are restrained, under forfeiture of their wages, from applying, in case of ill usage, to any one for redress, except to such persons as shall be nominated by the owners or the captain; and by others, to commence an action against the captain for bad treatment, incurs a penalty of fifty pounds. These restrictions seem to be a tacit acknowledgment on the part of the owners and captains, that ill treatment is to be expected.

Having stated the foregoing facts relative to the nature of this destructive and inhuman traffick, I shall leave those, whose more immediate business it is, to deduce the necessary conclusions; and shall proceed to give a few cursory observations on those parts of the coast of Africa already referred to; confining myself to such as tend to an elucidation of the slave trade, without entering minutely into the state of the country.

A short Description of such Parts of the coast of Guinea, as are before referred to.

BONNY, or BANNY, is a large town situated in the Bight of Benin, on the Coast of Guinea, lying about twelve miles from the sea, on the east side of a river of the same name, opposite to a town called Peter-forte-side. It consists of a considerable number of very poor huts, built of upright poles, plaistered with a kind of red earth, and covered with mats. They are very low, being only one story. The floor is made of sand, which being constructed on swampy ground, does not long retain its firmness, but requires frequent repair.

The inhabitants secure themselves, in some degree, against the noxious vapours, which arise from the swamps and woods that surround the town, by constantly keeping large wood fires in their huts. They are extremely dirty and indolent; which, together with what they call the *smokes* (a noxious vapour, arising from the swamps about the latter end of autumn) produces an epidemical fever, that carries off great numbers.

The natives of Bonny believe in one Supreme Being; but they reverence greatly a harmless animal of the lizard kind, called a Guana, the body of which is about the size of a man's leg, and tapering towards its tail, nearly to a point. Great numbers of them run about the town, being encouraged and cherished by the inhabitants.

The river Bonny abounds with sharks of a very large size, which are often seen in almost incredible numbers about the slave ships, devouring with great dispatch the dead bodies of the negroes as they are thrown overboard. The bodies of the sailors who die there, are buried on a sandy point, called Bonny Point, which lies about a quarter of a mile from the town. It is covered at high water; and, as the bodies are buried but a small depth below the surface of the sand, the stench arising from them is sometimes very noxious.

The trade of this town consists of slaves, and a small quantity of ivory and palm-oil, the latter of which the inhabitants use as we do butter; but its chief dependence is on the slave trade, in which it exceeds any other place on the coast of Africa. The only water here is rain water, which stagnating in a dirty pool, is very unwholesome. With this, as there is no better to be procured, the ships are obliged to supply themselves, though when drank by the sailors it frequently occasions violent pains in the bowels, accompanied by diarrhoea.

THE WINDWARD COAST of AFRICA has a beautiful appearance from the sea, being covered with trees which are green all the year. It produces rice, cotton, and indigo of the first quality, and likewise a variety of roots, such as yams, casava, sweet potatoes &c. &c. The soil is very rich, and the rice which it produces, is superior to that of Carolina; the cotton also is very fine. It has a number of fine rivers, that are navigable by small sloops, a considerable way up the country.

The natives are a strong hardy race, especially about Setrecrou, where they are always employed in hunting and fishing.[18] They are extremely athletic and muscular, and are very expert in the water and can swim for many miles. They can also dive to almost any depth. I have often thrown pieces of iron and tobacco pipes overboard, which they have never failed bringing up in their hand.

Their canoes are very small, not weighing above twenty-eight pounds each, and seldom carrying above two or three people. It is surprising to see with what rapidity they paddle themselves through the water; and to see what a distance they venture in them from the shore. I have seen them eight or nine miles distant from it. In stormy weather the sea frequently fills them, which the persons in them seem to disregard. When this happens, they leap into the sea, and taking hold of the ends of the canoe, turn her over several times, till they have emptied her of the chief part of the water; they then get in again, with great agility, and throw out the remainder with a small scoop, made for that purpose.

---

[18] For the Kru people see Diane Frost, *Work and Community among West African Migrant Workers*, Liverpool, 1999.

They sell some ivory and Malegetta pepper.

They are very cleanly in their houses, as likewise in cooking their victuals. The ivory on this coast is very fine, especially as Cape Lahoe. There are in this coast small cattle.

The GOLD COAST has not so pleasing an appearance from the sea, as the Windward coast; but the natives are full as hardly, if not more so. The reason given for this is, that as their country is not so fertile as the Windward coast, they are obliged to labour more in the cultivation of rice and corn, which is their chief food. They have here, as on the Windward coast, hogs, goats, fowls, and abundance of fine fish &c. They are very fond of brandy, and always get intoxicated when it is in their power to do so. They are likewise very bold and resolute, and insurrections happen more frequently among them, when on ship-board, than amongst the negroes of any other part of the coast.

The trade here is carried on by means of gold-dust, for which the Europeans give them goods, such a pieces of India chintz, basts, romals, guns, powder, tobacco, brandy, pewter, iron, lead, copper, knives &c. &c. After the gold dust is purchased, it is again disposed of to the natives for negroes. Their mode of reckoning in this traffic, is by ounces; thus they say they will have so many ounces for a slave; and according to the number of ships on the coast, the price of these differs.[19]

The English have several forts on the Gold coast, the principle of which are, Cape Corse Castle, and Anamboe.[20] The trade carried on at these forts is bartering for negroes, which the governors sell again to the European ships, for the articles before-mentioned.

The natives, as just observed, are a bold, resolute people. During the last voyage I was upon the coast, I saw a number of negroes on Cape Corse Castle, some of whom were part of the cargo of a ship from London, on whose crew they had risen, and, after killing the captain, and most of the sailors, ran the ship on shore; but in endeavouring to make their escape, most of them were seized by the natives, and resold. Eighteen of these we purchased from Governor Morgue. The Dutch

---

[19] The 'ounce' was the equivalent of the Sierra Leone 'bar' (see p. 35, *footnote* 32).

[20] At 'Cape Corse' (Cape Coast) Falconbridge had some conversation with the chaplain, the Reverend Philip Quaque, an African ordained in England (*House of Commons Papers, vol. 72*, p. 585).

have likewise a strong fort on this coast, called Elmina, where they carry on a considerable trade for slaves.

The principal places of trade for negroes, are Bonny and Calabar. The town and trade of Bonny, I have already described. That of Calabar is nearly similar. The natives of the latter are of a much more delicate frame than those of the Windward and Gold Coasts.

The natives of Angola are the mildest, and most expert in mechanicks, of any of the Africans. Their country is the most plentiful of any in those parts, and produces different sorts of grain, particularly calavances, of which they seem, when on ship-board, to be extremely fond. Here are likewise hogs, sheep, goats, fowls, &c. in great abundance, insomuch, that when I was at the River Ambris, we could buy a fine fat sheep for a small keg of gunpowder, the value of which was about one shilling and sixpence sterling. They have also great plenty of fine fish. I have often seen turtle caught, while fishing with a net for other fish. They have a species of wild cinnamon, which has a very pungent taste in the mouth. The soil seems extremely rich, and the vegetation luxuriant and quick. A person might walk for miles in the country amidst wild jessamin trees.

The Portuguese have a large town on this coast named St Paul's,[21] the inhabitants of which, and of the country many miles round, profess the Roman Catholick Religion. They are in general strictly honest. The town of St Paul is strongly fortified, and the Portuguese do not suffer any other nation to trade there.

THE END

[21] Luanda.

Index